Brad & Trisha

We wish you
and success in your
life together.

May God bless you
in all you wish
to accomplish.

Love
Bishop & Sister Hall
Brother & Sister Nielsen
Brother & Sister Belliston

Covenant
Hearts

Covenant
Hearts

Marriage and the Joy
of Human Love

Bruce C. Hafen

DESERET
BOOK

SALT LAKE CITY, UTAH

Photographs by Wal Richards, pages 4 through 6, used by permission of Maryborough-Midlands Historical Society, Inc., Maryborough, Australia.

Drawing by Käthe Kollwitz entitled "Kopf eines Kindes in den Händen der Mutter" ("Head of a Child in the Hands of Its Mother"), page 268, is a detail study for an etching from 1900.

Visit us at deseretbook.com

Library of Congress Cataloging-in-Publication Data

Hafen, Bruce C.
    Covenant hearts : marriage and the joy of human love / Bruce C. Hafen.
        p.   cm.
    Includes bibliographical references and index.
    ISBN-10 1-59038-536-5 (hardbound : alk. paper)
    ISBN-13 978-1-59038-536-4 (hardbound : alk. paper)
    1. Marriage—Religious aspects—Church of Jesus Christ of Latter-day Saints.   2. Marriage—Religious aspects—Mormon Church.   3. Mormon Church—Doctrines.   4. Church of Jesus Christ of Latter-day Saints—Doctrines.   5. Marriage.   I. Title.
    BX8641.H33   2005
    248.4'89332—dc22   2005022078

Printed in the United States of America
Publishers Printing, Salt Lake City, UT

10   9   8   7   6   5   4

FOR MARIE

*"The wife of thy youth, . . .
thy companion,
and the wife of thy covenant"*

Malachi 2:14

CONTENTS

PREFACE

For the joy of human love,
Brother, sister, parent, child,
Friends on earth, and friends above,
For all gentle thoughts and mild,
Lord of all, to thee we raise
This our hymn of grateful praise.[1]

The joy of human love gives us hope and purpose. It makes us want to live better. It makes us long for the day when we will take the hands that have held ours and enter our Father's presence together. There we will embrace not only Him but also our husbands, our wives, our children, family, and friends. There we will stay with them, always, to "go no more out" (Revelation 3:12).

We can sense a brief glimpse of that day when we taste love's deepest stirrings and God's Spirit brushes across our hearts. The promise of living together in love, both here and beyond time, is worth waiting for, worth trying and crying for, through all the days of life. No wonder we praise the Lord of all for this highest beauty of both earth and heaven.

The fountainhead of human love flows from a marriage between hearts knit together by covenants. When those head-waters run pure, children and grandchildren will later sing their own hymns of grateful praise: "For the love which from our birth, / Over and around us lies."[2]

Because I know these promises are true, I have watched with growing sadness over the last generation as our society has gradually but surely begun to replace an imperfect yet relatively stable "culture of marriage" with a disturbing new "culture of divorce." This is not just an American problem. As President Gordon B. Hinckley has said, "The family is falling apart. Not only in America, but now across the world."[3] On another occasion, he said the number of people hurt by crumbling families is "a matter of serious concern. *I think it is my most serious concern.*"[4]

Reflecting his concern, in 1995 the First Presidency and the Quorum of the Twelve Apostles issued the Proclamation on the Family. In a day when "people are confused" about life's most essential relationships, we need to hear the rest of that Primary song: "Follow the prophet, follow the prophet, / Follow the prophet; he knows the way."[5] The Family Proclamation helps restore the perspective the world is losing. The doctrine and principles expressed in that Proclamation are the foundation for what this book tries to say about marriage.

Just since the late 1960s, American law and culture have dramatically and tragically changed how most people now think about marriage, families, sex, and children. Drawing on my background from teaching family law, but much more fully informed by my Church experience, I attempt to explain here some of the reasons why today's culture no longer supports our traditional attitudes. As that support has dwindled, society does not always value what we do when we exert ourselves to nurture our own commitments. We may feel lonely or even strange, because we are going against the grain of a laid-back, permissive society in a countercultural way. But we cannot let the world's values dictate our own—there is too much at stake for that.

Part of what's at stake is that *our marriage really can be the most satisfying and sanctifying—and the most demanding—experience of our lives.* It is more than coincidence that the most *sanctifying* experiences of our spiritual lives should also be the most *demanding* experiences. Family life, with marriage at its center, is the homeroom of the earth school our Father created to give His children a place to learn and to grow. Our homes are laboratories where we test and develop our religion.

That makes it all the more risky that today's society no longer understands marriage the way God originally gave it to His children. Being married isn't easy. It isn't supposed to be easy. But when a confused culture confuses us about what marriage means, we may give up on ourselves and each other much too soon.

Consider five other brief points by way of preface. First, I include a number of stories as illustrations. The names in nearly all of these cases have been changed to protect personal privacy, even though the stories are based on actual experiences. I appreciate and admire these people. I have learned a great deal from them.

Second, I hope to convey accurate assumptions regarding "ideal" marriages and families in the Church. Once a couple is married in the temple, they are not yet living a celestial life. Rather, they walk out of the temple much the way Adam and Eve left the Garden of Eden—to enter a sometimes tough and lonely world. Their temple wedding gives them the authority of eternal marriage, but they will spend the rest of their lives working to create a marriage of celestial quality, striving and growing against opposition. As Elder Neal A. Maxwell once said, "*Authority* in the priesthood is given through ordination, but *power* in the priest-hood is received through righteous living."[6] That principle describes the sources of power in a true celestial marriage.

All marriages and all families struggle as we try to live up to the gospel's teachings about family life. That is both normal and expected. No, we're not perfect, but the very process of working toward that ideal is central to our personal growth. This makes me more interested in learning how to strive than in eliminating the need to strive. There is joy in the journey, not just in the destination.

At the same time, one reason we've seen more divorce in the last generation is that when our marriages struggle, we don't expect the same degree of idealistic conduct of one another. At least we're less openly judgmental, and much of that increased tolerance is desirable. But we must find ways to uphold high expectations even as we honestly acknowledge the heavy lifting and the exasperating personal weaknesses we all face in stretching toward our ideals.

Third, I realize from the experience of close friends that many faithful people do not now live in the kind of family situation they desire and for which they are fully qualified. Many factors can throw us off course—many of them beyond our control. Some people of exceptional faith live in the daily grinding effort of difficult marriages. Some are divorced after stretching themselves beyond the breaking point to improve their relationships and their lives. Some remain unmarried, despite years of conscientious searching.

People who seem to have achieved a "proper" marriage are not necessarily better or more faithful than those whose marriage still eludes them. We must learn how to talk about making stronger marriages without judging or losing compassion for those who as yet have no marriage.

As the prophets have always taught, the Lord will ultimately compensate the faithful men and women who are denied family fulfillment in mortality.[7] Until then, there are other, preparatory ways to grow spiritually, even to taste many of the joys of family life. I have known some people who feel like broken links in a family chain, yet who develop so much compensating spiritual depth that they help heal not only their own wounds but larger wounds in a family pattern. Of them, Isaiah wrote, "And they that shall be of thee shall build the old waste places: thou shalt raise up the foundations of many generations; and thou shalt be called, The *repairer of the breach,* The restorer of paths to dwell in" (Isaiah 58:12; italics added).

Fourth, this book is a personal expression and is not an official statement of Church doctrine.

Fifth, for their valuable suggestions on the manuscript, I thank Sheri L. Dew, Sarah H. d'Evegnee, Amy B. Hafen, David K. Hafen, Fran C. Hafen, Joy M. Hafen, Marie K. Hafen, Mark K. Hafen, Tom K. Hafen, Tracy T. Hafen, and Martha Johnson. I appreciate the resourceful production team at Deseret Book— Suzanne Brady, Rebecca B. Chambers, Richard Erickson, Tonya-Rae Facemyer, Doreen McKnight, Patricia H. Stokes, and Cory H. Maxwell. I also thank Tom Holman and Alan Keele for their advice, and I thank the Midlands Historical Society in Maryborough, Australia, for their kind permission to use the Wal Richards wedding photographs.

In summary, this book has two purposes. One is to describe recent changes in our cultural environment that have created enormous confusion about the nature and meaning of marriage. Chapters 4 and 20 through 23 address these themes, at times with language and historical context that necessarily have a little more academic tone than the rest of the book. These cultural shifts dangerously but subtly erode our desire, and therefore our ability, to sustain our own marriage commitments. Understanding them may help us reduce their influence on us.

My larger purpose is to explore how the restored gospel can help us transcend the modern chaos. Its teachings will keep us, realistically but securely, gathered in the arms of married love—the kind we imagine unfolding from wedding pictures or the kind we see in the story of Adam and Eve, the archetypal marriage story in which human love, blessed by God's love, does overcome all opposition and last forever.

PART I

LOSING THE PLOT

CHAPTER ONE

WEDDING PICTURES

I recently attended a temple wedding in which the bride's gentle grandfather performed the marriage. After the sealing, he invited the couple to kiss over the altar. Then they stood before him to exchange wedding rings, and they kissed again. All of us in the room felt their joy. The grandfather leaned toward them and whispered, "Well, how do you like married life so far?"

There is some pristine, unalloyed happiness in a wedding. I once occupied an office with a window that sometimes let me glimpse bridal parties who gathered for wedding pictures near the Salt Lake Temple. I have seen other scenes like that on the grounds of other temples, and it's always the same—the very sight of the couple's radiant faces transforms time into eternity, as the universe itself holds briefly still for just this bride and this groom.

A reception in our neighborhood once featured a display of mannequins adorned with the actual wedding dresses of mothers and grandmothers of the current couple. Some of the dresses were more than fifty years old. Near the dresses were old framed photos from the weddings of the couple's parents and grandparents. The dresses and the photographs connected both the generations and the guests, gracing the reception with the timeless, joyful spirit of weddings.

A few years ago an international news magazine shared the story of Wal Richards of Maryborough, a small town in southeastern Australia. Wal had just died—alone, in his modest home. He had never married. He had a terrible speech impediment and

other limitations that made him unable to communicate with people. Yet he was cheerful. He rode a bike everywhere. Some people in Maryborough thought of him as a kind of amiable village misfit.

For more than forty years, Wal came to local weddings to photograph the people. He just showed up carrying his camera, smiling and snapping candid, cheery shots of brides, grooms, their families and friends. He did it so often, people hardly felt married in Maryborough unless Wal came, though he was seldom actually invited. If the wedding were to be in Melbourne, three hours away, Wal would take the 5 A.M. train so he could be there with his camera as the bride and groom came out of the church.

Because no one ever saw his pictures, people assumed Wal had

no film or that his pictures never turned out. When he died in his mid-sixties, his family and friends were astonished to find in rows of carefully packed trays and boxes about twenty thousand wedding photographs dating back almost half a century. The city fathers published a notice to all the people who had been married in Maryborough during those years, inviting them to come and identify their own wedding pictures among the fruits of Wal's lifelong quest.

Not long after reading about Wal Richards, Marie and I found ourselves on a road trip that took us just south of Maryborough. We had been so taken by his story that we drove there and saw some of the photos for ourselves. We saw file after file—some of them out of focus, some at odd angles, but most

offering warm glimpses of fresh love. A number of them portrayed their subjects and their mood so memorably that the Central Goldfields Regional Art Gallery placed them on exhibit—in tribute to Maryborough, to Wal, and to the promise of married love.[1]

What does it say about weddings, and human nature, that this man in his utter loneliness would create and keep, as a sort of life's work, these artistic impressions of the way love gives birth to commitment? Time after time he came to weddings in all seasons, wanting somehow to "hold still" what he couldn't have and hold for himself. He found vicariously—in weddings— a sense of purpose and promise in his own life. For Wal Richards, as for all the rest of us, a wedding can be the sweetest of times—a day for dreams to come true. And wedding pictures do seem to capture glimpses of the dream.

Yet not all marriages turn out as well as the wedding pictures do. More and more, it seems, our neighborhoods and our extended families are full of people whose own dreams of family love fall short of their promise. Some of those dreams—too many, these days—end up torn and even battered, as in Fantine's mournful song from *Les Misérables:*

> *I dreamed a dream in days gone by when hope was*
> *high and life worth living.*
> *I dreamed that love would never die.*
> . . . .
> *But the tigers come at night with their voices soft as*
> *thunder,*
> *As they tear your hope apart, as they turn your*
> *dream to shame.*[2]

When the tigers do come at night, threatening our dream that love will never die, we instinctively reach for the gospel's perspective and teachings about marriage. Without that perspective, our frustration can lead us into the dark abyss of cynicism, not only about marriage but about life.

The gospel of Jesus Christ teaches us that our existence is like a three-act play and that mortality all occurs in the second act. Act one was the premortal life, where we lived as the spirit children of our Heavenly Father, preparing for our act two adventure. In act three, we may return to our Father's presence, depending on what happens in act two.

We marry, raise our children, and live our lives in act two. If we don't know about, or we lose contact with, act one and act three, our act two experiences can sometimes seem hopelessly hard. When we can't see with eternity's perspective on time, we are vulnerable to the pessimist's assumption that "life is no more

than a night in a second-class hotel"—and it can be a sleepless
night.[3]

Yet in the gospel's good news, those wedding photos really do
contain a taste of eternity, because they somehow "capture" and
keep alive the joy and vision of the wedding day. Making sure that
this joy both endures and expands is a cause worth fighting for, as
the complete vision of three full acts gives us power to hold on, to
keep giving and growing in married love. That big picture helps
us make sense of those mortal days when few things seem to make
sense. It pours meaning from both yesterday and tomorrow into
the hardest possible parts of today.

We can learn about the power of such a vision by looking at
other images that hold in place our moments most worth remembering, the way Wal Richards's wedding photographs do.
Glimpses like these can crop up in many places in the lives of
Latter-day Saints. In a typical cross-section of such lifespans, I
came across these spiritually photogenic images as I listened to
conversations among the members of an LDS ward I visited one
weekend.

A faithful and exhausted sister missionary travels twenty-four
hours from Eastern Europe to arrive home, having learned a language she once thought impossible, having fallen fully in love with
and having taught an oppressed people she at first couldn't understand. Imagine seeing her parents, her little sisters, and her brother
welcome her at the airport.

After four years of patient and childless waiting, two young
parents hold their newborn child. Imagine seeing them, their parents, and their brothers and sisters, all together in the hospital
room, beaming as the new baby cries.

After wandering for six years, the last of five children comes
to himself (see Luke 15:17) and is finally married in the temple.

Imagine seeing him and his wife in the temple with his parents and all of his married brothers and sisters.

An older man who years before made some mistakes that cost him his family, his priesthood, his temple blessings, and his self-confidence now remarries. His new wife, who has always longed for but never experienced having a priesthood holder living in her home, encourages him along each step toward rebaptism. Imagine being in their home the night his priesthood and temple blessings are restored, and his first official priesthood act is to give his wife a blessing. Weeping, his wife exclaims, "The priesthood is in my home! The priesthood is in my home!"

I listened as the ward members shared and discussed such joyful moments from their own lives, moments in which wedding days hold an honored place. One of them asked, "What is it about these experiences that makes them such treasures?" Some of them are full of exuberance, as when King David was so happy about reclaiming the ark of the covenant that he "danced before the Lord" (2 Samuel 6:14). Others are thoughtful, reverent times, such as crying quietly alone from the sheer comfort of being wrapped in the peace of the temple after a long absence.

How is it that these moments have the power to "make your heart swell so much it runs out your eyes and down your cheeks," as one sister said. These are *celebrations of meaning*—meaning found in the joy of human love. The joy we feel is from tapping into the deep roots of spiritual promise in our doctrine about that love.

One sister said, "These moments give us a taste of eternity, showing us what we can have—what waits for us." These are moments of power—staying power. Said another, "No matter what is coming (and often in these scenes we don't know what will happen next), this moment will always go with us and reassure us." Therefore, "cast not away . . . your confidence" (Hebrews 10:35).

Some of the joy is just from being together with the people we love most, as in a temple wedding party. Elder John Taylor called such times "a union of good feelings, good desires and aspirations" in a sense "of power, of faith, and of the Spirit of the Lord" in which the combination of many individual lights creates "a time of union, of light, of life, of intelligence, of the Spirit of the living God; our feelings are one, our faith is one, and . . . this oneness forms an array of power that no power on this side of earth or hell is able to . . . overcome."[4]

We must save these images, the group agreed, and write down our thoughts so we can preserve our clearest personal insights into our eternal nature and possibilities. As soon as they are over, these moments become the yesterdays that enfold our todays with purpose and give hope to our tomorrows—just like wedding pictures, which somehow do feel as if we've been granted a glimpse into a place of permanent light, where time will be no more and peace will never leave us.

How do the wedding pictures anchor our sometimes dreary act two lives in the larger perspective of act one and act three? They can touch eternal things, affirming them with the Spirit's own witness. Brigham Young said that when we "keep the Spirit of the Lord," we will feel "just as [if we] were again by our Father in Heaven before [we] came into the world."[5] To feel His presence now is to remember His presence then.

These are moments of such strong spiritual reality that they awaken within us the sure feeling of once more being at home, "with Him." They feel familiar and true because they stir our deepest longings and our oldest subliminal memories of our premortal life. In that core region of our hearts, no desire is greater than our longing one day to "be with" our Father and our eternal companions, families, and friends.

Brigham Young gave us this word picture about eternity's perspective on time: "He is the Father of our spirits; and if we could know, understand, and do His will, every soul would be prepared to return back into His presence. And when they get there, they would see that they had formerly lived there for ages, that they had previously been acquainted with every nook and corner, with the palaces, walks, and gardens; and they would embrace their Father, and He would embrace them and say, 'My son, my daughter, I have you again'; and the child would say, 'O my Father, my Father, I am here again.'"[6]

Mel and Helen left their Utah home for eighteen months to serve as temple missionaries in the Washington D.C. Temple. Their three-year-old granddaughter Ashley missed them terribly, having been very close to them in every sense before they left. For Christmas, they sent Ashley's family a picture showing Mel and Helen standing in front of the temple. When Ashley saw the picture, she pressed it against her cheek. Laughing, she called out, "Gamma! Gamma! I *have* you! I *have* you!"

Whether etched on paper or in our hearts, a wedding picture is a type and shadow of being able to say always, "I have you again. I am here again." Sensing that, Ashley could manage today because the picture showed her she would have Gamma tomorrow. That same assurance breathes life into the familiar and ancient male-female Love Story, the universal pattern that calls out to our very nature.

CHAPTER TWO

ADAM, EVE, AND THE GREAT LOVE STORY

If we don't move out of our comfort zone, said a friend, we won't grow. But if we don't grow, we won't find joy.

We may start off being married for comfort. But then problems come along. If we try seriously to solve them, we may not always be comfortable, but we will grow. Then we will end up being married not simply for comfort but for joy.

Joy is a higher, wiser form of existence than merely being comfortable. Elder Neal A. Maxwell said, "Pleasure takes the form of 'me' and 'now,' while real joy is 'us' and 'always.'"[1] Yet that kind of joy is not separate from trouble and pain, but is usually mixed with them, as if somehow it is not possible without them.

That's what Ammon and his companions found about being missionaries, as Ammon wrote of "their journeyings in the land of Nephi, their *sufferings* in the land, their *sorrows,* and their *afflictions,* and their *incomprehensible joy*" (Alma 28:8; italics added).

Paradoxically then, affliction can beget joy, as the story of Adam and Eve shows best. Our first parents chose to leave the comfort zone of Eden so that they, and we, might "be": live an earth life with its discomforts, its hardships, and along the way, its incomprehensible joys. They, and we, become mortal so that, by learning and choosing well amid the hard lessons of the earth school, we can taste, then finally comprehend, a life of eternal joy (see 2 Nephi 2:25). As W. H. Auden wrote, "The innocent eye sees nothing."[2]

Adam and Eve's story sets the pattern for our own lives. Their experience is the primal story about how the great "plan of happiness" (Alma 42:16) actually works—and the story is about a married couple. This story has six archetypal elements:

- Living before mortal birth with our Mother and our Father, God of the Universe.
- Living on earth, accepting its risks and its pain, with the promise that those who keep growing will return Home.
- Making choices, learning, hopefully marrying and becoming parents ourselves.
- Contending against the opposition of an Enemy who keeps trying to destroy God's plan and our happiness.
- Overcoming the Enemy through a Redeemer whose sacrifice, together with our efforts, allows us to go home.
- Returning home, mature and married, there to remain with our eternal Parents and to be *like* them, like God.

This pattern is how we attain our personal exaltation. Note the central place here of *marriage* between a man and a woman. God's plan consciously speaks to our deepest human instincts about permanent male-female love in the core meaning of joy.

The plan of happiness, then, deliberately includes the universal Love Story, history's most familiar and most hoped-for story line: boy meets girl, they fall in love, and then together they face trials and conquer their opposition, until they prove worthy of an eternal love, ultimately inheriting the right to be where love lasts forever. But getting there is very hard work. And even when they give that process every particle of their strength, the story couldn't have a happy ending without Christ's part in it.

The Love Story plot takes an honored place in many variations of what literary critic Christopher Booker has described in his *Seven Basic Plots: Why We Tell Stories.* Booker says that seven main plots are recycled through all literary genres, from novels and plays to operas and movies: "1. Overcoming the Monster, 2. Rags to Riches, 3. The Quest, 4. Voyage and Return, 5. Rebirth, 6. Comedy and 7. Tragedy." Five of these plots "all have happy endings, all trace a hero's journey from immaturity to self-realization and all end with the restoration of order or the promise of renewal." "In a sense," writes a reviewer of Booker's work, "these plots all represent variations on Freud's family romance— the process whereby a young person comes to terms with parental authority, ventures out into the wider world, faces assorted tests and eventually achieves independence. Along the way, confusion is dispelled; alienation gives way to a new sense of wholeness and well-being," unless the plot is a tragedy, in which the character's own flaws thwart what could have been a positive conclusion.[3]

The doctrinal elements of the classic Love Story were known in the world of ancient Christianity. As with the rest of the temple's teachings, prophets taught these doctrines whenever the fulness of the gospel was on the earth. Then the Great Apostasy gradually changed key parts of the doctrine, and the full religious meaning of the Love Story, like other key truths, was lost. In the meantime, however, fragments of the story, and the doctrine, have often reappeared.

The doctrines in the Adam and Eve story, for example, arise from the primary truth that man is the child of, and made in the image of, God. Adam's Fall was essential to God's plan, giving His children the pattern we just saw. Children are born to become like their parents, and our Heavenly Parents are married, deified beings.

Writing about man's being in God's image, the modern German religious historian Ernst Benz "traces the notion of the identity of humans and gods from the earliest times to the present day." He observes that "the concept of apotheosis," or deification—the idea that man can become as God is—"was once a widely held idea in the ancient world until it was forced underground by the doctrines of Augustine [a very influential fifth-century Christian scholar who] seemed nearly obsessed with the evil nature of all mortals."[4]

Augustine taught that Adam's Fall was a terrible mistake that gave mankind an evil nature. He also believed that the fallen, evil earth was a burning house from which man must bend every effort to escape. These ideas also led Augustine to create the first monasteries and convents, so that people with the highest religious aspirations could flee marriage and the burning house for the refuge of a monastic life. No boy-meets-girl love story there, let alone living together afterward as eternal companions in God's presence.

In Benz's words, "The concept of the apotheosis of man . . . disappeared from church doctrine in the fifth and sixth centuries . . . but it always remained alive in the tradition of Christian mysticism." A few Europeans still "dared to speak about apotheosis" in later years. But Benz admiringly found "the idea of deification" in its most fully flowered form in the teachings of Joseph Smith, a "complete reinterpretation" of "the orthodox Christian view of God."[5]

The European thinkers who dared to write about man's capacity to become like God were by no means Christian theologians, because their ideas ran directly counter to gloomy Catholic and Protestant teachings about human nature. Rather, they expressed their convictions about a premortal life, eternal marriage, and deification not as religious teachers but as poets, musicians, and artists.

Brigham Young University professor Alan F. Keele has summarized some of these expressions in *In Search of the Supernal: Preexistence, Eternal Marriage, and Apotheosis in German Literary, Operatic, and Cinematic Texts.* These texts contain ancient ideas about marriage and godhood that had been rejected by Augustine (and, hence, by Christianity). Yet the ideas clearly echo, even if only in fragmentary form, the original Adam and Eve story. They reinforce and reflect certain elements of the great Love Story, beginning with a premortal existence, seeing mortality as a time to learn and grow, and then viewing our progression toward eternal marriage and godhood as the highest possibilities of human life.

One celebrated example is Mozart's 1791 opera, *The Magic Flute,* still widely performed today. This story and its music are inviting enough that Marie and I helped our grandchildren perform a simplified version of it recently for their parents. These little watchers of Harry Potter and Star Wars know all about stories with heroes, villains, hardships, and romantic love— archetypes of our own earthly adventure stories—so they participated eagerly.

As the story begins, a giant snake is chasing Prince Tamino. He is saved by three mysterious women who tell their queen about him. They lead Tamino to rescue the queen's daughter, Pamina, after showing him a picture of her that makes him want to be with her forever.

In clear symbols of the personal growth that comes from overcoming adversity, the priest Sarastro then requires Tamino and

Pamina to satisfy three tests in a "Temple of Trials" to prove their purity and worthiness to be married eternally. Their ordeals require them to overcome all evil forces that oppose them.[6] Tamino and Pamina ultimately qualify as "a married god-couple who exemplify the highest kind of love and self-sacrifice" in their struggle to attain the highest virtues. This leads them to "that part of the temple where they [are] bonded [eternally] as . . . god and goddess."[7]

In contrast, Tamino's comedy sidekick, Papageno, is decidedly not willing to struggle enough to attain a love of virtue. His highest aim is food, drink, and sleep, though he does wish for a pretty wife. Comfort, not joy, is Papageno's goal. The price of joy is too high. Therefore, one singer tells him, "You will never experience the heavenly joy of the consecrated ones."[8] Eventually, Papageno raises his sights enough to succeed.

The Magic Flute shows married love as a universal force through which "a man and a woman can . . . become the most noble entity in the universe, capable of . . . [together] attaining godhood." As the characters sing, "Love sweetens every misery, . . . there is nothing more noble than a wife and a husband [reaching] upward [to attain] godhood." Another line notes the power of married love to motivate repentance: "And if a person has fallen, / love leads him back to his duty."[9] Is it possible that the inborn desire for permanent male-female belonging is a key source of the desire and energy we need to change ourselves for the better?

A second example of the power of the Love Story is Richard Strauss's opera *The Woman Without a Shadow*. This story also shows the connections between the premortal life, mortal troubles in marriage, and the mysterious, eternal strength of human love. One German musicologist calls this "possibly the most beautiful and moving of all" operas, partly for the way its characters "invite us to become different people, to exercise . . . repentance."[10] And the characters do this through love and marriage.

Keikobad, a God-like figure, allows his daughter to associate with mortals, but because she is a being from the premortal world, her body casts no shadow. She falls in love with and marries an Emperor, but their marriage may last only a year unless she can somehow become mortal. Then she will cast a shadow and bear children. If she does not succeed, he will turn to stone, and she will return to Keikobad.

Keikobad sends a Lucifer-like Nurse to look after his daughter, the Empress. As the deadline approaches, the Nurse, who despises the clumsy stupidity of all humans, exerts all her force to persuade the Empress not to become mortal. Facing an Eve-like choice, the Empress finally chooses mortal love—but must still find a shadow from a mortal woman.

Both to seek a shadow and to show the Empress the misery of earthly marriage, the Nurse takes her to the home of Barak and his wife—a decent but ordinary couple. They love each other, but their marriage suffers from typical mortal limitations—the intrusive presence of extended family members, the couple's painful inability to have children, the frustration of dealing with their own weaknesses, and their poignant efforts to behave better toward each other.

After one marital argument, Barak's house splits symbolically apart, as his Wife collapses into deep remorse, pleading with Barak for forgiveness. Seeing all of this, the Empress is unwilling to accept the Wife's shadow, which the Nurse has bargained to obtain, preferring to let the Wife learn from her error to make mortal progress.

In the final act, Barak and his wife are separated by a wall. She has heard the voices of her unborn children singing to her:

"Mother, Mother, let us come home! The door is bolted, we can't find the way in!"[11] Now she begs Barak's forgiveness even as he, unable to hear her, also sings her a longing apology.

The Nurse hopes that the mortal misery of Barak and his wife will persuade the Empress to return to the pain-free cocoon of her premortal comfort. But as she watches Barak and his Wife long for one another, the Empress sends the Nurse away, singing: "What humans require, you know too little. . . . At what cost they pay for everything, renewing themselves out of grievous guilt, like the phoenix, perpetually raising themselves up from eternal death to eternal life—they themselves hardly intuit it. . . . I belong to them."[12] The Empress has understood how married love, despite its inevitable discomforts, can draw man and wife to learn from hard experience enough to grow, and grow enough to find joy, together.

But because the Empress still has no shadow, the Emperor now turns to stone. She runs to him, feeling responsible for his fate. She needs only to say "I will" to take the Wife's shadow, but she refuses to take away Barak's Wife's mortality. In agony she cries, "I will—not." As she rises to return to Keikobad, miraculously her body casts a shadow. The Emperor rises from the stone. Soon their unborn children sing from above, thanking their future earthly parents for being willing to "strive and suffer, grapple and bear" enough that the children's "day of life" may yet "gloriously dawn."[13]

Premortal children did not first sing about their turn on earth only in the LDS production *Saturday's Warrior.*

Meanwhile, still separated from his Wife, Barak sings to her, "I'll find you . . . my eternal companion!" As she then sees him, her shadow bridges the abyss between them. They run to each other and embrace on the shadow-built bridge, the symbol of the

frail mortality that is also their promise. "Your shadow," sings
Barak, rejoicing, "it bears me to you."[14]

This story, like the archetypal Adamic Love Story, is not about
living happily ever after, if that just means being comfortable.
Rather, through the mixture of bitter and sweet experience, each
couple learns that their love is a source of power that helps them
change, grow, and become better. Something unique to married
love gives us motivation and strength, as our urge to lift the person we love helps us to face conflict and to overcome our own
weaknesses.

I see that instinct on the faces of Adam and Eve when I picture them leaving the Garden of Eden to enter an uncharted
world of misery mixed with joy. I see them stopping just outside
Eden, looking sadly back at the Garden, then peering anxiously
ahead to the unknown, and finally glancing at each other with
new, shared resolve. They can't know what awaits them. All they
know is that, whatever it is, if they can face it together, they can
face it.

As we consider the entire archetypal pattern, we may wonder
what marriage is doing in this grand doctrinal sequence. Why
couldn't our eternal progression be simply a matter of individual
process, with marriage playing some subordinate, even optional,
role? Today's world thinks so much in individualistic terms that a
strictly personal journey may seem to make more sense, even if we
need occasional help along the way. Besides, not everyone has a
realistic opportunity to marry during mortality.

Yet marriage can mysteriously empower personal growth and
fulness, so much so that the adversary helped hide marriage from
priests, monks, and nuns during the darkness of the early
Christian apostasy.

Some reasons for this power are more obvious than others. At the level of common sense, marriage fills the obvious need to pro-vide stable homes and lineages for the children who come to earth. Moreoever, by having children, we learn something of how our Father in Heaven feels about us, His children—no small discovery.

Further, the power of permanent male-female love is one of the strongest forces in humankind's experience. That force led the woman without a shadow to accept mortal marriage despite com-pelling evidence of its risks and miseries. The same force moved Barak and his wife to "renew themselves out of grievous guilt," growing, reaching, striving to live better. And the power of their married love depended not on easy resolutions, but on their con-stant striving, together, on the upward climb. "And if a person has fallen, love leads him back to his duty."[15]

In most modern discussions about love, we don't know quite where to put this classical power of marriage. Partly we struggle because the very idea of married love has seemed to become more trite and even hypocritical, as that love now so frequently fades into bitter disputes, collapses into hateful abuse, and may seem to endure only through pretense. But those unhappy realities are not inevitable, and they do not diminish love's inexplicable capacity to produce and sustain the deepest human drive to improve. Authentic married love, rare as that may seem today, still holds its ancient power of mutual sacrifice and striving, until "I lift thee, and thou lift me, and both ascend together."[16]

The Greeks knew three kinds of love—agape (the charitable, selfless love that motivates service to others), eros (the erotic feel-ings that can now seem independent of real relationships), and filia (the brotherly love of the sort known among kindly brothers and sisters).

Where does married love fit in this framework? The exquisite power of romantic love that we see in the historic love stories now often blurs into a cheap form of eros, having been severed from the context of permanent relationships and turned into a self-centered erotic commodity that can attach itself to a relationship of any duration or kind.

Still, the ancient meaning of married love is more than filia or agape, just as it is more than eros, if eros simply means erotic. Augustine didn't understand that. For him in his monastery, any romantic urge felt like an enemy of agape. Yet there is some kind of paradox, something about finding ourselves by losing ourselves, in the way genuine married love (like agape at its best) demands everything of us—even as (like eros at its best) it simultaneously brings us fulfillment. And somehow this combination nurtures the growth of a divine essence within us.

As part of the doctrine of apotheosis, married love also teaches us about becoming more Godlike by asking us to do Godlike things for those to whom we have committed our lives. Marriage asks us to be Good Shepherds for the sheep of our home, not leaving them when wolves and tigers come. It asks us to share the afflictions of those we love most dearly. When we respond to those invitations, we are doing something Christlike. And in that sense, our service to spouses and children teaches us by repetitive practice how to develop a more Christian—Godlike—character.

Christ Himself blesses that growth process with His atoning power. For example, the Empress finally saw her shadow because the sun shone on her. Without enough Light shining upon us, we mortals would cast no shadows. Sustained by that Light, our shadow can build a bridge between separated lovers or help us cross the shadowed valley in which one brings forth children.

The plot of the great Love Story is, then, an essential part of

the larger plot by which God's children may return to His presence and be like Him.

Today, however, despite the ancient pedigree of these ideas
and despite how the universal Love Story rings true even to a
child, we live in a world that is losing its way about all of these
connections. Today's culture does not really see the timeless point
of the wedding photos, for it is losing the plot of the Love Story
behind those hope-filled pictures.

CHAPTER THREE

NOW PEOPLE ARE
CONFUSED

Modern culture has, to use an expression common in Australia, "lost the plot" about marriage—the great Love Story. As our Primary children sing, "Now we have a world where people are confused. / If you don't believe it, go and watch the news."[1]

In November 2003, for example, the Supreme Court of Massachusetts bolted from all American precedents by upholding for the first time in history a state constitutional right to same-gender marriage. On 12 February 2004, in the turbulent wake of that decision, the Massachusetts legislature "adjourned in exhaustion after struggling for two days," unable to answer "a seemingly simple question: What is marriage?"[2] That same day, TV news cameras whirred as the city of San Francisco allowed scores of illegal, same-gender marriages in a bizarre protest against California law for not permitting what the Massachusetts court did. These simultaneous events "on both coasts demonstrated that marriage is in chaos."[3]

Later that same week, the *International Herald Tribune* ran a

front-page story on a trend among European couples who prefer
"marry me, a little"—a new concept of "marriage lite" that creates
a few contractual rights between live-in partners but without the
wedding bands or long-term commitments of legal marriage. This
"pragmatic approach" reflects "changing attitudes about the role—
and even the relevance—of marriage in contemporary life."[4] The
news that 82 percent of first children in Norway (and a similar
proportion in Sweden and Denmark) are now born out of wedlock also casts doubt on the relevance of marriage in Europe.[5]

A few months earlier, in a prime-time "reality show," ABC
Television paid $1 million to a former Miami Heat dancer if she
would marry one of twenty-four eager suitors—all of them total
strangers. She picked one, quickly but legally married him, and
they began living together—all before a national TV audience,
complete with a subsequent interview on *Good Morning, America.*

Soon afterward, pop celebrity Britney Spears spontaneously
married an old high school friend in Las Vegas—for fifty-five
hours. Tabloid publications paid $100,000 for photos of the wed-
ding. When asked why she married him, Britney said, "Just for
the hell of it." After the marriage was annulled, however, she told
MTV, "I do believe in the sanctity of marriage. I totally do."[6]

Just after the latter two events, though the timing was purely
coincidental, President George W. Bush proposed a $1.5 billion
federal program to promote healthy marriages, because he believes
the whole idea of marriage is in trouble today and he wants to
protect it as "one of the most fundamental, enduring institutions
of our civilization." A *New York Times* writer said of these events
and of the president's language:"But what civilization, exactly, is
he talking about? Since 1970, the percentage of American . . .
households containing married couples with kids [dropped] from
45 to 26 [percent]. . . . It says a lot about how out of touch Bush

[is] with this culture that he repeated [Britney] Spears's 'sanctity of marriage' language in the [2004] State of the Union only days after she had made the phrase a national joke. . . . .

" . . . It could be harder to restore the sanctity of marriage than to find weapons of mass destruction in Iraq."[7]

These bits of contemporary news are tiny tips of a very large iceberg. Since 1960, the divorce rate in the United States has more than doubled, though it has dipped slightly in the last few years. About half of today's marriages will likely end in divorce.[8] One in three American babies is now born out of wedlock—a thirteen-fold increase in nonmarital births since 1950.[9] These figures would be still higher if they reflected the breakups that take place among live-in unmarried couples, and the number of those couples in the United States has increased 760 percent since 1960.[10]

Giving historical perspective to these changes, Mary Ann Glendon, a Harvard legal scholar, believes Western society is now living through a "transformation of family law" so huge that it is the most fundamental shift in five hundred years in laws and attitudes about the family.[11] Historian Francis Fukuyama believes today's massive family disintegration is part of "the Great Disruption," a wave of history as big as the shift from the age of agriculture to the Industrial Revolution two hundred years ago.[12]

History means more when it becomes personal. I feel a more poignant pain about today's changing attitudes toward marriage when I know the people whose hearts are breaking in broken homes—my friends, my neighbors, their children.

I recall a visit with a capable woman whose family life was crumbling around her. She counted several people in her Utah neighborhood who were also dealing with marriage breakdowns. She cried as she shook her head and asked, "What is happening to us?"

In a BYU Education Week class a few years ago, we read in Malachi 4 and in Doctrine and Covenants 2 about the earth being "cursed" and "utterly wasted" at the Lord's coming, unless parents and children turn their hearts to one another. As we talked about the turmoil in modern family life, I asked the class members, all of them active Latter-day Saints, to think of the people they knew who had seriously troubled families. On an impulse, I asked how many of them thought we might already be living in the time of the curse these scriptures spoke of. I wasn't prepared for what I saw—heads nodding all over the room. I too asked myself, "What is happening to us?"

We Latter-day Saints seek prayerfully to avoid being "of the world." But we unavoidably live "in the world." And we live in a world that is fast losing its confidence that people can make marriage and parenting work successfully. That kind of cultural environment can't help but influence our own family lives.

If recent trends continue, LDS researchers project that about one-third of today's Latter-day Saint marriages in the United States will end in divorce. Temple marriages are generally far more stable than other marriages. LDS marriages outside the temple are "five times more likely to end in divorce than are temple marriages," partly because those who marry in the temple are more committed to the personal standards required for a temple recommend.[13]

The modern chaos does affect the way Church members think about their family life. One young returned missionary recently told his stake president that he had seen so much family dysfunction that he couldn't possibly get married unless someone would guarantee that his marriage and family life wouldn't fail.

An LDS mother of several children was expecting a new baby. Her Church assignment put her in close touch with a group of young single adult women. One by one, nearly all of these women found a private moment to ask the mother how she honestly felt about having another child. In a spirit of deep womanly trust, many of them told her their fears about being married, feeling bound to husbands, and taking on the burdens of motherhood. She was surprised to hear such questions from the lips of mature, active, honest Church members.

In response, she privately invited each young woman to do what she previously had allowed only her husband and children to do. She tenderly placed one of their hands on her abdomen and let them feel the baby's movements. Then, placing her hand on theirs, she taught them that despite the relentless demands of family life, marriage and children really were the source of her greatest happiness. The young women welcomed—they hungered for—her affirmation and mentoring. But many of those who lack such mentors today, in and out of the Church, remain disoriented about the most basic relationships in their lives: being married and having children.

At the same time, many people I have met in recent years have shown me the power of a covenant marriage that is grounded deeply in the doctrines of the gospel. Coming to know these people and their circumstances feels like a gift, because their experiences show me by real-life, personal examples how to restore permanent meaning to a marriage that needs it.

For example, I first met Meg, a Relief Society president, several years ago at a stake fireside where my wife, Marie, and I had been asked to share some thoughts about marriage. She was a woman of clear intelligence and unusual spiritual depth.

Two years later I saw Meg at another Church function. She surprised me by saying that on the night of that earlier fireside, she had just about decided to file for a divorce from her husband.

A few weeks before, he had been excommunicated for moral transgression, shattering her confidence in him, in their marriage, and in herself. She was wrenched by feelings of betrayal and failure. Both her common sense and her friends told her she didn't have to, and shouldn't, put up with the trauma his shame caused her family. The obvious answer was to leave him, take their children, and get on with her life.

But as she prayed and wept her way through a decision, she kept reading and thinking about Christ's teachings in the Gospel of John—a comparison between "hirelings" who flee when the wolf comes and "shepherds" who, like the Good Shepherd, do not flee (see John 10:10–15). She was feeling the hot breath of the wolves of adversity and disillusionment. The assumptions of the modern culture told Meg to flee. But an infusion of spiritual courage, her husband's desire to repent, and her commitment to the doctrinal foundation of covenant marriage gave her the strength to stay, to help him, and to keep their family together.

As we talked in that second visit, Meg did not minimize how hard it had been to stay with him, nor did she feel everyone should always do what she had. She had simply willed herself to keep trying, until gradually the doctrine of forgiveness and the power of the Atonement seeped like fresh spring water into the crevices of her heart. Like Eve, she had learned about the joy of her (and her husband's) redemption. She discovered a newer, deeper understanding of the way God will give eternal life to those who will learn from their experience (see Moses 5:11). Both he and she had grown in ways that surprised her. She hadn't known that the gospel of repentance and sacrifice had such practical power to heal and change. Incredibly, she said, the last six months had been the happiest of her life.

Meg's sense of her covenant marriage invited her to sacrifice beyond what many people would do. The Lord's words describe her:

"All among them who know their hearts are honest, and are broken, and their spirits contrite, and are willing to observe their covenants by sacrifice—yea, every sacrifice which I, the Lord, shall command—they are accepted of me. For I, the Lord, will cause them to bring forth as a very fruitful tree which is planted in a goodly land, by a pure stream, that yieldeth much precious fruit" (D&C 97:8–9).

Her heart had been broken, and her spirit was contrite. Then her choice to observe her covenants by sacrifice produced lasting fruit.

Meg's case illustrates a central theme of what marriage can mean: finding the strength and patience to sacrifice for our covenants blesses us, our families, and society—not just because it's good to endure challenges and misery but because loyalty to those covenants *helps us to grow,* both emotionally and spiritually. When we keep our "covenant with him [Christ]," he will "pour out his Spirit more abundantly upon [us]" (Mosiah 18:10). That is the "fruit" produced by observing our covenants *by sacrifice.*

One time, in an outburst of exasperation about one of our children, the ten-year-old with the freckles and the unruly hair, I said to Marie, "The Lord put Adam and Eve on the earth as full-grown people. Why couldn't he have done that with this child?"

In a flash of intuitive insight, Marie replied, *"The Lord gave us that child to make Christians out of us."*

Loyalty to our husbands and wives—as well as to our children—can help make Christians of us, because trying honestly to be true to those who mean the most, and ask the most, will stretch us into real growth. Marriage and family life are among

God's chief institutions for perfecting us, often through painful, incredibly demanding experience. No wonder we cannot be exalted without being married, because marriage is such a potent laboratory for helping us develop Christian character.

CHAPTER FOUR

HOW WE LOST THE PLOT

I have watched the universal marriage plot unravel over the last thirty years, as our society has experienced what some observers now call the "collapse of marriage." Writer Maggie Gallagher believes this pattern is "destroying American society" by creating fatherless homes and increasing single-parent families and births outside wedlock. These conditions all damage children's health, their psychological development, their social behavior, and their personal happiness. The ripple effects from so much personal harm then devastate the entire society. And yet, she notes, "we have refused to act, taking . . . bizarre comfort in the [new] belief that . . . marriage is ultimately a private matter, and therefore we can do nothing as a society to prevent its collapse."[1]

How did it come to this, that most people now see marriage—once widely perceived as the core structure of society—as "ultimately a private matter" that, being private, may now be beyond society's ability to repair? Looking back, we can now see that changes in United States divorce laws and attitudes about marriage in the 1960s and 70s were really part of a much larger historical change that moved many Americans to care more about their self-interest than about the interest of their families and communities.

Some of those changes will be explored a bit further in Part III, but consider here a few headlines about five trends that have contributed to the confusion that almost unconsciously perplexes us today about modern marriage attitudes—individual rights, no-fault divorce, same-gender marriage, the interest of others in our marriages, and optimism and pessimism as defining attitudes.

INDIVIDUAL RIGHTS AND THE "LIBERATION" MOVEMENTS

The individual rights causes that date back to the 1960s began with a compelling need to eliminate racial discrimination, which had become a shameful blot on the nation's conscience. This original civil rights movement was followed by an important women's rights movement that eliminated much unfair gender-based discrimination. But before long, some extremist critics went far beyond these much-needed movements, using "rights" language to challenge many laws and customs that had long supported traditional family relationships.

For example, a noted advocate of individual rights said in 1978 that he feared any kind of "domination" by one person over another. So he argued that American law should liberate "the child—and the adult—from the shackles of . . . family" commitments. In that way, "individual rights" attitudes began to challenge one spouse's right to keep a marriage together and parents' right to raise children as they thought best, claiming that traditional family ties interfered with the individual's right to be "free" from the demands or needs of other people, even in the family.[2] To these advocates, the right to be free was simply more important than the right to be together, because being expected to stay together seemed to them like bondage.

One illustration of how individual rights ideas influenced traditional family law was the famous 1973 abortion case, *Roe v. Wade*.[3] There the Supreme Court removed the historic right of state legislatures to say when a woman could choose an elective abortion. *Roe* gave that choice to individual women, rejecting long-held beliefs in our culture about the rights of the unborn child and society's right to define when life begins.

Building on such individualistic theories, some advocates of extremist radical feminism have more recently attacked the very concept of marriage, insisting that traditional ideas confine mothers and other women to stereotypes of subordination and oppression (see chapter 18).

Some court and legislative decisions also began to give individual rights priority over traditionally structured families. These included cases granting parental rights to unwed fathers, or giving child custody and adoption rights to people who lived in unmarried cohabitation or homosexual relationships. These decisions helped develop the legal theories that would one day support the more extreme idea of gay marriage.

Until the 1970s and 80s, American courts would never have awarded child custody to parents living in such "alternative lifestyles," unless the circumstances allowed no reasonable option. Nearly all of our judges and legislators had long believed that such custody awards were contrary to children's interests—verified by "several decades of social science evidence which strongly indicates that children do best when raised by a mother and a father."[4] That's why children born out of wedlock were considered "illegitimate," and social agencies tried to place them in two-parent homes. But as a more permissive cultural climate accelerated the momentum of ever-expanding personal rights, more and more judges allowed claims of adult personal liberty to trump children's interests.

When the liberation movements first started, I wondered if a children's rights movement would follow the civil rights and women's movements. Children had long enjoyed such "rights" as being entitled to a public education, parental protection, and protection against abuse. But soon the "kiddie libbers" began to urge children's liberation from any kind of "discrimination" based only on their age—even if that discrimination was designed for children's own (or society's) protection, like age limits for driving a car, drinking alcohol, or voting.

For example, I recall explaining in 1972 to our politically alert seven-year-old son that he was too young to vote in the upcoming national election between Nixon and McGovern. He was quite indignant, pointing out, "Hey, I know a lot more about the issues than Grandma and Grandpa do!" He did feel discriminated against—though he has since changed his view about when young people should be old enough to vote.

Since those days, American laws about "liberating children" have changed only somewhat, but many adults still came to favor "leaving children alone," often to the point of abandoning children to their "rights" to make their own lifestyle choices—everything from writing obscenities in the school newspaper to being sexually active. In 1989 the United Nations adopted a new Convention on the Rights of the Child, which the United States Senate still has not ratified, although most other nations have now accepted it. According to a UN document, this charter was designed "to protect children from the power of parents" and other adults in children's decision-making about their own lives.[5]

In a summary of how individualistic attitudes have changed American family law, professor Janet Dolgin says our society has now moved from an "outdated" world in which attitudes about women and children were "founded in a hierarchical ideology" to "an egalitarian ideology that presumes the autonomy of the individual in a world of contract."[6] Our laws thus increasingly recognizes a "right to be let alone," even in a family. We will see more about this "world of contract" when we compare legalistic "contractual" attitudes toward marriage with more spiritually based "covenant" attitudes (see chapter 7).

Professor Dolgin realizes that her new vision of family life leaves spouses and children "without a sense of ultimate responsibility within, and toward, any social group."[7] She also senses that the new spirit of individual freedom is unable to "anchor people in a social order that encourages responsible connection."[8] But in the world she describes, the priority of personal liberty remains, eroding our interdependence within families and leaving people unsure whether the natural bonds between spouses, parents, and children are valuable ties that bind or are sheer bondage.

No-Fault Divorce

I graduated from law school just before California passed the nation's first no-fault divorce law in 1968. That law tried to ease the pain of divorce, partly by creating new legal standards and partly by making divorce seem more acceptable. Then, like a fire raging out of control, this movement swept the country until it became easier to end a marriage in America than in any other nation—and the United States still has the world's highest divorce rate.[9] The wind that fanned that social prairie fire was individual rights theory.

Prior to 1968, someone who wanted a divorce had to prove

in court that his or her spouse had engaged in real misconduct, such as abandoning the family, adultery, or aggravated mental cruelty. It wasn't enough just to show that both spouses wanted to end the marriage, *because marriage was not understood as simply a private agreement between two people.* Rather, people saw marriage as a *social institution* that played the crucial role of rearing children and teaching all family members to obey unenforceable but vital moral and social obligations. When a truly "broken home" fell apart, society picked up the pieces and covered the costs. Theoretically, only a judge, who represented society's—and children's—interests, could determine if a troubled marriage met the standards for divorce.

These traditional divorce laws created strong incentives for couples to stay together and work out their problems; however, the old laws did have limits. Some people felt hopelessly stuck in miserable marriages, which aroused public sympathy, especially when no young children were involved. Women caught in messy divorces were often disadvantaged by economic inequalities that left them dependent on their former husbands for financial support. Many divorcing couples fabricated claims of abandonment and adultery to satisfy strict legal standards. The search for "fault" also increased the bitterness in already bitter disputes.

Some family law scholars thought this untidy situation wasn't so bad, because the old divorce laws were written strictly enough to keep the conservatives happy and enforced flexibly enough to keep the liberals happy. Nonetheless, California's 1968 no-fault law tried to remedy the problems by removing any requirement to prove misconduct on the part of either spouse. It also added a new, no-fault basis for divorce—irretrievable breakdown of the marriage, regardless of who or what caused it.

In theory, family court judges still represented society's interests in deciding whether a marriage was, in fact, shattered beyond repair. The new law never intended to let spouses end their relationship simply as a matter of personal choice. And it certainly never intended that one party alone could just announce a marital breakdown and walk away. In practice, however, no-fault judges soon found themselves simply unable or unwilling to impose their judgment about "marriage breakdown" against the will of the partners—or, eventually, even one partner—who had decided he or she wanted to get out of the marriage.

No-fault reform ultimately took on a life of its own. Blending in with the anti-authority mood of the 1960s, the movement gradually altered how society viewed the very nature of marriage. No-fault divorce was the first family law that no longer "looked at marriage . . . as an institution" that held parents and children together. Rather, the reformers came to view marriage as "an essentially private relationship between adults terminable at the will of either"[10] and with no one feeling much responsibility for the way a "termination" would affect other people, especially children.

This interpretation led to a fundamental change in attitude, sending married people the signal that, because their marriage was not society's business, no one had a right to *expect the marriage partners to keep striving* when their marriage ran into turbulence. It wasn't long, then, until judges' doubts about society's right to enforce wedding vows gave some couples the false impression that those promises held no great social or moral value.

Same-Gender Marriage

In July 2003, the United States Supreme Court overturned a Texas law that made it a crime for unmarried homosexual people to have sexual relations.[11] Five months later the Massachusetts Supreme Court, in a 4–3 vote, cited that precedent in concluding that the state could not constitutionally deny gay and lesbian couples the right to marry.[12] As recently as fifteen years earlier, no American court or legislature—in fact, no country in the world—had *ever* been willing to take same-gender marriage so seriously.

With visible support from the Church in the early 1990s, the citizens of Hawaii, Alaska, and California all adopted public initiatives that explicitly opposed same-gender marriages. Eleven other states joined this list in November 2004. The legislatures of more than thirty other states have enacted similar legislation. Still, a few European countries and the state of Vermont have recently authorized same-gender "domestic partnerships" that confer many legal benefits of marriage. By 2005 only Belgium, the Netherlands and Spain allowed gay "marriage," but a similar proposal was pending in Canada.

The current American tensions over same-gender marriage may not be resolved without amending the United States Constitution. On July 7, 2004, the First Presidency issued a statement that "The Church of Jesus Christ of Latter-day Saints favors a constitutional amendment preserving marriage as the lawful union of a man and a woman."

The dramatic 2003 cases were but the latest steps in an evolution in judicial reasoning that had long been gaining momentum. As described further in chapter 24, the radical "personal autonomy" theory behind the gay marriage case logically extends the same individualistic legal concept that created no-fault divorce in the 1960s. When the law upholds the individual's right to *end* a marriage, regardless of social consequences (as happened with no-fault divorce), that principle can also seem to uphold the individual's right to *start* a marriage, regardless of social consequences (as with same-gender marriage). That is how today's national debate on gay marriage is conceptually linked to no-fault divorce.

These ideas have clear implications for traditional marriage. When one believes that starting or ending a marriage is just a personal choice, one is less likely to think of one's own marriage as a serious social or moral obligation. Without even realizing why they assume and expect what they do, some people therefore feel less committed to making their marriages work and more willing to walk away when they're not getting what they want.

Same-gender marriage also alters society's judgment about preserving the best home environment for raising children. Once a couple of the same gender is entitled to a legal marriage, a family court would have more difficulty denying them the right to raise children. Until now, we collectively believed that, whenever possible, children should be raised by both a father and mother. As recently as 2004, for example, a twelve-judge federal appeals court upheld the constitutionality of a 1977 Florida law that forbids homosexual parents from adopting a child. The law was based on the state legislature's finding that children are better off in homes that have a mother and father.[13]

This pattern made allowance for such obvious exceptions as the death of a parent or a divorce. But until recent years, our experienced-based beliefs about the best interests of children would never have allowed a single person to adopt a child, much less simply make a trip to a sperm bank. Swept along by the currents of individual liberation, however, many judges are now simply unwilling to make judgments about the best moral and developmental home atmosphere for children.

THE INTERESTS OF OTHERS IN OUR MARRIAGE

The changes in recent decades have portrayed marriage as an individual adult choice, rather than as a crucial knot in the very fabric that holds society together. We have increasingly lost sight of how much every marriage, and every divorce, affects other people—especially children.

American writer Wendell Berry once described why relatives and friends come so gladly to wedding receptions. These happy gatherings have the feel of a community event—because that's what they are: *"Marriage [is] not just a bond between two people but a bond between those two people and their forebears, their children, and their neighbors."* Therefore, Berry continues: "Lovers must not . . . live for themselves alone. . . . They say their vows to the community as much as to one another, and the community gathers around them to hear and to wish them well, on their behalf and on its own. It gathers around them because it understands how necessary, how joyful, and how fearful this joining is. These lovers . . . are giving themselves away, and they are joined by this as no law or contract could ever join them. Lovers, then, 'die' into their union with one another as a soul 'dies' into its union with God. . . . If the community cannot protect this giving, it can protect nothing. . . . It is the fundamental connection without which nothing holds, and trust is its necessity."[14]

Picture the community silently saying to the new couple, "We need your marriage to succeed—for our sake!" And picture the new couple silently saying to the community, "We need your support to help us succeed—for our sake!"

Most people in the past understood Berry's insight enough to know that shattered families would damage children and parents and thus destabilize society. That's why G. K. Chesterton once remarked that we should "regard a system that produces many divorces as we do a system that drives men to drown or shoot themselves."[15]

The need to protect children from this kind of harm was traditionally the basis for the idea that marriage is a social institution, not just a private partnership—because *marriage brings into being an organization to serve interests beyond those of [the husband and wife],"* such as those of "the children of that marriage, the extended family," and society at large. "Marriage is the principal institution for raising children. . . . If it is undermined, children will suffer and are suffering. In the end, society and the state will be afflicted and are being afflicted."[16]

When divorce and illegitimacy rates began climbing in the 1970s, scholars argued about whether these trends would harm children. In more recent years, a flood of evidence has demonstrated the psychic and social harm of severe family disruption (see chapter 21). Primarily because of these findings, in 2000 a diverse group of leaders and scholars created a new, grass-roots "marriage movement."[17] President Bush's 2003 initiative to strengthen marriage drew directly from this movement. Partly through their efforts, partly because of an increased age at first marriage,[18] and partly because many of today's "children of divorce" want a different life for their children from the life their parents gave them, today's divorce rate has declined slightly from its historic high a decade ago.[19] Even so, the current United States divorce rate would have been dismissed as impossible had it been predicted during the mid-1960s when Marie and I were married.

As the children of the divorce culture now look at their own marriage prospects, the family trauma many of them personally endured has shaken their confidence in traditional family assumptions. This "relationship revolution" has changed "the whole language and concept of marriage. Where 1950s couples spoke of sacrifice, loyalty, unconditional love and hard work in marriage, those values have [now] become unfashionable." Today's unmarried live-in couples are "here for a good time, not for a long time." Yet, as psychologist Hugh McKay put it, this anti-marriage revolution destroys the motivation to "hang on and work it out." If marriage seems "too easy, and easy to get out of, maybe you never break through to a rock solid commitment."[20]

Optimism and Pessimism as Defining Attitudes

Ironically, many of today's undercommitted American couples still dream of "a big wedding," symbolizing their longing for the certainty of permanent ties. Some families risk bankruptcy just to throw a massive wedding party, and many of these weddings are second and third marriages. Said one news story, "here comes the bride—again and again."[21]

This reference to big weddings and a longing for permanence introduces an odd paradox about today's confusion: Just when their families have never seemed less lovable, many people today hunger for *eternal* family love. The public resonates to movies and books that develop the theme that love can outlast death.

For example, in the 1999 movie *What Dreams May Come,* a character played by Robin Williams dies in an accident and then joyously finds his family in a dazzlingly colorful "heaven" but only after going through a very ugly "hell" to save his wife.

The concluding scene of the popular musical *Les Misérables* reinforces a similar hope. In a moving depiction of life and love after death, Fantine returns in a white dress from beyond the veil to welcome the dying Jean Val Jean to her heavenly presence.

Mitch Albiom's best-selling book *The Five People You Meet in Heaven* explores how death lets us find explanations for life's mysteries from the people whose lives most deeply touched us in mortality—including, above all, our families.

Others have also documented this modern hunger for a heaven where people live forever with those they love. For instance, two scholars writing a history about the idea of heaven in Western society found that most Americans today believe not only in a life after death but that family life should continue beyond the grave. This popular belief persists, they said, even though churches other than the LDS Church offer little insight about the subject.[22]

For Latter-day Saints, of course, the dream of an eternal family is a natural as breathing. A few years ago our six-year-old granddaughter was with her family as they drove by an LDS temple one evening. The temple grounds were beautifully lit, symbolically and actually chasing away the dark night. As the car stopped, she looked at the shining temple and said, "When I get bigger, and bigger, and bigger, and BIGGER . . . I'm going to get married in the temple." Her dream makes us all want to stretch to be big enough for blessings so large.

At first it could seem contradictory that people today would yearn to take their family ties to heaven when so many of their own families are in disarray. In his book *Habits of the Heart*, Robert Bellah reported that many Americans have shifted their view of marriage from that of a relatively permanent social institution to a temporary source of personal fulfillment. So when marriage commitments intrude on people's preferences and convenience, they tend to walk away. Yet, ironically and significantly, Bellah also found that most of the people he interviewed still cling, perhaps in a hopelessly dreamy sense, to the nostalgic notion of marriage based upon loving and *permanent* commitments as "the dominant American ideal."[23]

Perhaps this modern "longing to belong"[24] is not really *in spite of* today's widespread family decay but *because of* the decay. Sometimes we don't appreciate life's sweetest gifts until we no longer have them or we seriously fear losing them. Nobody really wants to be lonely, but the lifestyles associated with today's frenzied search for "individual freedom" often lead, unsurprisingly, to loneliness. And the search to transcend loneliness is a theme of modern life. Elder Neal A. Maxwell once said that the laughter of the world is just a lonely crowd trying to reassure itself.[25]

Research on current American attitudes toward family life further illustrates the difference between what people accept and what they wish for. People today are more tolerant than previous generations about the lifestyle choices others make. Yet, in spite of this new tolerance, most people still don't believe that everything they tolerate is a wise choice. One survey found that "while there were marked shifts toward permitting previously [socially prohibited] behavior, there were no significant shifts toward believing that remaining single, getting divorced, not having children, or reversing gender roles were positive goals to be achieved. . . . [T]he vast majority of Americans still value marriage, parenthood, and family life. . . . [W]hat has changed [is] an increased tolerance for behavior not previously accepted, but not an increase in the active embracement of such behavior."[26]

James Q. Wilson said of such data: "Half [of] us approve of *other* people's daughters having children out of wedlock, but hardly any of us approve of that for *our* daughters." In today's "widening tension between tolerance and belief," we "don't wish to be 'judgmental,' unless [we are judging] something we care about, [like] the well-being of the people we cherish."[27]

Despite society's increased tolerance for behavior once considered immoral, most people today—paradoxically—do still long deeply for permanent, loving marriages in their own lives. Yet despite those private hopes, the cultural changes of the last generation have also created a widespread pessimism about binding commitments. Such pessimism collides with the popular personal dream of family fulfillment, and that very pessimism is one of the biggest obstacles to fulfilling the dream.

In earlier years, most people worked hard to reach high ideals, such as stable marriage, even when they didn't achieve their hopes "except at the high points of their lives." And in those days, the ideals still served as "signposts pointing the way for man's endless *striving*,"[28] even in the presence of common human weaknesses.

Striving is a crucial word when the subject is marriage. Marriage, like religious faith, is no more satisfying than we are *willing*—striving—to make it. William James said: "Belief and doubt are living attitudes, and involve conduct on our part." If you are climbing a mountain and must jump a chasm to survive, you must "have faith that you can successfully make [the leap. For if you do,] your feet are nerved to its accomplishment. But mistrust yourself . . . and you will hesitate so long that . . . all unstrung and trembling . . . you roll into the abyss. . . . Refuse to believe, and you shall indeed be right, for you shall . . . perish. But believe, and again you shall be right. . . . You make one . . . of two possible universes true by your trust or mistrust. [Thus] optimism and pessimism are definitions of the world, [and often we create the kind of world we live in because] our faith beforehand in an uncertified result is the only thing that makes the result come true."[29]

This principle applies to marriage with uncommon force. Whether we "strive" to make the marriage work may be the most important ingredient in whether it does work. As President Spencer W. Kimball taught, marriage is never easy:

"Happiness does not come by pressing a button. . . . It must be earned. . . .

"One comes to realize very soon after the marriage that the spouse has weaknesses not previously revealed or discovered. The virtues which were constantly magnified during courtship now grow relatively smaller, and the weaknesses that seemed so small and insignificant during courtship now grow to sizeable proportions. . . . The habits of years now show themselves. . . .

"Often there is an unwillingness to settle down and to assume the heavy responsibilities that immediately are there. . . .

"[Still,] while marriage is difficult, and discordant and frustrated marriages are common, yet real, lasting happiness is possible, and *marriage can be more an exultant ecstasy than the human mind can conceive. This is within the reach of every couple, every person . . . if both are willing to pay the price.*"[30]

Because this is a true principle, the survivability, the happiness, even the "exultant ecstasy" that is possible in a marriage may depend—more than it depends on any other single thing—on whether spouses (and their family and community) *expect* their marriage to succeed.

Most ordinary people, despite their disappointments, are still willing to believe that marriage can, or at least ought to, work. But as the pessimistic strains of modern culture stir their doubts, more and more people are losing the confidence they need to *make their dream possible* by their conduct. Then their own doubts will confirm that they were right.

As a silver lining to these modern clouds of confusion, the changing attitudes of the last thirty years may at least help us appreciate the clarity and power of the gospel's teachings about marriage more than we did when society supported our assumptions. In this world of bewildering lifestyles and compromised commitments, the gospel is our surest hope for gaining the perspective and the discipline we need to fill our heart's longing for the fulness that marriage can provide.

PART II

PERSONAL
COVENANTS

CHAPTER FIVE

MARRIAGE IN ETERNAL PERSPECTIVE

The gospel's core doctrines teach us how to think about marriage and children because marriage and family are at the heart of why God sent us to earth. We will receive our exaltation as married people, or not at all. "It is not good that the man should be alone" (Genesis 2:18). "Neither is the man without the woman, neither the woman without the man, in the Lord" (1 Corinthians 11:11). "In the celestial glory there are three heavens or degrees; and in order to obtain the highest, a man must enter into this order of the priesthood [meaning the new and everlasting covenant of marriage]; and if he does not, he cannot obtain it" (D&C 131:1–3). This framework places marriage at the very center of act two and of act three.

Not long ago I heard a talented soprano, a Church member, sing Dvorak's "Songs My Mother Taught Me," accompanied with equal exactness on the piano by her mother. Having long tried to coach a few of our children through their music lessons, I found myself thinking about the mother's perspective on her daughter's performance that night.

I felt a vicarious satisfaction as I tried to imagine how the mother felt now, having watched her child develop her voice and musical skill. I wondered how early the mother had sensed her child's talent, what it must have been like to hear her early attempts—perhaps like watching a newborn colt awkwardly trying to walk. Then I wondered if the singer might also be starting to teach music to her own children. Would she someday hear one of them sing, at her mother's standard of quality, "Songs My Mother Taught Me"?

Hearing her was like watching a small act two scene. Probably no one but her mother really understood the prior scene, though the daughter would remember her own version. The subsequent scene was yet to come, when the student becomes a teacher.

Life is like that, and so is marriage. Both develop in stages, both are concerned with growing, learning from experience, going someplace—like the character development in a fine play or novel. In marriage, of course, each partner is both a student and a teacher, each learning and supporting the other's learning. But because society has lost the plot about the marriage drama, people today too often see marriage as a brief act-two-only *event,* not enough as part of a long term *process,* especially not as the growth process God means it to be. Too many today have no comprehension of where family life comes from, where it has the potential to go, and what kind of sacrifices, what trial-and-error grit, it will take to go there.

Shakespeare's *Macbeth* hauntingly confines marriage—and life—totally to the second act. After Lord and Lady Macbeth have successfully schemed to take a king's life, in order to take his throne, Lady Macbeth gradually goes insane and then dies from maddened guilt. Upon hearing of his wife's death, Macbeth offers the chilling cynicism that sees mortality as the entire drama:

Seyton: The Queen, my lord, is dead.

Macbeth: . . . .
Tomorrow and tomorrow and tomorrow
Creeps in this petty pace from day to day
To the last syllable of recorded time,
And all our yesterdays have lighted fools
The way to dusty death. Out, out, brief candle!
Life's but a walking shadow, a poor player
That struts and frets his hour upon the stage
And then is heard no more. It is a tale
Told by an idiot, full of sound and fury,
Signifying nothing.[1]

There is no place for the meaning of either "tomorrow" or "yesterday" in Macbeth's dark world, where there is no future, and the past has no point. Then life is "but a walking shadow." Lacking either origins or ultimate destination, the "poor players" in this single act "strut and fret" their lonely "hour upon the stage" and then are "heard no more." Because it came from nowhere and goes nowhere, this sad and senseless story means no more than an idiot's babbling, "signifying nothing."

During my high school days we sometimes said "like there's no tomorrow" to describe someone who ran or sang his or her heart out: that girl sings (or that guy runs) like there's no tomorrow. A popular song from that era used the same phrase. I remember the words:

> *There's no tomorrow when love is new.*
> *Now is forever when love is true,*
> *So kiss me and hold me tight.*
> *There's no tomorrow,*
> *There's just tonight.*

That's one way to think of love—or marriage: "like there's no tomorrow." And every relationship, whatever its length, is therefore disposable.

Yet because of the Restoration, we know there *is* tomorrow. And because there is, all of our yesterdays have meaning, and all of our dreams have hope. So true love is never wasted, and our sacrifices for family relationships signify everything. We are willing to work in the now because we have such confidence in the future. We do not strut and fret for but an hour on life's stage, and our candles do not go out by darkness. As the Indian poet Rabindranath Tagore wrote, "Death is not extinguishing the light; it is putting out the lamp because the dawn has come."

The Restoration's doctrine of eternal families is just such a light in a very dark world—and the light is beginning to be noticed. Ours is the religion that understands not just *family history*, though we're well known for that. We also understand the *family's future* with unmatched clarity. Because of what we know about the past and the future, our insight, then, about the *family's present* is truly unique and a source of real power.

Consider how some thoughtful people from outside the Church are coming to view the LDS family across three dimensions. With a nod to Charles Dickens, let's call this family past, family future, and family present—a perspective that puts the present in a unique light.

First, regarding family past, I was present when the Church gave a large personal family history to the prime minister of Australia, John Howard. The PM, as the Aussies call him, was delighted to learn all about his ancestry, which included true Australian convicts sent there from England. Then he asked, "Do I correctly understand that your Church has the largest collection of family history records in the world?"

We gladly said yes. We also told him that the Church has now made many of those records freely accessible on the Internet through FamilySearch.org. People everywhere feel a growing hunger to understand themselves better by understanding their ancestral roots. Church members pursue these roots and records partly to know their ancestors but also to help build eternal bonds across the generations.

The spirit of family past in our doctrine also includes our appreciation for Adam and Eve, our first mortal parents, and our role models for what life and marriage are about. Yet our understanding of family past reaches even further back, prior to Eden, prior to the earth's creation—to our family relationship with God Himself. Through the Restoration, we know that each of us lived in a premortal life with God, the literal father of our spirits. If we could recall all we learned there, we would be able to sing "songs my father taught me."

I recently met a bright and vivacious new Church member from the Midwest whose discovery of the doctrine of our premortal life was the turning point in her conversion. These ideas rang so true and meant so much to her that she just kept telling everybody, "We lived with God before! We lived with God before!"

This is why we pray to God as "Heavenly Father." It's why we refer to one another as "brother" and "sister." Our Father gave us the opportunity of coming to earth to develop through demanding experience the personal qualities we need to live permanently with Him. Then the Atonement of Jesus Christ makes it possible for us, if we are faithful, to live eternally "at-one" with our Heavenly Father and with our mortal families.

The most beloved of all LDS children's songs captures this idea in childlike clarity: "I am a child of God." A few years ago in Australia's Northern Territory, one of the most remote places on earth, I visited the Church's only branch in which all of the members are Aborigines. Because the branch is so isolated—five hundred miles from its district priesthood leaders—I wanted to know what the members there were learning. On impulse, I asked the children if they could sing that song, unrehearsed. I was reassured as they all came forward and sang every word earnestly, their faces full of light: "Teach me all that I must do / To live with him someday."[2]

As that song teaches, our earthly home is an extension in both purpose and pattern of our premortal home. And mortality prepares us for our eternal home. This plan of happiness is all about marriage and life in families. Elder Dallin H. Oaks said: "The fulness of eternal salvation is a family affair. . . . The gospel plan originated in the council of an eternal family, it is implemented through our earthly families, and has its destiny in our eternal families. Small wonder The Church of Jesus Christ of Latter-day Saints is known as a family-centered church."[3]

Next consider family future. When I was teaching at Brigham Young University a few years ago, I received a phone call from Kenneth Woodward, the religion editor of *Newsweek*. After we talked about family law issues, he wondered if I were a Mormon. When I said yes, he said, "I see where the Mormons got some pretty good play in the new book on heaven out of Yale."

Not knowing that Yale was into books about heaven, I asked him to tell me more. He said the book, *Heaven: A History,* was written by two non-LDS scholars and published by Yale University Press. It traces the history of beliefs about heaven in Western culture. It concludes by reporting how people, and religions, think of heaven today. The authors found that the public feels a widespread hunger for heaven—and families in heaven. The majority of Americans still believe in life after death *and* in the eternal nature of love and the hope for heavenly reunion with their families.[4] Yet, most Christian churches offer little response to this inner hunger. Rather, today's "ideas about what happens after death are only popular sentiments and are not integrated into Protestant and Catholic theological systems."[5]

Then the authors describe one "major exception" to this religious vacuum about heaven—"the theology of the Church of Jesus Christ of Latter-day Saints." They describe our teachings about temples and eternal marriage, concluding that "the understanding of life after death in the LDS church" offers the most complete concept of heaven in our day.[6]

What a discovery! Most people today long for eternal families, and the Restoration fulfills that longing better than any other known set of ideas. I wish the whole world could hear LDS children singing the glad news: "Families can be together forever."[7]

This understanding places family present—our mortal family and our own marriages—within the *eternal* perspective of a family past and a family future. Without the vision gained from acts one and three, act two could seem too short, too long, too hard, or too confusing. When we do know about all three acts, act two has infinite significance.

I've sometimes been asked by people of other faiths why so many LDS families seem to thrive during this age of family decline. We clearly have our share of troubled homes, but still they ask, "How do you explain the amazing *confidence* in marriage and family life that I see in the Mormons I know?"

For example, a law professor from Tokyo visited the United States to explore his concerns about the damaging effect of American law and pop culture on traditional Japanese family attitudes. But after he'd been in Provo on the BYU campus for several days, mixing in the dorms with students, he said, "Tell me about these students. This campus is an island of hope in the land of the apocalypse. What is the secret behind all the shining eyes?"

I said his questions can't be fully answered in behavioral terms, because a Latter-day Saint's understanding of family past and family future make family present more a matter of religion than of social behavior. To paraphrase President Boyd K. Packer, family life is a case where our understanding of our doctrine will influence our behavior much more than talking only about behavior will influence our behavior. And those who lack eternity's perspective on time and on human relationships can too easily believe, like Macbeth, that "there's no tomorrow."

It isn't easy to translate our doctrinal framework into daily reality, because mortal family life is by its nature a continual struggle between the ideal and the real. Yet the gospel's full-length perspective does influence our attitudes about marriage and children—and everything associated with them.

For example, imagine with me a young man named Jared, who learned how his understanding of family past influenced his sense of the present. Jared's parents had tried to teach him the gospel in their home, but as he got older they felt they hadn't reached him. They wanted him to go on a mission and marry in the temple. But Jared wanted to live his own life. He enrolled as a freshman in a college far from home, where he could be his own person and do his own thing. He was tired of seminary and what he called "cheesy Church kids." Jared got involved with the wrong kind of music, movies, and girls. He was on his own, and he loved it. His relationship with Stephanie got very physical very fast, and Jared found that exciting.

One night Jared and Stephanie were approaching serious intimacy. Impulsively, Jared asked, "What if you get pregnant?"

She replied, "I'm on the pill. And if that doesn't work, it's no big deal. I know how to get an abortion."

"An abortion?" Jared asked. "Wait a minute." It hit him hard that they were now talking, even if only hypothetically, about a baby that could be his own child. Suddenly he felt confused and uncomfortable. He tried to explain the connection he was seeing between sex and children and where children's spirits come from, something he hadn't focused on before. And it bothered him that what she was willing to do with him, she had probably done with others.

Stephanie was hurt. She didn't understand what he was talking about, and she asked him not to push his religion on her. Jared didn't think he'd said anything about the Church. He took her home and then drove off feeling angry at himself but not quite sure why. Close to tears, he kept on driving, trying to settle down. He kept thinking about what he'd almost done. After driving around for an hour in an aimless sort of way, Jared called his cousin, a returned missionary who was married and attending his same college. As they sat together in the cousin's little apartment, Jared told him about Stephanie. With a very serious look, he said, "I need to date girls who see the whole family thing the way I do. Why couldn't I see that?"

To illustrate the influence of family future on the present, I recall the experience of a group of Young Women in a new temple in Australia. When the temple there was nearly finished, the stake Young Women leaders invited some girls to put "some finishing touches" on the building. Their task was to place small pieces of clear crystal on each rung of the huge chandelier that would hang from the celestial room ceiling.

The workmen lowered the giant frame to the floor. The girls unwrapped each piece of crystal and polished it to be clear and clean, like the temple. Then they lay on the floor and reached up into the rungs to carefully hang each piece. It took about two hours to hang all the pieces.

The girls felt reverent as they worked in the celestial room. They didn't really know what the room meant, though some had heard it was something about God's presence. They didn't feel like talking as they worked; they spontaneously sang a few Church songs together. When they finished the careful work, the workmen lifted the chandelier up to the ceiling and turned on the lights.

Light filled the room, glistening from the crystal and into the huge mirrors on the walls. The girls didn't want to leave. After a time, the leaders told them their work was done and they could go home. Even after hearing that pizza was waiting for them outside, the girls still lingered, until the leaders gently led them out of the temple.

One of those girls wrote in her journal that night that in the celestial room she felt a deep desire to be with her Father in Heaven, always, and to be there with her family—more than anything. She went straight home and asked her family if they could have family home evening, even though it wasn't Monday, and could they read the scriptures and then pray together. She told them what she'd felt and asked each one to promise that they would live so they could all be together, always, with their Heavenly Father.

Her feelings and her mental picture of the future stirred her well beyond her level of present understanding about the doctrines of the temple. She didn't need to understand more, because she knew what she needed to do.

When I was about seven, I was riding in the backseat of our family car on a bumpy gravel road. Somehow the door came open, and I fell from the car. I landed on my elbow and banged it up. I jumped to my feet, crying, and ran after the car, fearing my family would leave me. My father stopped the car, and I climbed in. My older brother pointed out how stupid I'd been to fall out of the car. Then he looked at me and said, "What happened to your elbow?"

I looked at my arm and saw it bleeding from a nasty abrasion. Suddenly it began to sting as we looked for a way to bandage it. I have since wondered why I didn't feel that pain when I was running. Now I understand that I wanted to be with my family so much that my intense desire to join them was greater than my pain.

The power of our doctrinal vision of family future is strong enough that it will outweigh whatever sacrifice and pain we may need to bear during our days of family present. That is how our distant memories of what was—and a mental picture of what will be—puts everything about today into perspective, as it did for those girls in the temple.

I remember a bright fall afternoon in Idaho when I went fishing with our seven-year-old son, Mark. As I splashed up the shallow stream in my waders, I carried him on my back. He held his feet above the water and hugged me tight around the neck, laughing in my ear when I stumbled on the rocks. He said he hoped we'd fall into the water.

We stopped at one spot to fish. I looked up at the blue sky, almost tasting the crisp fall air. I saw early snow on a distant mountain peak. I drank in the color of autumn leaves in the backlighting of the sun. I saw Mark downstream, skipping rocks on the water. The sun caught the pure whiteness of his hair, and his agile form stood out against the shadows of the wooded background.

I sensed a sudden rush of feeling that I suppose only a father or mother can know. My heart reached out to touch him as the thought struck me—he is my son, my own little boy, my posterity, and I am his dad. He is filled with a child's love. I am responsible to God for my conduct as his father. He and I are sealed together, if we are faithful. He is the fruit of the deep love I feel for his mother. The constancy of her daily life is teaching him about truth and light. That's why he is so secure, so mentally healthy. Thank God for such a child. What miracles are worked by the laws of nature and of nature's God. In that moment, I felt in harmony with everything I saw. It was a witness to me of the Lord's love—and it came from simply seeing my child in the context of my eternal marriage.

CHAPTER SIX

THE DOCTRINAL PATTERN OF ADAM AND EVE: NO MISERY, NO JOY

In the scriptures and in the temple, we learn that the primal doctrinal story that links the three-act plan of salvation with marriage is the story of Adam and Eve. From earth's first day, the purpose of marriage and the purpose of mortality have been tightly interwoven. First, God Himself commanded that "a man leave his father and his mother, and shall cleave unto his wife: and they shall be one flesh" (Genesis 2:24).

Lehi also taught his children that if Adam and Eve had not transgressed, they would have remained in the Garden of Eden. Had that happened, Adam and Eve *"would have had no children; wherefore they would have remained in a state of innocence, having no joy, for they knew no misery; doing no good, for they knew no sin. . . . Adam fell that men might be; and men are, that they might have joy"* (2 Nephi 2:23–25; italics added).

Astute parents will notice an interesting little connection here: No children, no misery! There is actually some truth to that point. For without being expelled from the innocent comfort of Eden into the turbulence of mortality, Adam and Eve would not only have had no children, and no misery, but they would never have found joy; hence, the very meaning of life would have been lost on them. There really is a deep connection between the hard things of life and the best things of life.

The Lord taught Adam and Eve not only that they should "cleave" to one another but that they must live and bear children in the sorrow, sweat, and thorns of mortality—not as some kind of punishment for disobedience but so that through sometimes bitter experience, they could come to really understand life and meaning and joy. "They taste the bitter," the Lord explained to Adam, "that they may know to prize the good" (Moses 6:55). In fact, He said, "If they never should have bitter [experiences] they *could not know the sweet*" (D&C 29:39; italics added). In other words, sometimes the twists and turns of life *are* the straight and narrow path.

The story of Adam and Eve is the pattern for our own marriages, our lives, and the personal meaning of the Atonement. The story of Christ's life is the story of *giving* the Atonement. But the life story of Adam and Eve is the story of *receiving* the Atonement. Especially in that sense, their lives and their marriage set the pattern for our own.

Because they received the Atonement of Christ, Adam and Eve were able to learn from their experience without being condemned by it. "For God sent not his Son into the world to condemn the world; but that the world through him might be saved" (John 3:17). If, therefore, God allows us to learn from our experience without condemning us for it, how much more should we be willing to let our companions learn from their experience without condemning them for it.

The poem "Lamentation" breathes life and sinew into the story of Adam and Eve. It was written by Arta Romney Ballif, a sister to President Marion G. Romney. Here she imagines Eve's experience as a mother and wife—her honest questions, her hunger to understand the Lord. Note the symbols of mortality here—the "fruit" of both the garden and of the body; the "storm," the repetition of "multiply" and "sorrow." Here in all its sometimes furious opposition—part of the plan for all of us—is act two:

> *And God said, "BE FRUITFUL, AND*
> *   MULTIPLY—"*
> *Multiply, multiply—echoes multiply—*
>
> *God said, "I WILL GREATLY MULTIPLY*
> *   THY SORROW—"*
> *Thy sorrow, sorrow, sorrow—*
>
> *I have gotten a man from the Lord*
> *I have traded the fruit of the garden for the*
> *   fruit of my body*
> *For a laughing bundle of humanity.*
>
> *And now another one who looks like Adam.*
> *We shall call this one "Abel."*
> *It is a lovely name, "Abel."*
>
> *Cain, Abel, the world is yours.*
> *God set the sun in the heavens to light your*
> *   days*
> *To warm the flocks, to kernel the grain*
> *He illuminated your nights with stars*
> *He made the trees and the fruit thereof yield-*
> *   ing seed*
> *He made every living thing, the wheat, the*
> *   sheep, the cattle*
> *For your enjoyment.*
> *And, behold, it is very good.*

Adam? Adam,
Where art thou?
Where are the boys?
The sky darkens with clouds.
Adam, is that you?
Where is Abel?
He is long caring for his flocks.
The sky is black and the rain hammers.
Are the ewes lambing
In this storm?

Why your troubled face, Adam?
Are you ill?
Why so pale, so agitated?
The wind will pass
The lambs will birth
With Abel's help.

Dead?
What is dead?

Merciful God!

Hurry, bring warm water
I'll bathe his wounds
Bring clean clothes
Bring herbs
I'll heal him.

I am trying to understand. You said, "Abel is
    dead."
But I am skilled with herbs
Remember when he was seven
The fever? Remember how—

Herbs will not heal?
Dead?

And Cain? Where is Cain?
Listen to that thunder.

Cain cursed?
What has happened to him?
God said, "A fugitive and a vagabond"?

But God can't do that.
They are my sons, too.
I gave them birth
In the valley of pain.

Adam, try to understand
In the valley of pain
I bore them
> *fugitive?*
> *vagabond?*

This is his home
This soil he loved
Where he toiled for golden wheat
For tasseled corn.

To the hill country?
There are rocks in the hill country
Cain can't work in the hill country
The nights are cold
Cold and lonely, and the wind gales.

Quick, we must find him
A basket of bread and his coat
I worry, thinking of him wandering
With no place to lay his head.
Cain cursed?
A wanderer, a roamer?
Who will bake his bread and mend his coat?

Abel, my son, dead?
And Cain, my son, a fugitive?
Two sons
Adam, we had two sons
Both—Oh, Adam—
        multiply
    sorrow
Dear God, Why?
Tell me again about the fruit
Why?
Please, tell me again
Why?[1]

Eve. Mother Eve. Your sorrow and your faithful questions bring a hush across my heart.

I wonder if Adam and Eve ever worried about how much fault was theirs for losing Cain and Abel. Did Lehi and Sariah ever wonder that about Laman and Lemuel? What does it tell us about what we could face in our own marriages, our own families, that these two "first couples" from the scriptures had to contend with so much family sorrow?

We may not have ready answers to all of these questions, but we do know that because they accepted the Atonement of Christ, Adam and Eve, Lehi and Sariah, could all grow from their experience without suffering irreparable damage. With their family life as their main place of spiritual schooling, they learned from both misery and joy, discovering firsthand that "God . . . shall consecrate thine afflictions for thy gain" (2 Nephi 2:2).

Adam and Eve didn't understand all of this just by tasting the forbidden fruit. That fruit was but the beginning of a lifelong quest for meaning—not an event but an extended process, marked by having children and discovering misery, sin, goodness, joy, and the very meaning of eternal life. After all of this, then, when Adam and Eve returned "home" to God's presence, being with Him in act three was very different from their having been with Him in act one. They didn't simply return to the innocence of Eden, as if the Atonement wiped out their very experience.

Rather, they *progressed,* until they reached the Lord's presence. But this time they understood what they could never have known in Eden—now they *knew what it meant to be there, with Him, and with each other.* This journey, in polar opposition to the blank drawn by Macbeth's idiot, *signifies everything.* T. S. Eliot captured Adam's process of discovery:

> *We shall not cease from exploration*
> *And the end of all our exploring*
> *Will be to arrive where we started*
> *And know the place for the first time.*[2]

Doctrinally, the experience of Adam and Eve makes clear that the Fall was not a terrible mistake, as most Christian religions portray it. Without the Fall, we couldn't know good from evil, we couldn't know joy—we couldn't even have been born.

Our understanding of covenant marriage is all bound up, then, with the doctrines of the plan of salvation, the Fall, and the Atonement. Since Augustine's day, traditional Christianity has wrongly viewed the Fall as a preventable disaster. But the Restoration views it as an essential step in our Heavenly Father's plan for His children. The Fall introduced the process by which we can *learn from personal experience the central meanings of existence.*

Our prototype for this learning is in the marriage and experience of Adam and Eve. Much of our essential learning is together *as a couple,* like Adam and Eve *together* facing the opposition that "must needs be" (2 Nephi 2:11). Thus marriage—and overcoming troubles together—has a religious, doctrinal significance so powerful that we often underestimate it.

Before their temple marriage, each couple learns through the temple endowment about the perspective of eternity on the opposition they will encounter in this world of time. The endowment will also show them, as Elder Bruce R. McConkie explained, that "the marriage of Adam and Eve . . . [is] a pattern for all others."[3]

Married people who sense all of this try instinctively to sustain and lift each other, as Adam and Eve did. But most newly married couples can hardly grasp what awaits them when they happily walk, arm in arm, from the gardenlike temple grounds. If they did realize what lies ahead, they would probably walk more slowly, like Adam and Eve, driven from Eden, bowed down in unspoken sorrow. Do they know it is only a matter of time until trouble comes and that it will keep returning, because learning from hard things is what life is about?

I liked the honesty and insight with which our six older children and their spouses shared their own Adam-and-Eve-like perspectives with their youngest sister and her fiancé the night before their wedding. On this, her "last night as a single person" (the theme of the evening!), with no platitudes allowed, each person shared one insight he or she had learned, from experience, about marriage. Some samples:

Don't try to make him into what you want him to be. You fell in love with what he is. He will still grow. But you'll learn from experience to trust what he does rather than jumping to negative conclusions when you don't understand something.

I don't agree with whoever said don't go to sleep when you're upset. Most things that have me upset by bedtime aren't really a problem by morning. We all have moods; we all get tired. A good night's sleep really helps.

I agree with Sister Marjorie Hinckley. Someone asked her the secret of her happy marriage, and she said, "I lowered my expectations."

I have found that, as a mother, my spiritual mood really does set the spiritual tone for my home. If I'm stressed, my kids are stressed, my husband is stressed. So I try to control myself more than I try to control others.

Communicate. Say what you're thinking, in a kind way. Don't make the other person read your mind, and don't let unspoken things build up until some event triggers a reaction that's out of proportion.

Up to now, your first question has naturally been "what is best for me"—how to use your time, money, school, work, whatever. But after your wedding, the biggest question is, "What is best for our marriage, our family?" And *that is a very hard thing to learn.*

As you hear all this advice, remember that each couple is unique, so different things work for different people. But whatever you do, show in every action that your spouse has the highest priority in your life. If one of you does things that suggest you give higher priority to other things or other people, that undercuts the confidence your marriage has to have.

For us, being married to each other has often been very hard. Yet I've learned that our relationship is still the best thing for us, because our particular match pushes both of us to develop in the ways we each need most.

Don't expect immediate perfection—in him, in marriage, in the relationship. You're entering a big transition, and it takes time to grow into a whole new way of living.

I read somewhere that loyalty is greater than love—and now I know it is, as hard as that can be. Your loyalty to each other is what gives power to your covenants—and you have to *learn* how to do that. It will take time. Marriage will show you more about your weaknesses than his; but it's worth it.

The experiences of these couples, with fresh thoughts from lives still very much in process, showed me how much marriage does help us learn, just as Adam and Eve did.

CHAPTER SEVEN

A HIRELING'S CONTRACT
OR A SHEPHERD'S COVENANT?

When Brian was fourteen years old, he heard a puzzling radio talk show. A woman called to talk about her marriage problems. Her husband had lost his job, he wasn't much fun to live with anyway, some of her children were sick, they couldn't pay their bills, and she was getting tired of all the miserable pressure. When she asked for advice, the talk show host said, "Hey, you're entitled to a little happiness. You don't have to stay in this mess. Jump the fence. Get out. Let your old man solve his own problems. You go find greener pastures."

Brian felt sympathy for the woman, but the host's advice bothered him. He asked his parents, "When you get married, don't they say something like, 'for richer or poorer, for better or worse, in sickness and in health'"?

His mother said, "You're right about that, Brian. Good for you."

Brian wasn't satisfied. "So why would that guy on the radio tell her that?"

Replied his father, "Because that's the way people are starting to think these days. The pop psychologists are telling everybody to just look out for themselves."

About ten years later, I watched Brian and Kathy emerge from a sacred temple. They laughed and held hands as family and friends gathered to take pictures. I saw happiness and promise in their faces as they greeted their reception guests, who celebrated the creation of a new family.

I wondered that night how long it would be until Brian and Kathy faced the opposition that tests every marriage. Maybe their problems wouldn't be the same as those that hit the woman in the talk show. But I knew their trials would come. And only then would they discover whether their marriage was based on a contract or a covenant.

As Elder Robert D. Hales said, "An eternal bond doesn't just happen as a result of the sealing covenants we make in the temple. How we conduct ourselves in this life will determine what we will be in all the eternities to come."[1] Our conduct, guided by our response to the sealing covenants, also determines *whose* we will be—whether we will belong to each other, whether we will belong to Christ.

Consider the general distinction between contractual and covenant attitudes toward marriage. One bride sighed blissfully on her wedding day, "Mom, I'm at the end of all my troubles!"

"Yes," replied her mother, "but at which end?"

When troubles come, the parties to a *contractual* marriage seek happiness by walking away. They marry to obtain benefits and will stay only as long as they're receiving what they bargained for.

But when troubles come to a *covenant* marriage, the husband and wife work them through. They marry to give and to grow, bound by covenants to each other, to the community, and to God. *Contract* companions each give 50 percent. But *covenant* companions each give 100 percent. Enough and to spare. Each gives enough to cover any shortfall by the other. Double coverage. Because their covenant is unqualified, they simply plan on solving their problems *together*—whatever trouble comes, no matter what it is, how long it takes, or what it costs.

A covenant marriage in the highest sense will begin as a temple marriage. When the partners are then sufficiently righteous, the marriage will be sealed by the Holy Spirit of promise (D&C 132:7), "which the Father sheds forth upon all those who are just and true" (D&C 76:53). Such a marriage will then be not only eternal in duration but also celestial in quality, for it will be a marriage that partakes of God's quality of life. As President James E. Faust said:

"When the covenant of marriage for time and eternity, the culminating gospel ordinance, is sealed by the Holy Spirit of promise, it can literally open the windows of heaven for great blessings to flow to a married couple who seek for those blessings. Such marriages become rich, whole, and sacred. Though each party to the marriage can maintain his or her separate identity, yet together in their covenants they can be like two vines wound inseparably around each other. Each thinks of his or her companion before thinking of self."[2]

In addition, the term *covenant marriage* also carries echoes of the ancient Old Testament pattern of "covenant," which gave high and sacred meaning to religious covenant-making performed in "a shrine or sacred place" and was accompanied by a sacred oath intended to yield divine blessings or cursings based on obedience to the oath.[3]

Covenant marriage can also have a more general meaning. People of other faiths can approach their marriage with the sense of wholehearted reciprocity that creates the attitudes and commitments of a covenant marriage. When they do, their relationship, their family, and society will be richly blessed, even if they do not yet enjoy the eternal fulness of celestial marriage.

Even a Church member who marries in the temple but who approaches his or her marriage as a "contract" partner rather than a "covenant" partner is not really living in a covenant marriage. Those of the half-hearted commitment are by definition not among those who "overcome by faith, and are sealed by the Holy Spirit of promise" (D&C 76:53). Hence their marriage will be neither eternal nor celestial in duration or quality.

How soon does opposition come to test the covenant assumptions, and does it even come to a temple marriage? Warning of the opposition that faced the Saints in building holy temples, Brigham Young said that we never undertake to build a temple but what the very bells of hell begin to ring.[4] And as soon as temple wedding bells begin to ring, so may ring the bells of hell.

The way new couples approach their rough spots, small or large, really does depend on whether they *expect* that they've made a contract or a covenant. As God first established it, marriage was by its nature a covenant, not a commercial-style contract one may cancel and pay the damages when the going gets tough. And our commitment to a real covenant can be tested with the earliest irritations.

For instance, Matt took Lisa on a horseback ride, excited at the novelty of his plan to offer her an engagement ring that was under some secret flowers he had tied to a tree some miles away. Then Lisa's horse took a tumble, she hurt her hip, and the clever trip was over. Matt had to propose as Lisa sat happily but tenderly on her bruises, far from the flowers.

Another couple I know had several hundred engagement photos printed, only to discover that the photographer printed the wrong picture and there was no time to print again before the invitations had to be mailed. I watched them decide, after working hard to resolve their differing opinions, to just use the wrong picture rather than demand an overnight reprinting job.

I remember the groom at the Idaho Falls temple who was so lost in bliss during a photo session that he didn't realize he was standing on the hem of his bride's white dress, mashing it into the muddy grass. That night they stood bravely through the reception, concealing as best they could the little smudge that symbolized that their real life journey had begun.

These are samples of the mildest and earliest tests. The bigger ones come later.

Jesus gave us the best possible definition of the difference between a covenant and a contract in His parable of the Good Shepherd. Notice here the difference between a hireling (a paid servant) and a shepherd:

"I am come that they might have life, and that they might have it more abundantly.

"I am the good *shepherd:* the good shepherd giveth his life for the sheep.

"But he that is an *hireling,* and not the shepherd, whose own the sheep are not, seeth the wolf coming, and leaveth the sheep, and fleeth: and the wolf catcheth them, and scattereth the sheep.

"The hireling fleeth, because he is an hireling, and careth not for the sheep.

"I am the good shepherd, and know my sheep, and am known of mine.

"As the Father knoweth me, even so know I the Father: and I lay down my life for the sheep" (John 10:10–15; italics added).

The hireling performs his job only when he receives something in return. So when the hireling sees the wolf—any kind of serious trouble—coming, he leaves the sheep and "fleeth," because his "own the sheep are not." He doesn't really "care" for them. In utter contrast, the "shepherd" cares for the sheep so much that he will "lay down [his] life for the sheep."

Because of today's "me first" misconceptions about marriage, more people now marry with a hireling's contractual expectation. They too easily assume that if being married cramps your style and you're no longer happy, you just move out of your "starter marriage."

So when the wolf comes, they flee. It seems natural to flee these days, when one sees so many others in flight. Their movement is like that of a frightened, scattering army. The new soldiers desert the battlefield, not because they know for themselves that they're beaten but because they see the other soldiers running away. To give up so easily is wrong. It curses the earth, turning parents' hearts away from their children and from each other. It also lets a shallow desire for comfort deprive people of paying the price to discover real joy.

A covenant marriage differs from a contractual one in scope, duration, intensity, and conditions. *Covenant* marriage is unconditional, unlimited, and eternal, a reflection of the kind of love and commitment on which it is based. *Contractual* marriage, by contrast, is subject to conditions and limited in the breadth of its demands as well as its expected duration.

The text for one rendition of "The Lord Is My Shepherd" says of the Good Shepherd, "With blessings unmeasured my cup runneth over."[5] "Unmeasured" means He is not counting my blessings, even if I am—and naming them one by one. He has no sharp pencil, no quota, no limits. That is why "I shall not want." Like the well of Living Water, the fountain of His love is a spring that never runs dry (John 4:14). And because He is not counting how much He will give, neither do we count how much we will offer in return.

Father Flanagan's Boystown used the motto "He ain't heavy— he's my brother." It really doesn't matter how heavy my brother is. What I owe him or how long I'll carry him is based on a permanent sense of mutual belonging, not on my having agreed to carry him as long as I can manage it. In the same way, covenant marriage is, like kinship, without limits. And to those who understand the unspoken covenants of close kinship, the very nature of the relationship means that the load of carrying "my brother" can never become heavier than I will keep trying to carry.

The Savior drew on this concept when, during His agony on the cross, He asked John to care for His mother, Mary, after His impending death. He didn't give John a list of things He wanted him to do for His mother, and He didn't need a lawyer to draw up a contract covering all of the details. Rather, He drew on the unmeasured meaning of terms handed down through the ages— *mother* and *son:* "When Jesus therefore saw his mother, and the disciple standing by, whom he loved, he saith unto his mother, Woman, behold thy son! Then saith he to the disciple, Behold thy mother! And from that hour that disciple took her unto his own home" (John 19:26–27).

A Russian writer named Pitirim Sorokin once distinguished between covenant and contract marriages, though he used "familistic" to describe what we here call covenant marriage. In his terms, familistic partners share a "mutual attachment" that eclipses each partner's self-interest. Their unqualified commitment to one another can yield endless joys, but it also requires "sorrow and sacrifice." Because of its "unlimited ethical motivation," the "sacrifice" of the covenant partner is "regarded not as a . . . personal loss . . . , but as a privilege freely and gladly bestowed." And even though this open-ended sense of duty may at times seem to impose a "frightful" limit on one's personal freedom, it blends "discipline with freedom" and "sacrifice with liberty" to the point of high personal fulfillment.[6]

Contractual attitudes, on the other hand, rest on very different assumptions. A contract is *always limited* in its scope and duration. It never involves a contracting party's "whole life or even its greater part." Moreover, people enter contracts for reasons of self-interest, "uniting with the other party only so far as this provides him with an advantage (profit, pleasure, or service)."[7] Today's society wrongly but fully expects the contracting parties to interpret their marital differences according to what is in their personal interest—like a hireling.

One example of a contract marriage is the growing number of couples who write their own wedding vows, which many officials who perform marriages these days are glad to use. In customized marriage vows, every "contracting" couple consciously holds something back, determined to remain free to define the nature, purpose, and bounds of their relationship in whatever way they choose—with or without some degree of "binding" commitment.

To the modern mind, a covenant marriage may seem not only sobering but incomprehensible because its limits are beyond us, out of sight. How else could it be, when the Good Shepherd's devotion is so utterly limitless as "I lay down my life for the sheep." This covenantal soberness makes for better marriages by encouraging people to be far more careful about whom, when, and how to marry. Conversely, if one makes the contract assumption that marriage is easy to end, one will be much less cautious about starting it.

No other relationship could possibly be as meaningful—or as demanding—as a marriage based on covenants without limits. As

President Boyd K. Packer taught: "No relationship has more potential to exalt a man and a woman than the marriage covenant. No obligation in society or in the Church supersedes its importance."[8]

M. Scott Peck wrote in *The Road Less Traveled* that the development of genuine, loving relationships within marriage and the family is the highest hope of which honest, disciplined, human love is capable. We can't truly "love" huge groups, much less "humanity" in general, he said, because actual love is truly extending oneself to nurture another individual's growth.[8] With that premise, "if one can say that one has built genuinely loving relationships with a spouse and children, then one has already succeeded in accomplishing more than most people accomplish in a lifetime."[9]

A small, lighthearted example of the "blessings unmeasured" in a covenant marriage occurred one winter morning. A young man I know couldn't budge his car from his frozen, snow-bombed Utah driveway. After trying to dislodge it until he was late for work, he caught a ride with a neighbor. Later in the day, his wife melted away the ice by carrying pan after pan of hot water to the driveway. When she called him at work to say his car was no longer stuck, he said with relief and gratitude, "Thanks. I really owe you one." She replied, "You know why we're married for eternity, don't you?"

He didn't catch the implication. "Why are we?" he asked.

"Because," she responded with her gentle, knowing laugh, "that's how long it's going to take for you to pay me back all the ones you owe me."

In that little exchange is the spirit of a covenant marriage. It is not a "pay me back" contract, and nobody keeps score. Both the blessings and the commitments are unmeasured.

As his first sentence in the classic *Anna Karenina,* Leo Tolstoy wrote, "Happy families are all alike. Every unhappy family is unhappy in its own way." In the same sense in which I believe Tolstoy meant it, the spirit of unlimited commitments in a covenant marriage makes all such marriages alike; but every contractual marriage is contractual in its own way, because one way or another, its commitments are qualified, its partners each holding something back.

CHAPTER EIGHT

GOOD SHEPHERDS

The parable of the Good Shepherd contains many clues for understanding covenant marriage. The parable is not only about Christ's love for us. It is also about the love of marriage partners or parents who give themselves to others in covenants so deep that they may fairly think of the other as their "own" and "mine"—even though their companion's freedom and personal growth are, paradoxically, as precious to them, perhaps more precious, than their own.

The sheep in this story are those for whom Christ has given His life, and they have accepted His sacrifice by hearkening to Him. He is known of them, because they follow Him. He "owns" them because He redeemed them. He bought them with His blood in the two-way covenants of the Atonement. They are His covenant people. He is their covenant Shepherd. He lays down His life for them—that they might have a more abundant life.

The partners in a covenant marriage also give their lives for each other, a day or an hour at a time. They sacrifice and hearken to each other as equal partners. Each gives wholly to the other;

each receives the other fully to himself or herself. They *belong* to each other—never as property but as souls willingly entrusted to each other's keeping. By caring passionately about their partner's personal spiritual growth, a central part of their life's work is to help their partner develop a more abundant life.

As with most analogies, the parallel between Christ as the Shepherd and a husband or wife as a shepherd is limited. What Christ did for us is unlike anything we could really do for each other. He is divine and we are human, His sacrifice beyond serious comparison with ours.

Yet there are parallels between our relationship with Christ and our relationships in marriage. Jesus suggested as much when He compared His second coming to the coming of a bridegroom and the people who await Him to ten virgins preparing for a wedding (Matthew 25:1–13). Moreover, Paul wrote, "Husbands, love your wives, even as Christ also loved the church, and gave himself for it" (Ephesians 5:25). A man "nourisheth and cherisheth" his wife, "even as the Lord the church" (Ephesians 5:29).

And marriage partners who help carry one another's afflictions (see Chapter 10) are doing something Christlike. By living more as He does, they will become more as He is.

The wolf in the parable is any serious threat to a marriage or to one of the marriage partners. Because of the hireling's limited commitment, when he "seeth the wolf coming," he flees.

Why does the Lord speak in such matter-of-fact terms about this wolf that always seems to show up? Because life is hard and full of problems—wolves. Dealing with the wolves is central to life's purpose. For a husband and wife to deal with the wolves together is central to the purpose of marriage.

Some of the wolves are so frightening they can scatter the sheep or catch them and kill them. Still, a good shepherd will not flee, even if that means he must give his life to protect the sheep. Yet we now live in an undisciplined society in which too many people think of marriage as a contract between two hirelings who can too easily give up and get out.

Covenant attitudes ask us to get over the self-absorption that produces hirelings and replace it with a shepherd's self-mastery. Only "after much tribulation come the blessings," the Lord said (D&C 58:4). "For ye receive no witness until after the trial of your faith" (Ether 12:6). President David O. McKay's philosophy about spirituality was focused keenly on such practical forms of discipline and sacrifice. His words describe the kind of spiritual work required to sustain a vision of covenant marriage:

"Every noble impulse, every unselfish expression of love, every brave suffering for the right; every surrender of self to something higher than self; every loyalty to an ideal; every unselfish devotion to principle; every helpfulness to humanity; every act of self-control; every fine courage of the soul, undefeated by pretense or policy; but by being, doing, and living of good for the very good's sake—that is spirituality."[1]

Many wolves come at us today from every direction. And many of the meanest ones snarl and pound on the doors of young married couples. But before we consider some wolves, let us be clear that *just because you're having tough problems in your marriage and your family doesn't mean there is something wrong with you.* Quite the opposite. You're just seeing the wolves, and they always come.

Our doctrinal perspective on mortality and the plan of salvation teaches us that life is supposed to be full of problems—story problems. We learn about life and we discover hidden satisfactions by solving one personal story problem and then moving on to the next one.

Earlier we caught a glimpse of Brian and Kathy on their wedding day. After they had been married about ten years, I heard Kathy talking about the problems in her life as she and Brian shared their recent experiences with a small circle of intimate friends in a matter-of-fact blend of realism and hope. The second of their six children, Melissa, has cerebral palsy. She will never walk or talk; yet when she smiles, her countenance can fill a room with light. Because Melissa has severe problems with eating, her parents feed her by carefully draining a container of liquid food into a tube surgically implanted directly into her stomach. Each of her four daily feedings takes ninety minutes. When she gets a respiratory infection, sometimes she can't control her tongue, which may then block her breathing. One of Melissa's relatives recently looked at her and said, "Not a lot of people want to trade places with you now, Melissa, but you just wait."

Kathy and Brian had been living in a large city for several years while he was attending school. To finance their education, Kathy taught part-time, and they worked day and night together as university dorm parents. With the end of his education now in sight, it appeared impossible to find a job in his field.

She and Brian had been waiting for conditions to get better for what seemed like as long as they could remember. Kathy told her friends it had recently dawned on her that life will always be hard, but she has discovered that a hard life is okay. More than that, she has discovered an unexpected connection between the hard things and the best things of life. She has also found that although she enjoys traveling and getting away, she really is happiest when she's just at home with her children, as demanding as that often is.

Others in Brian and Kathy's little circle that day also shared their own stories about the helpless feelings that accompany a miscarriage, about failed applications for schools and jobs, about struggling to hang on in demanding Church callings, the surprises of health problems, and their worries about whether their children will ultimately accept what their parents teach them about life and eternal life day by day.

As the friends talked, a theme emerged—*life's problems never seem to cease, but trying hard to deal with the problems somehow makes you dig deep enough that you learn things you'd never understand without the digging.* A happy life isn't about getting what you want; it's about the attitude you develop toward whatever happens to you, an attitude that lets you grow. Faith and sacrifice are no longer abstractions about the pioneers or people in the scriptures; now those are the principles we must live to get through each day, and they are sometimes as essential as food and water. There is something mellow and enriching about living this way as husband and wife, trying to discover what's behind life's problems, together, as a team.

Scott Peck wrote that once we understand that life is difficult, rather than just whining about it, we'll be willing to accept "discipline" as "the basic set of tools we require to solve life's problems." Solving problems can still be painful. Yet "it is only because of problems that we grow mentally and spiritually." Thus "wise people learn not to dread but actually to welcome problems" rather than avoid them. The "tendency to avoid problems" and their attendant suffering can eventually shrivel the human spirit.[2]

People who learn the value of facing life problems directly, with all their discomfort, will develop the discipline and the tools needed to solve problems, "learning and growing in the process. When we teach ourselves and our children discipline, we are teaching them and ourselves how to suffer and also how to grow."

The use of these tools is enormously enhanced by our developing "the will to use them, which is love."[3]

Those who therefore apply the life-altering patterns of covenant marriage will become good shepherds for their wives or husbands. As they experience life together, they will encounter wolf after wolf, not because they're necessarily doing something wrong but because applying the gospel to those encounters fulfills the very nature and purpose of the human experience.

To the extent that they can be shepherds for each other, they will not merely guard against the wolves but they will also extend themselves for the purpose of nourishing the eternal spiritual growth of their companion. When that happens, though at times they may feel they are giving up their lives to some degree, they will ultimately discover that by living the Christlike life of the shepherd who will not flee, they will have found—and given to each other—the abundant life of authentic joy.

CHAPTER NINE

THE WOLF OF ADVERSITY: ON BEING AFFLICTED IN ANOTHER'S AFFLICTIONS

Every marriage is tested repeatedly by at least three kinds of wolves: natural adversities, the personal imperfections of each partner, and the self-centered individualism that has spawned today's belief that marriage is just a contract.

Consider first the wolf of adversity, or, to use Lehi's apt word, "opposition," which "must needs be," he said, "in all things" (2 Nephi 2:11). Most couples find this wolf at their door so often that he is no stranger, even though his arrival always, somehow, surprises us.

President Gordon B. Hinckley once described how all marriages taste adversity: "Stormy weather occasionally hits every household. Connected inevitably with the whole [marriage and family] process is much of pain—physical, mental, and emotional. There is much of stress and struggle, of fear and worry. . . . There seems never to be enough money. . . . Sickness strikes periodically. Accidents happen. . . .

"It has been so since the beginning."

He cited a favorite quotation from Jenkin Lloyd Jones:

"'There seems to be a superstition among many thousands of our young who hold hands and smooch in the drive-ins that marriage is a cottage surrounded by perpetual hollyhocks to which a perpetually young and handsome husband comes home to a perpetually young and ravishing wife. When the hollyhocks wither and boredom and bills appear the divorce courts are jammed. . . .

"'Anyone who imagines that bliss is normal is going to waste a lot of time running around and shouting that he has been robbed.' (*Deseret News,* 12 June 1973, p. A4.)"[1]

Elder Joe J. Christensen echoed that marital adversity is natural: "Occasionally, we hear something like, 'Why, we have been married for fifty years, and we have never had a difference of opinion.' If that is literally the case, then one of the partners is overly dominated by the other or, as someone said, is a stranger to the truth. Any intelligent couple will have differences of opinion. Our challenge is to be sure we know how to resolve them."[2]

Marie's and my first encounter with the wolf of adversity came shortly after our marriage began. A few weeks before the wedding, we had fasted and prayed to decide when we should start our family. We read the teachings of the prophets encouraging young couples to have children. We wanted to follow those teachings, but we couldn't figure out how to do that and still make our financial ends meet while we both finished school.

We finally felt at peace that we should let nature take its course. Two months after our wedding we got the big news. To use the standard Australian term, Marie "fell pregnant." And the joyous news of the pregnancy fell upon us in an odd way. In sharp contrast to the spiritual peace we had felt when we first accepted the idea of welcoming our children, Marie was suddenly hit hard with morning sickness. The pregnancy remained bumpy to the end. She was bedfast for the last two weeks, her final exams were due, and then the baby's delivery was complicated. The whole experience was much harder than we had expected.

When Marie was cuddling our new little redheaded son in her hospital room, our salty obstetrician bounced in to greet her with his cheery portent of the opposition yet to come: "Well, how does it feel to have the easy part over with?" He knew how hard the pregnancy and delivery had been.

Puzzled, Marie asked, "Easy part?"

"Sure," he said. "It's the next twenty years that will be hard!"

He was right, especially when six more children followed. Through all the diapers and dishes, the frustrations and the outbursts, the nights without sleep and the days without peace—and the multiple moments of laughter, insight, and delight—we saw in Alma's words the real-life version of marriage and parenting: fatigue, labor in the spirit, journeyings, suffering, sorrows, afflictions, and yet laced through all of this was "incomprehensible joy" (Alma 28:8; see also 17:5). We would never trade those forty hard years for forty easy ones.

Incomprehensible joy because you can't explain it, you can't imagine it, you can hardly believe it—until it is your own experience. Much of it you just wouldn't do, unless your solemn covenants made you feel you *must* do it. Paradoxically, we often learn only after the fact that what we've learned and grown through is worth whatever it cost. Which is why we can't learn the things Adam and Eve did until we learn them the same way they did: the hard way, in the earth school—much of it in marriage, the homeroom of the earth school.

This earth is not our home. We are away at school. As Theodore Roethke wrote:

I wake to sleep, and take my waking slow.
I feel my fate in what I cannot fear.
I learn by going where I have to go.[3]

The Atonement of Christ is a central element in the doctrinal flow that joins the story of Adam and Eve about opposition, marriage, children, misery, and joy with our learning for ourselves about tasting the bitter that we may know to prize the sweet.

The doctrines of the Fall and the Atonement place us in the earth school for the very purpose of teaching us to prize—to really grasp the meaning of—the good. These doctrines put act two's wolf of adversity into the big-picture perspective of acts one and three. Hard, unexpected, and undeserved problems challenge all marriages. Yet problems of that kind are among the most vivid illustrations of the "opposition in all things" without which we would never experience "holiness nor misery, neither good nor bad" (2 Nephi 2:11).

The Atonement somehow gives a kind of life-energy to our covenants, with power to turn the burdens into privileges "through the joy of his Son" (Alma 33:23). Of course we experience adversity in mortality. Yet the Savior's healing and compensating power will sanctify the effects of that experience for our gain and growth.

Helping to carry the afflictions of our loved ones is also a Christlike thing to do, because that process follows the pattern of the Lord's being afflicted in our afflictions, even to the point of giving our lives for our sheep, a little or a great deal at a time. Trying honestly, even if imperfectly, to carry another person's burdens over an entire lifetime really can help make Christians of us.

I saw one poignant but not uncommon example of adversity's wolf in Tyler and Anita's marriage. Having both come from large families, they hungered for children of their own. After years of patient pleading and medical searching, they learned excitedly that their baby was on his way. But their boy was born with a serious congenital defect, literally a broken heart. Following a three-week struggle, which included a search for a possible heart transplant, Anita and Tyler lost their little Ryan, and they couldn't help fearing that he would be their only child.

Just before Ryan's death, his parents were in the temple, pleading for him. Anita wrote that there she "felt as Adam and Eve must have felt upon leaving the innocence of the Garden of Eden. They had known they could never return to the peace and security that the Garden had provided them" but were "obligated to face their lone and dreary world together."

On a warm and windy day in a small Utah cemetery, a large family "circle of crying faces" surrounded the chair that held Ryan's small casket. Tyler and Anita stood close together, holding each other up in every way. "A violin duet filled the air with the soft strains of 'I Am a Child of God,' . . . a bittersweet melody." That day, wrote Anita, was "the beginning of many weeks and months of aching, soul-searching reaching, pleading, pondering, growing, and understanding. It was a time to weep, a time to mourn."[4]

Now, years later, Ryan is like a pioneer advance party to the other side of the veil for his family. His life beckons to his younger brothers and sisters, for whom he and his heavenly home are tangibly real. I have watched them return to his grave annually on his birthday. I have seen them mature, grow closer together, as they have also sustained other grieving parents with their hard-won perspective on life and death.

Tyler and Anita's ripening together makes me think of Adam and Eve's growth process. In the beginning, Eve was for Adam simply "the woman thou gavest me" (Moses 4:18). Then later, together, they lost Abel. And, perhaps with even more sorrow, together they lost Cain, who "listened not any more to the voice of the Lord" (Moses 5:26). By then, their shared adversity turned Adam and Eve toward each other in a way that only couples who have struggled together can know: "Adam and his wife mourned before the Lord, because of Cain and his brethren" (Moses 5:27).

The seamless sense of shared support in a couple's grief mirrors the Lord's moving words when assigning Peter Whitmer to be Oliver Cowdery's missionary companion. *"And be you afflicted in all his afflictions,* ever lifting up your heart unto me in prayer and faith, for *his and your* deliverance" (D&C 30:6; italics added).

In other words, let his afflictions be your own, no matter what they are or where they come from. Absorb them. Accept them. They are yours because they are his. Then your prayers will be not only for him but for "his and your" deliverance.

Isaiah's use of this same scriptural phrase shows how shared tribulation brings the Savior into a marriage relationship, as He consecrates our mutual afflictions for our mutual gain: *"In all their affliction he was afflicted; and the angel of his presence saved them: in his love and in his pity he redeemed them: and he bare them, and carried them all the days of old"* (Isaiah 63:9; italics added; see also D&C 133:53).

The comparison between these two scriptures suggests that when we allow ourselves honestly to be afflicted in the afflictions of our marriage partner, we are doing something Christlike—absorbing another's pain, carrying another's burden. We are then Good Shepherds, not hirelings.

Being afflicted in the afflictions of a marriage partner can range from trivial afflictions to major ones, but in either case, the attitudes of unqualified sharing are essentially the same. At any point along the spectrum of severity, the partner to a covenant marriage gets into the boat of affliction with his or her partner rather than just watching the partner's affliction from a distance. In a contract marriage, each individual's problems are his or her own. In a covenant marriage, "each man's grief is my own."[5]

Before looking more at shared affliction, we should note that the fulness of empathy that animates this principle has a positive side: rejoicing in one another's joys. In the misguided competitiveness of modern society, we sometimes envy the happiness of other people rather than rejoicing in their happiness. That competitive spirit can deprive us of one of empathy's real delights—honestly sharing our companion's happy experiences as we "live joyfully with the wife whom thou lovest all the days of . . . life" (Ecclesiastes 9:9).

We saw one poignant example of the power of vicarious satisfaction in the way Wal Richards felt about taking pictures at other people's weddings. Parents also learn about basking in another person's satisfaction when they discover that they "have no greater joy than to hear that [their] children walk in truth" (3 John 1:4). Vicarious joy is also well known to teachers who see their students learn and to coaches whose players succeed.

I've seldom seen a more ecstatic facial expression than that of Sarah Hughes's coach when she hugged her gifted student as sixteen-year-old Sarah glided off the rink to discover in shocked surprise that she had just won the gold medal in the ice-skating competition at the 2002 Olympic Games in Salt Lake City. The tears of joy on both faces had differing motivations, but both rejoiced in the same achievement.

The Lord Himself knows these feelings: "How great is his joy in the soul that repenteth!" (D&C 18:13). This satisfaction in another's growth must be among our Father's highest realizations. Our growth is, after all, His work and His glory. Thus a central feature of celestial life is to rejoice in someone else's joy (Moses

1:39). This positive divine empathy is also the inverse image of the sadness our Father feels when His children slide into irretrievable misery: "Behold, they are without affection, and they hate their own blood. . . . wherefore should not the heavens weep, seeing these shall suffer?" (Moses 7:33–37).

For much of my adult life I enjoyed the mentoring friendship of Harry Blundell, twenty years my senior, who recently passed away. One of Harry's gifts was that he could honestly rejoice in the good things that happened to other people to whom he felt a closeness, in and out of his family. His heart reached out in shared joy, just as it did in shared sorrow.

In my last conversation with Harry, his physical infirmities were giving him a blue day in a hospital. As we visited, I thanked him for helping teach me how to fish for trout with nymphs. Then I told him about recently catching a few German browns with Harry's favorite nymph in a stream where I knew Harry loved to fish. His delighted expressions at the story's every detail were a story in themselves. Then he said with dancing eyes, "I enjoyed that as much as if I'd caught every one of those fish myself."

Applying that principle to marriage, we learn about both sides of shared empathy in the Lord's instructions to Emma Smith. He told Emma to "be for a comfort unto my servant, Joseph Smith, Jun., thy husband, in his afflictions, with consoling words, in the spirit of meekness" (D&C 25:5). But hers was not the only supporting role: "And thou needest not fear, for thy husband shall support thee" (D&C 25:9). Then, as Emma would "let thy soul delight in thy husband," the Lord assured her that Joseph's promised reward was also hers: "And a crown of righteousness thou shalt receive" (D&C 25:14–15).

I've seen many a marriage partner rejoice in the other's unique interests, even when that activity held little or no direct charm for the supporting spouse: A husband warmly encouraged his wife's foray into competitive horse shows after their children were grown because he knew what horses had meant to her childhood. A non-aviator wife recognized how much it meant to her husband that she support his desire to learn to fly airplanes, his childhood dream. In each case these spouses sensed that if it was important to the other, it was important to them.

This same spirit of reciprocity will bless the wife who can, even in the tears of her own sacrifice, rejoice when her husband is called as a bishop. Then before long, she might be called as Relief Society president, and it will be his turn. The Church has a way of teaching each of us what Emma Smith knew: fear not, for thy husband will support thee—and sooner or later, those supporting roles will probably be reversed.

Companions can delight in a spouse's gifts in ways that bless their entire family. Pam said that soon after she married Kelly, she was sorting through some of his personal papers as she organized things in their first apartment. She found a list he'd once made of the qualities he wanted in a wife. As she scanned the list, she felt reassured until she saw "must play a musical instrument" on his list. Her only experience with music had been when the ward choir director asked her not to attend practices any more, because her monotone voice did more harm than good.

Pam thought of Kelly's passion for music, his years of developing his musical gifts. She could have felt a twinge of envy. Even though her tin ear had not kept him from marrying her, that didn't end the story. She decided by herself that music mattered enough to him that she would make sure each of their children learned to play an instrument. Over time, her commitment bore musical fruit, and the family made music together, and even Pam learned eventually to play a simple recorder in the family orchestra.

CHAPTER TEN

SHARED AFFLICTION:
SOME STORIES

We begin with what may seem a trivial illustration. She leaves her purse at a service station while the couple is traveling a long distance on a tight schedule. Thirty minutes after leaving the station, she suddenly realizes her loss. "Oh, no! I left my purse in the restroom when we stopped for gas!"

He might justifiably chide her for not remembering, as he wheels the car around and begins to backtrack along their travel route. He could point out, perhaps more than once during the day, that her failure to remember the purse made them late for an important commitment. He could exonerate himself to the people who are waiting for them by telling them that the reason they're late is because she, not he, forgot the purse.

But if he accepts the idea of "be you afflicted in all her afflictions," he will know that she is at least as embarrassed as he is, and she really doesn't need him to point out her oversight. When he remembers this perspective, he will behave as if he had left his wallet in the men's room; and that will change the tone and spirit of all their conversation. Neither the purse nor the failure to remember it is just her problem—it is their problem. Once this is clear, both will lift up their hearts.

At the other end of the spectrum of seriousness, husbands and wives must deal with each other's illness or emotional turmoil. During the long illness of Claire Hunter, her husband was a member of the Quorum of the Twelve Apostles. One late afternoon Elder Howard W. Hunter left a meeting as soon as it concluded, rather than waiting to visit as he sometimes did. Someone asked where he was going in such a hurry. The reply was that at this hour each week, Elder Hunter always hurried home to take his wife to her hair appointment.

On this day, as had been the case for months, Sister Hunter was a bedfast invalid, unable to speak. Knowing this, one of those in the meeting asked why Elder Hunter took his wife for her regular hair appointment when she might not even be aware that the hairdresser was caring for her hair. One of the Brethren who knew Elder Hunter well replied, "Because he knows she might be aware. And even if she isn't, he is aware—and he knows how much that weekly appointment always meant to her. Because it mattered to her, it matters to him."

I thought of this sense of shared affliction when reading a letter from a longtime friend. After commenting on other topics, he wrote about his wife's difficult chronic illness:

"We are fine. Jan suffered a terrible breakdown a few years ago, which led to her [early] retirement. She is a pioneer patient, one of many to sadly learn that [a certain drug] alone will not control manic-depression more than 10–15 years. Her recovery has been very slow. We finally found a new doctor who brought together a combination of drugs that works, [for now]. These times are never easy for us as a family. But these episodes of heartache and even fear fuse our feelings for each other and have brought our children even closer to us. I think, in a strange, miraculous way, our heartache has saved our family. I owe so much of my own survival training to my mission—the mother lode I continue to mine every year of my life."

The tone of these lines is unexpectedly peaceful yet candid. The references are not singular but plural: "*We* are fine." "*We* found a doctor. "*Our* feelings for each other." "*Our* heartache." Whatever their trauma has been, they have shared it together. The affliction is theirs, not just hers.

At almost the same time I received this letter, I heard from another friend, Rick, whose story of shared affliction gives perspective to his letter. His story centers on Thursday Island, which is located off the northeastern tip of Australia. On its west is Wednesday Island, and on its east is, of course, Friday Island.

Rick grew up in New Zealand. He never knew his father. His mother, who never did marry, lived with a series of men to whom Rick looked in vain for fatherly guidance. When he was ten, his mother's boyfriend would come home drunk and beat her. By the time Rick was twelve, this boyfriend had introduced him to alcohol; and within a couple of years, Rick was into hard drugs. In his late teens, Rick left New Zealand for Australia, where he joined a drug gang and spent all his time and energy feeding his drug habit. Eventually he ran out of money and could no longer steal enough from his drug friends. So he prepared himself to rob a stranger. For the first time in his life, he was ready to kill someone.

Rick waited near a train station on a dark street in Sydney. He approached a well-dressed man leaving the station. He flashed his crude knife and ordered, "Give me your money or I'll kill you." The frightened man pulled his wallet from his pocket. As he opened the wallet, trembling, Rick saw there a photograph of the man's family. The picture hit Rick with a piercing thought: "Look at that beautiful family. I'm about to kill somebody who has what I've always wanted."

Rick suddenly felt such shame that he turned and ran away, throwing his weapon into nearby bushes. The astonished man gasped and ran the other way. Rick kept running until he reached a city park. There he fell to the ground crying and breathless, pounding the earth in frustration and self-doubt. He kept thinking how worthless, how pointless, was his life. Having hit bottom so hard, Rick resolved that his only choice was suicide.

He climbed to the top of a nearby skyscraper and found a place where he could leap to his death. As he poised to jump, a strange thought filled his mind. Like his impression about the family picture, this reaction showed that some inner light still flickered in his soul: "If I land on that sidewalk, I'll die; but my last earthly act will leave a mess for somebody else to clean up." Finding relief in his confidence that he could find a better way to die, Rick raced back to his apartment. He decided to go to Thursday Island.

When he first saw this little island as a child, he thought it was the most peaceful place he'd ever seen. His memory invited him back now. There he could take his life without disturbing anybody. So he gathered his few possessions and flew to Thursday Island. He hired a boat, agreeing to meet the owner the next morning at dawn. The owner would deliver him to a tiny uninhabited island nearby, where he could die in peace. And nobody would have to clean up after him.

Rick spent his last night in a local hotel. As he vacantly ate his final meal, he noticed three women singing on a small stage. One of them had an especially mellow voice. He stayed and listened.

Grateful, he offered the singers a drink. Two accepted, but Moana, the one with the mellow voice, politely said she didn't drink.

Feeling drawn to Moana, Rick stayed and talked. They kept talking as he walked her home. He didn't tell her his plans. They talked until daylight broke the darkness. Rick looked at his watch. He told Moana he had to go. He thanked her for what had been the most peaceful night of his life and then hurried away.

Suddenly Moana called to him. "Stop, Rick," she said. "I don't know where you're going, but don't go." Rick looked back, noticing a light in her face that matched her mellow voice. But it was too late; he had made up his mind. He looked at her again and then toward the sea, hesitating between life and death. Her voice pulled him back to her.

She asked for no explanation. He sat down while she cooked breakfast. As he finished eating, two young men in white shirts came to the door. They were missionaries. Moana was a new convert, and they often came to see her. That's why she didn't drink. She asked Rick to listen to the missionaries.

Within a short time, Rick was baptized, and he stayed on Thursday Island. He married Moana and created his own family picture. I met Rick and Moana some years later when they served together as a missionary couple.

Rick had heard Moana's call to live. He left the path of addiction and death and returned to her. She fed him, both physically and spiritually. She sang to him what Alma called "the song of redeeming love" (Alma 5:26). She knew the song by heart, because the Savior's love had lodged there. As she called to Rick, the song and the love also lodged in his heart. This story teaches the power of a woman's moral influence and the power of a family picture to begin a change of heart that gives purpose to being alive.

Rick told me this story when we first met him and Moana. A couple of years later we saw them again. Prompted by that second visit, he wrote us a letter. Its tone, even its content, are strikingly like the letter we saw earlier from Jan's husband. Happy families, covenant marriages, are alike—in sunshine and in shade:

"Moana is always a blessing to me. In her humble way she lives the gospel. She is currently going through a trial of memory loss, and it gives her much anguish. At times I feel I am helpless to put her at ease. Then I remember how she cared for me as I went through withdrawals from drugs and the nights she sat up till daylight comforting me as my mind wandered with its fears. Love and patience, selfless service and faith in the Savior—that is how she helped me. I pray as often as I can. I love my wife and desire to be her strength. The Savior is helping us."

A story from Leo Tolstoy also reveals how allowing oneself to be afflicted in another's afflictions can completely change us—and deliver us—from our own afflictions. In *War and Peace,* we meet Natasha, a happy and romantic teenager in the Rostov family. Natasha falls in love with Andrew, who is more mature than she is. After they are engaged, Andrew goes to war, telling Natasha to take a year to be sure about the engagement. She pledges her unconditional devotion but is soon swept off her feet by a manipulative charlatan with whom she almost elopes. Hearing this news, Andrew calls off the engagement. Natasha tries fervently to repent of her foolish mistake, but she doesn't hear from Andrew.

Two years later, Natasha's family leaves Moscow to escape the approaching French army. As the Rostovs assist injured Russian soldiers who are also leaving the city, Natasha discovers Andrew among the wounded. As she nurses him back to health, she begs his forgiveness. They eventually renew their love for each other, but Andrew's wounds are so serious that he does not survive.

Nastasha is despondent. She withdraws from her family, from all of her interests, from life itself. She feels it an insult to Andrew's memory even to think about the future without him.

Then comes word that Natasha's beloved and cheerful younger brother, the fifteen-year-old Petya, has been killed in battle. This news depresses Natasha even further. But her sorrow is eclipsed by that of Natasha's mother, who is wild with despair over losing her child. Others in the family try to help, but only Natasha has the power to really reach her mother. Instinctively sensing her mother's desperate need, Natasha rushes to her side and stays with her night and day for three weeks, feeding her, talking to her, and comforting her, until she restores her mother's will to live. Of Natasha's experience, Tolstoy writes: "The dreadful ache [Natasha felt upon hearing about Petya] was immediately followed by a feeling of release from the oppressive constraint that had prevented her taking part in life. The sight of her father, the terribly wild cries of her mother that she heard through the door, made her immediately forget herself and her own grief." Natasha turns her attention fully to her mother, repeating, "'My darling Mummy!' . . . straining all the power of her love to find some way of taking upon herself the excess of grief that crushed her mother."

As the three-week vigil concludes, "Natasha's wound healed in that way. She thought her life was ended, but her love for her mother unexpectedly showed her that the essence of life—love—was still active within her. Love awoke and so did life."[1]

Though Tolstoy does not say so, Natasha seems to act here as something of a Christ figure, giving all she has, spiritually and emotionally, "taking upon herself the excess of grief that crushed her mother." The effect of losing herself in this way is that she finds herself, unintentionally and indirectly renewing her own spiritual will to live and to love, which had seemed mortally wounded.

I once attended a Sunday evening meeting for priesthood leaders and their wives. The subject was how to strengthen temple work in a particular region. Just before the concluding talk, a man was invited to sing "I Need Thee Every Hour." I learned after the meeting that he had experienced some serious problems in his life and had only recently been returned to full Church fellowship. This song was his first act of Church participation since his return. Learning about his circumstances helped me understand what happened during the song.

He began singing with an earnestness that invited the Spirit's presence. Toward the end of the third verse, his focus on the meaning of the song's words caused him to lose his composure. After singing, "I need thee, oh, I need thee," his voice broke and he couldn't sing, despite two or three attempts. The woman at the piano played a little bit, wondering what to do. When he began to sing again, his voice was unsteady. "I need thee . . ." A woman seated on the stand spontaneously but quietly began to sing with him. "I need thee, oh, I need thee . . ." Her singing gave him the strength to move on; then she stopped to let him finish the verse.

He continued singing until he neared the end of the last verse. Again he was unable to continue, having even more difficulty than before. The pianist hesitated. Again the woman on the stand began to sing with him and for him. As he joined her, this time she continued to sing with him. Soon others began singing, until all of us in the congregation were singing the last few words together:

> *Every hour I need thee!*
> *Oh, bless me now, my Savior;*
> *I come to thee!* [2]

"I Need Thee Every Hour" is about our need for Jesus Christ. But that night I discovered that in a sense, perhaps it can also refer to how much we need one another, how much our mutual support can sustain and lift when we allow ourselves to follow the Good Shepherd by being afflicted in another's afflictions.

Paul taught all husbands to "love your wives, even as Christ also loved the church" (Ephesians 5:25). And how much did Christ love the Church? In all their afflictions He was afflicted.

In a covenant marriage, she is afflicted in all his afflictions, and he in hers. Together they bear each affliction and carry each other all their days. Their pattern is that of the Good Shepherd, who "shall consecrate thine afflictions for thy gain" (2 Nephi 2:2).

Chapter Eleven

The Wolf of Personal Imperfection

The second wolf is personal imperfection. The best of us have weaknesses, and the worst of us have strengths. And in the daily closeness of marriage, we see each other at our best and at our worst. How we deal with these inevitable disclosures affects the spirit within our homes, our ability to understand and help each other, and our own sense of who we are and what we can become.

Good marriages (and the individual growth of each marriage partner) actually thrive on a couple's ability to share gentle and loving correction with each other when needed. Most of us are not always aware of our weaknesses or the way we affect other people. We need the help of an honest, caring spouse to provide corrective vision for our blind spots. That correction helps most when we really extend ourselves to communicate with kindness and a charitable spirit.

So whether our suggestions help or hurt our partner (and our marriage) usually depends on the way we choose to give advice, not on whether we give it at all. There are many effective techniques for saying what needs to be said. The "feedback sand-wich," for example, consciously looks for ways to mix needed correction with specific, deserved praise—all in the same paragraph and with the same supportive tone.

One time early in our marriage I was so preoccupied with university homework that I forgot to take out our massive old garbage can two weeks in a row. The lid on top of the battered can bulged higher each day. That was one household chore I knew how to do—but only if I remembered to do it. We drove into our wintry driveway very late the night before the early morning garbage pickup was due. Marie remembered what I needed to do and thought about how to tell me.

"It's a special day in the neighborhood tomorrow," she said with cheerful mildness.

"Special day?" I said. "What is it?"

"Think about it," she said. "It's something special right on our street."

I still missed it. "Is it a parade?" I asked innocently.

"Well, kind of. Yes, it *is* a parade. Do you think we need to do our part to be in it?"

Suddenly I grasped her point. "Oh, garbage!" I said.

"You've got it!" she replied.

As I dropped off to sleep that night after performing my mighty labor, I smiled as I realized with what deliberate care Marie had coached her errant husband.

It is beyond the scope of this book to say much about how-to methods, except to underscore the doctrinal point that an overly critical spirit can eventually destroy a marriage. "He that hath the spirit of contention is not of me," said the Savior, "but is of the devil, who is the father of contention, and he stirreth up the hearts of men to contend with anger, one with another" (3 Nephi

11:29). King Bejamin taught that those who seek to "be filled with the love of God" will "not have a mind to injure one another, but to live peaceably. . . . And ye will not suffer your children [to] fight and quarrel one with another" (Mosiah 4:12–14).

That's why the problem of our own imperfections can be such a big wolf—not just because we're imperfect but because our imperfections are such a large target that the wolf of ugly criticism can easily drive away the Spirit and blow our spiritual house down.

The spirit of raw criticism between husband and wife is a common theme in the early chapters of many stories of marriage breakdown. When it becomes intense and frequent, such criticism can be a serious form of emotional abuse. As President Gordon B. Hinckley said:

"Who can calculate the wounds inflicted, their depth and pain, by harsh and mean words spoken in anger? How pitiful a sight is a man who is strong in many ways but who loses all control of himself when some little thing . . . disturbs [him]. . . .

"A violent temper is such a terrible, corrosive thing [that] only feeds evil with resentment and rebellion and pain."[1]

I have also seen how bitterly destructive, yet how often practiced, this habit is. I understand why the Lord's prophet would feel that while "most marriages in the Church are happy," there is "enough of the opposite to justify what I am saying" about the harm of harsh criticism.[2]

One LDS woman told me through tears of great sorrow how her husband's constant complaining finally destroyed not only their marriage but her entire sense of self-worth. At first he corrected her in off-handed ways about this or that small thing. As time went on, he gradually lost any sense of restraint. His language took on a kind of mean-spirited tone, as she felt he sat in judgment on her not just with bluntness but with contempt.

He complained about her cooking and housecleaning. Then it was how she used her time, how she talked, and the way she looked and dressed. He reserved his ugliest tone of voice for the way she reasoned. Eventually his harsh insistence convinced her that she was utterly inept and dysfunctional, with or without her marriage. My heart ached for her and for him. I thought of Jacob's plea on behalf of women who "instead of feasting upon the pleasing word of God have daggers placed to pierce their souls and wound their delicate minds" (Jacob 2:9).

Contrast this woman's experience with Deb's. I heard her describe her precious three years of temple marriage to Sam at his funeral after a fatal car crash. She had grown up as a shy person with a low sense of worth and little self-confidence. During their brief marriage, Sam was constantly amazed at all the good things she did. He would say, "How did you know how to cook that?" "How is it you always know the right thing to say?" "I don't have a clue what to do with this baby, but you just know how to do everything he needs. Who taught you all these things?"

A few days before the accident, Deb had caught herself looking in a mirror and smiling at herself. "I'm a good person," she said. "I can do things! Sam tells me so—it must be true!" "Now that he is gone," she said at the funeral, "I will miss him terribly, constantly. But the sense of my own worth that Sam gave me, no one can take from me now. And it will only keep growing." Because Sam constantly affirmed Deb's value with honest, specific, deserved appreciation for her, she believed more in herself, and more in God's acceptance of her, than she had ever before thought possible.

One can spot someone of Sam's maturity early in the dating

process. A young woman I know was dating two capable returned missionaries. One day she realized a big difference between the two. One of them enjoyed making jokes at her expense, putting her down in front of his friends to make them laugh. Then it dawned on her that her other friend would never do that, as a matter of principle. "In fact," she said, "he would protect me from that if anybody else tried it." She soon lost interest in the first young man.

The wolf of personal imperfection really rattles our home's timbers when the imperfection is a serious, sinful one. I have seen several cases in which a husband's or wife's inability to cope with such weaknesses led to marriage breakdown. In talking about these cases, I do not minimize the seriousness of chronic bad habits or major sins. I acknowledge the transgressor's primary responsibility to repent and change. My heart goes out fully to the faithful, disciplined partner who would never consider doing what his or her spouse has done. But as a matter of doctrinal principle, if the Atonement of Christ allows us to learn from our experience without being condemned by it, there must a way for married partners to give each other room to learn while refraining from condemnation.

The problem of the prodigal spouse is not unlike the problems of prodigal sons and daughters, and the comparison here between kinship and marriage is helpful. You show me the temple-married parent of an adolescent engaged in serious drug, alcohol, or sexual misbehavior, and I'll show you a parent who has probably thought seriously about asking the ungrateful child to leave home—or worse. After surviving the initial shock, the parent will feel embarrassed and then angry that the child would reject the parent's years of sacrifice, teaching, and exemplary living.

But in many cases, after what can be exhaustingly long nights and months of prayerful searching, the parent usually realizes that simply banishing the child isn't really an option. When the parent's anger and bewilderment turn into a desire to really listen and understand, an entirely new relationship with the child can develop. The process may take years. It may take a bishop's intervention and/or professional counseling. But if the parent communicates love and commitment more than the understandable but now consciously muffled desire to judge, the prodigal may come to himself and return and repent (Luke 15:17)—not simply to please the parent but because the child has discovered that he can, and wants to, claim his own spiritual blessings, and he needs a warm place to return to.

Frequently, a turning point occurs when the parent comes to understand that the child is searching for his own identity or is perhaps grasping to satisfy some deep unmet need created by gaps or trauma from an earlier time in his life. As Sterling Ellsworth writes:

"Children need love like fish need water. If [because of what happens at home or in other relationships during childhood] they don't get the real thing, they reach for love substitutes such as food, sexual self-gratification, and pornography. Some love substitutes are even worse. . . .

"When true love is given to a child, he grows up sensitive to his own identity. . . . He doesn't need to go looking for love because his 'love bucket' is full."[3]

If the search for "love substitutes" is indeed at work in a child's rebellion, the truly attentive parent may, with great effort over a period of time, begin to restore some of the love, the attention, and the security the child may have missed—whatever the cause.

What does this comment about parents and children have to do with a spouse who has behavioral problems as an adult?

Because parents can't divorce their children and because everybody knows that children must learn to grow up, parents usually make more allowances and try harder to help their children than they try to help their spouses.

Yet our homes are full of adults who are also still growing, still learning, and still making mistakes—some of them very serious—as they, too, vainly and perhaps unwittingly search for substitute forms of love. In such cases, the same general principles that help us nourish an adolescent may help us nourish a married adult. As President Spencer W. Kimball taught:

"Jesus saw sin as wrong but also was able to see sin as springing from deep and unmet needs on the part of the sinner. This permitted him to condemn the sin without condemning the individual. . . . We need to be able to look deeply enough into the lives of others to see the basic causes for their failures and shortcomings."[4]

This insight reminds me of a woman who lost her husband in a plane crash when both were about forty years old. A few months after his death, she said that part of what helped her find peace was that there was no unfinished business between them, no regrets, no unresolved problems. As she reminisced, she said he had never lost his temper with her, and she had lost hers with him only twice. And both times, instead of replying in kind, he patiently sensed that her frustration was not really because of him but because of other things that had been going wrong for her—and he found nonjudgmental ways to support her in dealing with those things.

I once interviewed a married father who had been excommunicated for a pattern of transgression that began with a pornography habit he had developed well before his marriage. Repentance from such addiction can be unusually hard, but I concluded, as had the man's priesthood leaders, that his repentance and progress were genuine. He cried as he told me that the most significant factor in his recovery was the loving yet demanding patience and support his wife had given him during their years of trial together.

When I spoke with her before restoring his priesthood and temple blessings, I found her to be a realistic idealist. What she had been through was really miserable, and she had often almost given up. I asked her how she had been able to sustain him as she had. She said quietly, "I just prayed that I could look at him the way Christ looks at me. I thought that was the least I could do."

This woman reminds me that if we insist on a God of justice, chances are we'll only know a God of justice. But when we dig deeply enough to extend mercy to someone else, seeing him or her as the Savior would, we are more likely to recognize God's mercy when He extends it to us. The Savior said, "Blessed are the merciful: for they shall obtain mercy" (Matthew 5:7). Because the wolf of personal imperfection is so prevalent in our marriages, learning to extend mercy (which will teach us how to obtain it) is a natural part of the core curriculum in the homeroom of the earth school. Learning to be merciful makes Christians of us.

The value of learning to sense the "deep and unmet needs" of a companion applies not only in trying to understand a partner's poor choices but also when coping with other baffling behaviors. For example, Craig would sometimes become irrationally angry at Lucy when she needed to leave home at night—regardless of whether she needed to run a simple errand or to fulfill her duties as a Young Women leader. The couple would find themselves in emotional arguments that neither one could understand, and they blamed each other and the Church in a descending spiral of criticism.

The problem frayed their nerves until their sheer determination to understand each other led them to discover something

Craig hadn't realized any more than Lucy had. They found that during his childhood, his mother, a single parent, had frequently left him at home alone for prolonged absences. This pattern had continued long enough that it left Craig deeply traumatized, and in the emotional attachment of his marriage, his subliminal fear of Lucy's leaving him alone had triggered an entrenched emotional scar.

Kate and Rob had a similar but more complex problem. During his childhood years, Rob was abused by a parent, then his parents were divorced, and then his mother died in an accident. Kate knew all of this but assumed it was all in the past. It bothered her when Rob continually carried the trauma of his early years "almost like a suitcase" into their present interactions. She wanted him to just get over his past and move on with their marriage.

However, Rob was very thin-skinned whenever he felt corrected, much less really criticized. Her mildest suggestions at times triggered such angry responses that she felt forced into silence. Rob also objected with irrational intensity whenever she was late coming home. So one night she decided to be very direct, describing some of his faults and telling him to stop letting his past rule him—words she later realized were the worst she could have said to him. With a flash of angry sarcasm he said, "Well, thank you! Obviously you're so perfect."

Kate was furious. She turned around and stomped out. She decided to drive to her parents' home for the night to teach him a lesson. As she drove, a strong spiritual impression told her to stop, turn around, and go home. Kate stopped the car and burst into tears of exasperation. But the prompting continued. She didn't know what it meant, didn't know what to say, didn't want to swallow her own pride, but she drove home. Inside, she found Rob on their bed crying like a frightened child. He wasn't angry. He was afraid and hurt. She ran to him, held him, and whispered her love as they both cried.

As they worked harder to understand each other, Kate found that when Rob saw her leave in anger, she seemed to confirm what he dreaded most—that he wasn't capable of living in a way that would keep her close. He thought she had left him permanently, just as his mother had.

Rob's childhood home had been a cauldron of bitter criticism. Most conversations he could remember between his parents were loud, biting arguments. Then one day his mother left in a mighty huff. Soon there was a divorce. And the cauldron in Rob's young life boiled with grief and confusion. No wonder criticism and anger were, for Rob, triggers of unexplainable despair.

Kate soon discovered that you don't just marry a person in the present—you marry that person's past. And often the past will control the present in ways a partner could never understand without knowing the past. We must refrain from judging the present until we have a better sense of what it means in the light of the past, as hard as that may be to uncover.

Kate found a story that captured her discovery. Someone driving across a back road in Morocco came upon the scene of an accident. A car had carelessly hit and injured a sheep from a small, nearby flock. Local custom required the driver to pay to the shepherd one hundred times the sheep's value, and then the sheep would be slaughtered and divided among those present. As the shepherd approached and the driver prepared to make his payment, an experienced observer said to his companion as they watched, "The shepherd will not accept the money. They never do."

The two men watched the bearded old shepherd pick up the

injured animal and place it in a pouch at the front of his robe. Walking until he disappeared in the desert, the shepherd stroked the sheep with his hand and repeated the same word several times. The word was the sheep's name.[5]

Kate was the shepherd, and Rob was her wounded sheep. That realization came only gradually, not easily, but as it came, her responses to him became ever more like the old shepherd's. And what she had thought were Rob's faults somehow came to feel a good deal like her view of her own faults. She learned to judge less and listen more, until her understanding of what President Kimball called Rob's "deep, unmet needs" helped her discover new ways to help her pour into him the love and security he had never known as a child. That process included hours of gospel conversations together, which led them to Atonement doctrine as a major source of the love and peace Rob hungered for. The healing he gradually experienced was then not just his but theirs.

CHAPTER TWELVE

CHARITY: SEEING A SPOUSE'S IMPERFECTIONS FROM THE CENTER

A good shepherd will respond to a spouse's imperfections by giving up the spirit of negative criticism. Removing the weeds of criticism, however, is only the beginning. Once we have cleared the land on which our marital home rests, then we must begin planting the positive seeds of cooperation and support.

In addition, a real covenant marriage asks us to replace the wolf of ugly criticism not only with cooperation but finally with the lamb of true charity. Then our *motive* is more toward our companion's interest than our self-interest. Whatever we say or do is to seek our partner's blessing, growth, and happiness—just as the Good Shepherd desires those things for each of us. So we must move across the complete spectrum—from negative criticism toward constructive cooperation and, finally, toward charity, the pure love of Christ. Loving as He loves is at the heart of what it's like to see others as He sees them.

Jesus taught His disciples to love "as I have loved you" (John 13:34). This was "a new commandment" (John 13:34), going even beyond "love thy neighbour as thyself" (Mark 12:31). To love *as Christ loves* is a higher, deeper form of love that reflects our having become *like Him.* When we taste that love, we will extend Christlike compassion not only because we think we should but because that is the way we are becoming.

For all that charity means as an attitude toward the mass of humanity, for all that it means about the worth of souls in missionary work or family history or sustaining the poor and needy, charity never reaches a higher meaning than it does in marriage.

It isn't that difficult to be pleasant, even quite charitable, toward those with whom we have essentially contractual associations at church, at work, in our neighborhoods. But when we extend true charity to those who share our name, our checkbook, our possessions, our home, and our covenants, we are especially likely to emulate Him whose love we seek to have. When partners strive to qualify for the spiritual gift of charity, their covenant marriage can make Christians—Christlike beings—out of them. That is the very nature of charity: for it is "*bestowed*," that is, given as a spiritual gift, "upon all who are *true followers of . . . Jesus Christ; . . .* that when he shall appear we shall be *like him*" (Moroni 7:48; italics added).

For that reason, the quest to find charity in a covenant marriage is coupled with—usually even the result of—our quest to become better followers of the Savior. With such motivations, our love for Him is not in competition with, or going a different direction from, our love for our companion. Indeed, the more we extend true charity to a husband or wife, the more we love the Lord; and the more we love the Lord, the more the love we extend to our partner will carry the spiritual essence of charity.

Marie once compared making Christ the center of our lives with the old flying saucer ride in the Fun House at Utah's Lagoon

Amusement Park. As children, Marie and her friends would clamber onto the moving saucer (which looked like a large upside-down plate) and then crawl toward the middle so they wouldn't be thrown off as the saucer spun faster and faster. Some riders found excitement by riding close to the edge and grabbing a friend from the middle until they pulled her, sliding and sprawling, completely off the saucer.

Marie's favorite spot was sitting at the center of the spinning saucer, where its centrifugal force didn't affect her, no matter how fast the saucer spun. She found it great fun to pull a friend into the center with her. There they would hang on to each other, laughing and fighting off the stretching hands and feet of those who tried to knock them off their secure perch. Applying the saucer analogy, she said:

"We must be vigilant in holding on to the Savior and staying with him in the center. When Christ is the focus of our lives, we know he will help us if we have the spiritual maturity to stay with him no matter what is swirling around us. And when we are secure and watchful in the center, we can stretch out our hands to pull others, in charity, into the center with him, too. . . .

". . . I desire that gift [of charity]. I am willing to be a 'true follower.' Instead of sprawling off the saucer from the centrifugal force of daily temptations and distractions, I desire to move myself more completely toward the center. . . . [R]emaining steadfast in that focus requires constant vigilance—constant faith, constant prayer. Yet as I seek to love him more fervently, I feel myself loving others without constraint . . .

"When we come so fully to Christ that we have true charity, his pure love will flow through us into other people."[1]

Marie has further observed: "This binding tether—she is His, and He is hers—brings security no matter what gales blow about her. Because she is bound securely to Him, she is free to have a buoying, stabilizing influence on others—an influence that is uniquely hers, uniquely a woman's, and uniquely Christian. Those of us who are wives or husbands therefore have the challenge of becoming celestial individually in order to be celestial together."

I have felt Marie's loving pull toward the Center in the whirling of our lives. I know no safer place than being with her, holding each other as close to the Center as we possibly can.

Julie discovered what her personal crawl toward the Center could do for her shaky marriage. She yearned for a closer relationship with her husband, but the two of them had been judging each other's imperfections with increasing harshness. She was feeling neither listened to nor loved. The fabric of their relationship was beginning to fray. Angry and frustrated, Julie poured out her feelings in a letter she started writing to her husband. However, "the longer I wrote, the more I began to have a feeling come over me that what I was writing was false. The feeling continued growing until I could no longer squelch it, and I knew intuitively that the feeling was coming from God, that He was telling me that what I was writing was false. 'How could it be false?' I asked angrily. . . . But the feeling became so powerful . . . that I could no longer deny it. . . . So I tore up the pages . . . , threw myself down on my knees and began to pray, saying, 'If it is false, show me how . . .' And then a voice spoke to my mind and said, 'If you had come unto Me, it all would have been different.'

"I was astounded. I went to church; I read the scriptures often; I prayed pretty regularly; I tried to obey the commandments. What do you mean, 'Come unto You?'

" . . . And then into my mind flashed pictures of me wanting to do things my own way, of holding grudges, of not forgiving, of not loving as God had loved us. I had wanted my husband to 'pay' for my emotional suffering. I had not let go of the past and had not loved God with all my heart. I loved my own willful self more.

"I was aghast. I suddenly realized that I was responsible for my own suffering, for if I had really come unto Him, as I outwardly thought I had done, it all would have been different.

" . . . I . . . did not mention to my husband anything of what had transpired. But I gave up blaming. . . . And I tried to come unto God with full purpose of heart. I prayed more earnestly, and listened to His Spirit. I read my scriptures and tried to come to know Him better.

"Two months passed, and one morning my husband awoke and turned to me in bed and said, 'You know, we find fault too much with each other. I am never going to find fault with my wife again.' I was flabbergasted, for he had never admitted he had done anything wrong in our relationship. He did stop finding fault, and he began to compliment me, and show sweet kindness. It was as if an icy glass wall between us had melted away. Almost overnight our relationship became warm and sweet. Three years have passed, and still it continues warmer and happier. We care deeply about one another and share ideas and thoughts and feelings, something we had not done for the first 16 years of marriage."[2]

What Julie found was charity. When her vertical relationship with the Lord changed, her horizontal relationship with her husband changed—but not as the direct result of her mechanical effort to change it. Rather, her spiritual quest to draw closer to the Lord "wrought a mighty change" in her heart, creating a desire "to do good continually" (Mosiah 5:2). Thus her covenant relationship with the Lord breathed spiritual life into her covenant marriage.

Our young friend Wendy knows that this vertical dimension

is the primary source of her spiritual identity. In a conversation about relationships between men and women in the Church, I expressed my concern that when the men in a woman's life do not seem to value her, her sense of worth may be undermined. Wendy shook her head in disagreement. She spoke with conviction, "A woman's sense of self-worth depends not on how much other people seem to value her, but rather on how well *she* is spiritually grounded. To depend on what others think of us lets them determine our sense of worth."

When our happiness is based on someone else's choices rather than our own, we become prime candidates for "hazardous hope," a hope based entirely on what other people do. Such hope is hazardous for an unsettled marriage, because it can kill our dream of reconciliation, even when we have done everything within our control. Ultimately, we can't control what other people do, but we can control what *we* do, including developing our own relationship with the Lord. If we walk one step toward Him, He will always run at least two steps toward us. Hope based in Christ is not hazardous but full of life and light, for ourselves and for those we love.

A few years ago we came to know Nicole and Geoff. Nicole had made a discovery very similar to Julie's and Wendy's. She wrote in a letter to us that she had been feeling discouraged and unworthy because of the "gap between the ideal of married life and the reality of [her] marriage." A few years after their temple marriage, Geoff began losing interest in the Church, which left Nicole feeling spiritually very alone. "Somehow," she wrote, "I had come to believe that I had to become righteous all by myself . . . to be worthy of God's love and blessings."

As she searched for guidance, Nicole ran across a book about the Atonement. In its pages she found "truth and hope and light being unfolded . . . and [her] life changed." Instead of continuing to worry about her husband's choices, she gave priority to putting her own "spirituality back on track." She prayed for changes in her marriage, in her husband's choices, and in her own choices. She was surprised when the changes didn't come in big ways, but they did eventually come—"in the most subtle ways and through obedience to promptings." Then, she wrote, "last Sunday, with no forewarning and with no apparent catalyst, Geoff woke up and casually announced he was coming to church."

She had learned to stop working on trying to force his Church activity. Rather, she had focused on being "faithful regardless of others' decisions" and on making herself "the kind of wife and person that Geoff wants to be with forever." Her new understanding of the Atonement and her growing closeness to the Savior helped her be able to say, "[Even though] I have wanted to give up [many times, and] many times I questioned my testimony, it has [nevertheless] been a good test for me. The Lord has blessed me with strength, understanding and healing. He has become my friend and my support."

Nicole was strengthened and healed independently of what her husband chose; yet when she decided not to criticize him, he chose on his own to come back to church. No matter what his choices were, she trusted in the Savior and in His Atonement.

Sometimes a couple must pay a high price before they discover what it takes to replace criticism with charity. Rolf and Marianne had five children and were married twenty years before making their discovery. Their temple marriage was tolerable, but Rolf said he wasn't really happy, so he assumed other marriages were as dull as his own. He simply accepted Marianne's habit of being initially opposed (so it seemed to him) to whatever he might suggest on almost any subject. She would sometimes come around but only grudgingly, after contention.

Then he was assigned to a Church calling in which he began working with a widow named Molly. She simply had a welcoming spirit, listening carefully to his ideas, responding to his sense of humor. With Molly, Rolf said, "everything we needed to do together glided smoothly, easily—we just understood each other." He began looking forward to his meetings with Molly, the opposite of how he felt about facing Marianne.

Rolf wanted to confide his frustration to Marianne; he knew he should, but he simply dreaded it. When he finally found the courage to talk, he told Marianne he was wondering about a divorce. Instead of trying to understand what was behind his startling question, she chastised him for even thinking such a thought, underscoring how wrong divorce was. Rolf withdrew from Marianne and fell into deep emotional and then physical intimacies with Molly—serious enough that he was disciplined by a Church council. He still wanted a divorce, but he couldn't bring himself to demand it.

Then Rolf was in a temple visitors' center with relatives. Near the statue of the *Christus,* he saw these words: "If ye love me, keep my commandments." The words pierced Rolf's heart. He couldn't get back to Marianne fast enough, though the dread of facing her remained.

Meanwhile, Marianne had been praying for some kind of answer for Rolf, for her, for their family. She had decided Rolf wouldn't change, so she tried to become interested in another man. But that didn't feel right either. She had run out of ideas when Rolf came back in tears and pleaded for her forgiveness. She asked him to live away from the house for a few months while she thought about what to do.

One day Rolf called and asked if they could take a long drive together. When they stopped at a place for lunch, Rolf left the car to pick up something from a store. Marianne said that as she watched him walk away, she unexpectedly felt a strong, warm spiritual impression, something she'd felt only once before. It was exactly the same feeling as when she first knew that the Book of Mormon was true. This witness changed her, made her more willing to trust Rolf, more willing to look inside herself.

That day, Rolf and Marianne talked and talked. As time went on, he consciously looked for specific ways to help her more. She began asking herself in each conversation how things looked to him, rather than assuming her view was correct. Like once-disabled people who'd found a miracle surgery and now needed to learn to walk again, Rolf and Marianne began to practice trying to understand each other. They stopped contending over every little thing and learned gradually to discuss their differences in a quiet spirit, and that made all the difference.

The last time I saw them, they said they were wiser, happier, and growing more than ever before. Now they wonder why it took so long and was so hard to reach this point.

This pattern occurs with enough frequency to demonstrate that like a good recipe or scientific formula, it is a consistent, repeatable spiritual process. Bruce and Jo Erickson, for instance, had been married in the temple, but Bruce believed that this high level of sacred formality was somehow enough to ensure a happy marriage. In their early years, Bruce thought his way was "the only correct way to do things, whether it had to do with food preparation, how our home was cleaned, how our children were disciplined, or a hundred other things." He sensed trouble in their marriage but "blamed Jo for all the problems." He criticized "everything from the way she cooked to the way members of her family spoke and acted."

Jo's version of this same experience was "every day I wondered what he would criticize me or the girls for next. I never knew what I should or shouldn't say to him, and . . . I had to justify and explain everything I did." With this stressful relationship as a backdrop, the Ericksons had three children who developed excruciating physical handicaps. Bruce "resented God's unfair treatment" when they were unable to heal their children, which compounded their marital strains until he "thought divorce was the only escape."

Bruce felt pushed beyond his limits by their family's adversity. Through an extended and agonizing search for understanding, he gradually experienced a complete kind of spiritual conversion. The change began with his earnest repentance and an all-absorbing effort to "center my life on God and Christ." His primary quest had been to understand the unfairness of his life circumstances. But as he began to see those circumstances in a clearer spiritual light, his relationship with Jo was also transformed—as something of a by-product of his more basic change of heart. He discovered, by himself, that his "judgmental and critical attitude" was ruining his marriage. He also stumbled onto something their marriage had lacked—real romance. And "the paradox was that romance came because of my repentance and change of heart, not by getting away on an exotic vacation."

For Jo, Bruce's change was "like the difference between day and night." Now, instead of issuing decrees and criticism, "he sincerely recognizes the difficulty of my tasks, and he appreciates and compliments me for what I have done rather than criticize me for what I haven't done."[3]

There really is a pattern for replacing the wolf of criticism with the lamb of charity.

A woman from Utah captured her version of it this way: "I was miserable and didn't think our marriage could last.

"Then I felt the hand of Heavenly Father guide me, through a friend, to hear a talk about charity in marriage. The speaker suggested being charitable toward your spouse for just one month. I knew it would never work with *my* husband! But because I wasn't going to let it be my fault if we got a divorce, I determined to stop nagging and fighting with [him] for the next four weeks. . . .

"I turned to the scriptures and read about charity in Moroni 7. I learned that charity belongs more in marriage than anywhere else. As I changed, my husband began to change too. After the month was over, my husband was a different person!"[4]

As I think about Julie, Nicole, Rolf and Marianne, the Ericksons, and the woman from Utah, the pattern is clear and consistent. In the most fundamental ways, despite differences in the details, all happy families—and all covenant marriages—are much alike. The principles for moving from criticism to cooperation to charity in a marriage are consistent. They flow from the same process by which each of us comes unto Christ. When we do, we receive His pure love, which includes the gift to see others more the way He sees them. And as we become more like Him, we begin seeing them with His eyes.

"And charity suffereth long, and is kind, and envieth not, and is not puffed up, seeketh not her own, is not easily provoked, . . . beareth all things. . . . pray unto the Father . . . that ye may be filled with this love, which he hath bestowed upon all who are true followers of his Son, Jesus Christ" (Moroni 7:45–48).

CHAPTER THIRTEEN

THE WOLF OF
EXCESSIVE INDIVIDUALISM

The third wolf that tests our marriages is the excessive individualism of the "me" generation, which has spawned today's contractual attitudes. For example, a young woman is in love and wants to be married, but some fears hold her back. One fear, she says, is that she will "lose her freedom." Well, what is marriage—a flight *from* freedom or a flight *to* freedom?

People today are not so sure how to answer that question, because they're being influenced by the broad cultural changes we have seen. Let's look at a brief general perspective on this waning of belonging.

A friend's young daughter came home from school one day, crying and upset. "Is it true that I don't really *belong* to you, Mom?" she asked. Knowing this was her natural child, the startled mother asked what she meant. The girl said her teacher had told their class that everyone is free to control his or her own life and that no one "belongs" to anyone else. Children don't belong to parents; husbands don't belong to wives; nobody belongs to anybody.

Then, still crying a little, the child asked, "I *am* yours, aren't I, Mom?" Her mother hugged her close and whispered, "Of course you're mine—and I'm yours, too." As the two embraced, they both felt the love and the security of really belonging to each other.

A man and woman who love each other also feel joy and meaning in the thought that they could "belong" to each other. Indeed, many phrases from the language of romantic love draw on this idea. "Be mine" invite the little candy hearts we see on Valentine's Day. Possessive case. "I'm yours" proclaimed a hit song of the 1950s. And the opening line of another once-popular song goes, "If I give my heart to you, will you handle it with care?"

In everything from bumper stickers to billboards, we see red hearts as a symbol for love. In its highest form, this symbol represents the ultimate gesture of giving our hearts to those we love. To offer our hearts is to offer our innermost selves. And if the offer is accepted, there may one day be a wedding—that ancient, sacred ritual in which a man and a woman gladly give themselves to each other in the permanent bonds of matrimony.

We have always known that people who offer their hearts to others take the risk of getting them banged up and sometimes of getting them broken. These days, however, a fear more bewildering than the risk of a broken heart clouds our willingness to give ourselves to one another. The teacher's comments to her young class fairly remind us that family members are neither slaves nor inanimate objects. But her approach also illustrates how ours is the age of the waning of belonging.

The sense of possession implicit in the idea of "belonging" to another person can imply relationships as beautiful as eternal love—or as ugly as slavery. In earlier times, our common sense told us the obvious difference between these opposite ends of the spectrum of human relationships. But the "set me free" spirit in this age of liberation often can't distinguish between bonds of love and bonds of slavery. That liberating spirit seems to say, You're not really free until you break loose from the relationships and commitments that tie you down. Thus many people today are wary of long-term personal obligations and commitments.

The adversary has long cultivated this overemphasis on self-focused autonomy, and now he feverishly exploits it. Our deepest God-given instinct is to run to the arms of those who need us and sustain us. But using wedges of distrust and suspicion, Satan tries to drive us apart from each other. He exaggerates the need for having space, getting out, and being left alone. Some people believe him and get out—and then wonder why they feel so lonely.

We should not be surprised that the Evil One would twist a true value such as individual freedom in ways that render suspect the mutual belonging of covenant marriage. He was a liar from the beginning, and he seeks to destroy the happiness of mankind.

As soon as Adam and Eve realized the joy of the Lord's plan of happiness for them, centered on Christ's redemption, they "blessed the name of God, and they made all [these] things known unto their sons and their daughters." Instantly, "Satan came among [Adam and Eve's children], saying: . . . Believe it not; and they believed it not, and they loved Satan more than God. And men began from that time forth to be carnal, sensual, and devilish" (Moses 5:12–13).

That same pattern has mushroomed to a very large scale in the modern world. We've always had temptation, always had challenges within families. But the new plague of modernity is that Satan has crossed the threshold of our homes more fully than ever before. Chapter 18 will examine how the sexual revolution and the "emancipation" of both men and women from a sense of responsibility to, or for, each other have lowered the protective barriers of all our moral thresholds. But for now, the point is a simple one: Lucifer huffed, and he puffed, and he blew down the doors of our houses of family belonging.

As he stood at the door, he somehow looked disarmingly attractive. Satan is too clever to appear as the ugly wolf he actually is. The devil who shows up in Dostoyevsky's *Crime and Punishment,* for example, is "fashionably liberal, and politely skeptical. Hell, it turns out, is just like our world—it has adopted the metric system—and the devil himself is, remarkably enough, an agnostic."[1] Thus, his devious enticements begin with a truth and end with a lie, and many people today, like the children of Adam and Eve, have believed him: "Be your own person. You need space. You don't want anybody telling you what to do. Be free, run free, love free. Don't let them tie you down." And they love him more than God—enough so that our society is now more carnal, more sensual, and more devilish than in many centuries, perhaps more than any society since the Flood.

The notion that we can become "free" by ridding ourselves of our ties to others is a basic element in Satan's most ancient plot. After "Cain loved Satan more than God" (Moses 5:18), he killed Abel to get gain. Then "Cain gloried in that which he had done, saying: I am free"! (Moses 5:33). Yet Cain was never more in bondage than in that moment. And he was never more distant from the blessings of belonging to the human family than when God asked him, "Where is Abel, thy brother? And he said: I know not. Am I my brother's keeper?" (Moses 5:34).

"Now Satan knew" what Cain was doing in all this, "and it pleased him" (Moses 5:21). Because he seeks our misery, Lucifer wants to prevent everlasting relationships of family love. When he can't do that, he tries to disrupt and destroy them. He envies those relationships in which procreation occurs, for that is a power beyond his own. As President Boyd K. Packer said, "The adversary is jealous toward all who have the power to beget life. He cannot beget life."[2] He resents the joy of married love, because he can never have it and because it foils his plans to ensnare us. Doug Brinley put it this way: "Because Satan will never marry, he is determined to destroy our relationship. . . . He wants each of us to be alone and separate as he is."[3]

In the eternal misery that is his, he preaches the glory of "being left alone," as if that should be humanity's highest aim. But in fact, his motivation is that "he seeketh that all men might be miserable like unto himself" (2 Nephi 2:27). Contemplate the misery of his infinite banishment from all fully satisfying human relationships.

At the same time, on some days, most of us could imagine some relief in being left all alone—no one making demands on us, no one judging us, calling us, bugging us, needing us. And on such days, one could be tempted to believe that the greatest eternal reward really might be to find some little corner of the universe to just be by yourself, alone forever.

But the Savior of mankind did not come to work out the great *alone-ment*. He came to work out the great *at-one-ment*, overcoming our separation from God and from each other. He did this so we can forever be "at one" with those we love most: our husbands, our wives, our children, our parents, and the Lord. Without the Atonement, there could be no eternal marriage, no eternal togetherness.

This simple idea is at the very core of both the gospel and our nature—the human part and the divine part of that nature. Most every child senses its truth in our best one-line descriptions of the celestial kingdom: "You get to be with your family." "You get to be with Heavenly Father forever!" We don't *have* to be with them; we *get* to be with them. We respond to this idea because it responds to our soul's deep longing to belong. We are incomplete beings when alone, because our highest nature is complete only in being together.

We do not live by bread alone, and we were not made to be alone. The life of alienation and distance from God and from other people leads away from eternal happiness. The life of faith, hope, and charity keeps us within the arms of the Holy One of Israel. When in His presence, we will embrace not only Him but also those we loved and served on earth. And in all these bonds of belonging is the fulness of our joy. The gospel not only recognizes the longing to belong but offers the most complete means of fulfilling that longing.

Before marriage, each partner sings alone. But we are not two solos. We are two parts to a duet, each looking for the other part. That "half of a duet" part of our nature wants nothing more than finding the other half. We also yearn to have the Lord's Spirit to "be with" us. That's why no pain is more exquisite than being cut off from His presence. We taste that pain when, because of sin, God withdraws His Spirit from us (D&C 19:20). Because of these instincts to belong, embedded deep within our eternal nature is the innate desire to "be with" the ones we love—in the temple, at Christmas, at home, together—to share, to cling to, to lean on.

CHAPTER FOURTEEN

ABIDING ALONE, ABIDING TOGETHER, AND BRINGING FORTH FRUIT

Seeking to fulfill our longing to belong does not ask us to extinguish our personal identity. On the contrary. No understanding of human nature values the uniqueness and potential of each individual soul more than does the gospel of Jesus Christ. Through its teachings, we know we are eternal beings—each a child of God, for whose personal growth and development the entire plan of salvation was created. Each of us seeks to fulfill that plan by the exercise of *individual* agency and *personal* responsibility. No one else can do our part for us, even though we are dependent on others, especially the Savior, to complete our salvation.

Reflecting this insight, Kahlil Gibran wrote of marriage:

> *But let there be spaces in your togetherness,*
> *And let the winds of the heavens dance between you.*
>
> . . . .
>
> *Sing and dance together and be joyous,*
> *but let each one of you be alone,*

Even as the strings of a lute are alone
though they quiver with the same music.

. . . .

And stand together yet not too near together:
For the pillars of the temple stand apart,
And the oak tree and the cypress grow
not in each other's shadow.[1]

The great trees *grow* not in each other's shadow. To grow—
that is the point, the eternally inborn human need to become
whatever we're capable of becoming. And it is exactly to enable
our personal growth that our Father gave us the plan and the doctrine that bring us together, to each other, and eventually to Him.
It is only when we lose our lives in that sense that we find our
highest *personal* meaning—received, paradoxically, in our most
generous giving. "For whosoever will save his life [the urge of a
hireling for unfettered freedom] shall lose it: but whosoever will
lose his life for my sake [the shepherd is willing to give his life for
the sheep], the same shall save it" (Luke 9:24). We lose our lives
and then find them through following the Lord's commandments,
which include marriage—a pattern designed precisely to promote,
not to prevent, our personal growth and spiritual freedom.

Seeing our individuality within this gospel framework avoids
the excesses of today's self-oriented approach. Without that framework, the quest for being left alone can run away with itself. For
example, one important arena that sometimes fuels a myopic passion for personal freedom is the "therapeutic culture"—the culture of pop psychology, which is mostly a way of drawing on ideas
from today's secular therapeutic psychology to explain life through
human behavior alone.

This trend is everywhere now, from talk shows to self-help
books and everyday conversation. As Mitch Albom wrote:

"America [has] become a Persian bazaar of self-help" but with "no clear answers. Do you take care of others or take care of your 'inner child'? Return to traditional values or reject tradition as useless?"[2] Influenced by popular TV shows and magazines, many people feel equipped to explain life's issues through such psychological mysteries as "bonding," "boundaries," "healing our shame," and "self-actualization."

I value the benefits, even the blessings, made possible by psychotherapy. I know many people whose lives and whose marriages are both richer and more responsible because of competent professional therapy. In some severe cases, therapy has quite literally prevented death and given people the tools to live. I am especially grateful for therapists who are both competent and faithful—those who study the behavior of man in light of the doctrine and behavior of God.

But like other powerful tools, from fire and lawyers to TV and the Internet, therapy can be either valuable or dangerous, depending on who uses its tools and how. I mention the therapeutic culture here primarily because some of its practitioners, pop or otherwise, today reflect the culture of individual liberty to the point of taking some of psychology's valuable principles to harmfully self-centered extremes.

For example, the preoccupation with the self in some popular versions of "look out for yourself" (there is, symbolically, even a magazine called *Self*) can easily cause us to think like hirelings. When one is thinking superficially and primarily of oneself, the appearance of any wolves on the horizon can make it feel like a good time to abandon the flock.

More broadly, some proponents of the therapeutic culture simply begin their thinking with anti-religious and/or anti-marriage biases. William Kilpatrick has found that much of "the therapeutic culture has no God." These agnostic approaches, he believes, are "well on the way to dismantling the moral structure of society through semi-sincere appeals to tolerance, compassion, and diversity." This misuse of psychology has damaged Christianity more than has militant atheism, because "the more insidious attacks of the therapeutic culture" have terribly eroded "the sense of guilt, the sense of sin, the sense of the sacred, the sense that there is another order of [spiritual] authority by which we are judged."[3]

Specifically regarding marriage, some non-LDS professionals in such fields as therapy, law, and social work have urged society to recognize a category of relationships they call "nonbinding commitments." The very term is an oxymoron. A nonbinding commitment is like a parachute that opens only some of the time.

The search for noncommittal forms of "marriage" arises, understandably, from the belief that deep personal commitments can lead to the painful, even irreparable, harm of broken hearts and broken promises, either the promises we make or those made to us. For such reasons, Dr. Albert Ellis, a psychiatrist who describes himself as representing the mainstream of his profession, questions the "emotional stability" of people who commit themselves to "unequivocal and eternal fidelity or loyalty to any interpersonal commitments—especially marriage."[4] People of that view would have real trouble with the idea of eternal marriage.

Whatever the source of our preoccupation with self, an understanding of the gospel will show us how "losing our lives" actually leads to "finding our lives" in a covenant marriage. When this happens, "where one door closes, another opens."[5]

Our family once enjoyed a weekend of "the three white dresses." One granddaughter was named and blessed. Another granddaughter was baptized and confirmed a member of the Church. And our daughter was married. The three white dresses a young woman wears as she grows in the gospel—all on one wonderful weekend!

In these three sacred events, we realized that each girl also received a new name—a name that represented giving up one stage of life and accepting a new one. The baby girl received her name for mortality, "by which she will be known upon the records of the Church . . ." The baptized girl took upon herself the name of Christ, a covenant she will renew each time she takes the sacrament. Our newly married daughter took the family name of her husband.

Significantly, the marriage also gave the husband's name a new meaning. Now his name means the head of a little republic called a family. He is all finished with his unattached status as a free-as-the-breeze "young single adult" male. Their common family name means not only that she belongs to him but that they belong to each other. Perhaps in that same sense, President Spencer W. Kimball said of Adam and Eve, "Adam was their name. And I suppose that the name Adam was the family surname, just as Kimball is my name and my wife's name."[6]

A couple I know, Kevin and Paula, helped me learn about a scripture that teaches the principle behind giving up the single stage of life to find the more fruitful stage of marriage. This experience also taught me about the unexpected spiritual fruits a temple marriage can bring to an extended family.

Because they both loved a French story called *The Little Prince,* in which wheat is an important symbol, Kevin and Paula used a wheat motif in their wedding plans. A tasteful sketch of wheat graced a corner of their invitations. At the table for their guest book, tall jars of clear glass held sprays of wheat on either side of their wedding photo.

Their wedding was in the Salt Lake Temple. Only some of Kevin's extended family could attend, because most relatives on his mother's side were not members of the Church. A few days later, the couple flew to Kevin's hometown for a reception that could include his non-LDS family and friends. Just before the reception, they hosted a small gathering of friends and relatives in the LDS chapel where Kevin's family attends church. His stake president conducted the meeting. The program included music, a talk on marriage, lighthearted life sketches for the group by Paula's sister and Kevin's sister, and then a brief response from the two of them—he in his crisp tuxedo, she in her handcrafted white wedding dress.

Because I am one of Paula's relatives, they had invited me to attend this pre-reception gathering and give the marriage talk, including a perspective on temple marriage for Kevin's non-LDS relatives. We all knew this was a rare opportunity, and I needed guidance about what I might say. So the night before, I asked them about Kevin's family. We talked over a few ideas, but finally, at Kevin's suggestion, we just prayed for spiritual guidance. He described his Aunt Barbara, a devoted, religious mother whose baby had just been diagnosed with a serious illness. "She is the one I especially hope might be touched by the Spirit," he said, "because she is so good, and she really needs a blessing right now."

I went to the chapel the next day still unsettled about just what to say. As the meeting was about to begin, I noticed that Paula had placed her two tall glass jars with the sprays of wheat on either side of the pulpit. "Wheat," I thought. "Paula and Kevin will probably say something about *The Little Prince* and the wheat. I need a scripture on wheat."

I thumbed quickly through the Topical Guide, rejecting "wheat and tares" and a few other things. Then I saw a verse I had never noticed before. It felt just right, so I included it in my talk: "Verily, verily, I say unto you, Except a corn [seed] of wheat fall into the ground and die, it abideth alone: but if it die, it bringeth forth much fruit" (John 12:24).

I said the Savior's words in this passage tell us what happens when people marry, as Paula and Kevin had done. Each one is leaving forever his life as a single person who is not accountable to a companion. In that sense, marriage represents a burial of the self, like a kernel of wheat falling to the ground where it must die to bring forth fruit. This burial allows husband and wife to join their souls through temple vows into a new life, with a new and permanent accountability to each other and to the Lord. Like sprouted wheat, they will never again be like that hard and tiny kernel, which "abideth alone." Now, as was never possible before, their lives are full of the promised fruit of their covenants—children, personal growth, and the blessings of family life.

That evening as we finished the wedding dinner, Kevin's Aunt Barbara and her family approached our table. She carried her sick child over one shoulder. In her other hand was a small pot filled with rich soil but with nothing growing in it. She said, "It is Easter Sunday tomorrow. So our family took time this week to fill some pots like this with soil and seeds. We're giving them to friends and relatives. We thought you'd like to have one. If you water it, the seeds will sprout. You might be interested in the verse of scripture our family wrote on each of the pots yesterday. We liked what Jesus said there about himself and the Resurrection."

We thanked Barbara, took the little pot, and read these hand-written words on the pot near the top edge: "Except a corn of wheat fall into the ground and die, it abideth alone: but if it die, it bringeth forth much fruit. John 12:24."

As my eyes moistened and then met hers, she smiled and said, "When you quoted that verse today in the church, one of our girls whispered to me, 'Mom, how did he know our family's scripture for this week?'" I thought of Kevin's prayer the night before.

These two meanings of John 12:24 also remind me that marriage, like the experience of Christ, really is like a burial and resurrection. Mortal death makes eternal life possible; and when we stop abiding alone, we can bring forth the human fruit made possible only by abiding together. One more example of At-one-ment echoes in the meaning of marriage.

CHAPTER FIFTEEN

THE BONDS THAT LIBERATE: I DIDN'T KNOW I HAD IT IN ME

Brian and Kathy's temple wedding day was like what the Aborigines call their "dreamtime," or creation period. They were so fresh, so young—a new couple "just starting out in life," like Adam and Eve. Their dreamtime gave them a context of doctrine that taught them, through the temple endowment and the sealing ceremony, the principles, the purpose, and the promise of the marital mortality they now faced together.

I did wonder how long it would be until their marriage would be invaded by the wolves of adversity, imperfection, and excessive individualism. They had promised each other in their ceremony to accept the vows of the ages, but their shining eyes were fixed that day mostly on each other. Neither was thinking about the wolves that waited for them out of sight over the next hill. Then they embarked on the journey from their Eden-like innocence down into a world of sorrow and thorns. Only if they faced up to that world's risks, as Lehi taught, could they potentially find joy. If they reacted to their wolves as shepherds would, not as hirelings, Kathy and Brian would discover that theirs was a covenant marriage. If they could do that, they would also find insight into life's meaning and Christ's redemption which, as Eve said, "God giveth to all the obedient" (Moses 5:11). But only after the trial of their faith (Ether 12:6).

Kahlil Gibran put it this way: "Your joy is your sorrow unmasked."[1] When the times of sorrow are upon us, if we are faithful, the Lord will help us unmask the sorrow. The blessings of joy are behind adversity's disguise. They're often hiding, masked, like buried treasure or hidden springs of water. And to find what is buried, we must endure and keep digging, sometimes with very hard, deep digging, even pick and shovel work. And we don't always recognize the treasure when we've found it, covered with grit—another layer of the mask.

How does this discovery process occur? When we observe the covenants we make at the wedding altars of sacrifice, we uncover hidden treasures of personal strength.

For example, one night Marie exhausted herself for hours encouraging one of our children to finish a school assignment. He'd been a challenge to his teacher, who had warned us that if our boy didn't complete this project by the next day, he would be in deep trouble. (This was also the child of whom one kindly seminary teacher said, "He's a good boy. But I think he learned to whisper in a sawmill.")

His task was to build his own diorama of a Native American village on a cookie sheet—and he had to do it all himself. It would have been far easier for us to build it for him than to see that he did it himself. Getting him to do it was a test no hireling would have endured.

At first he fought his mother's efforts. And as I kept hearing that sawmill voice directed in frustration at her, I was ready to toss him out of the room. But Marie made a deal with me. If I would finish family home evening with the other children, she would oversee the diorama project. I quickly agreed. Then, just at bedtime, he brought "his" diorama into his bedroom, carrying it as proudly as if it were a birthday cake. He pointed out to his little brothers the trees, the pond, the wigwams—and the wolves. He laid it carefully on a shelf and started for his bed.

Then he turned around, raced back across the room, and hugged his mother, grinning up at her face with his large fourth-grade teeth, the freckles sprayed across his boyish cheeks like dandelion seeds tossed from the wind. As she ruffled his hair with her hand, the two of them looked at each other in an affectionate hug of much unspoken meaning.

As we left the room, I asked Marie in amazement, "How did you do it?"

"I'm not sure," she said. "I just made up my mind that, no matter what he did, *I wouldn't leave him.*" Then she added her most important discovery: "*I didn't know I had it in me.*"

Marie had dug deep enough to discover the deep, internal wellsprings of her own compassion. Tapping into that underground source, she found within herself a well of energetic charity whose capacity far exceeded her expectations. In this way, her bonds to the child of our covenant gave her strength to lay down her life for her sheep, even an hour at a time.

Michael Novak applies that experience, and others like it, to marriage: "People say of marriage that it is boring, when what they mean is that it terrifies them: too many and too deep are its searing revelations. . . . They say of children that they are . . . brats . . . , when what they mean is that the importance of parents with respect to the future of their children is now known with greater clarity . . . than ever before.

" . . . No tame project, marriage. The raising of children . . . brings each of us breathtaking vistas of our own inadequacy.

" . . . [So,] we want desperately to blame [family life,] the institution which places our inadequacy in the brilliant glare of interrogation. . . .

"The quantity of sheer . . . selfishness in the human breast (in *my* breast) is a never-failing source of wonderment. I do not want to be disturbed, challenged, troubled. Huge regions of myself belong only to me. . . . Seeing myself through the unblinking eyes of an intimate, intelligent other, an honest spouse, is humiliating beyond anticipation. Maintaining a familial steadiness whatever the state of my own emotions is a standard by which I stand daily condemned. . . .

"[Yet] my dignity as a human being depends perhaps more on what sort of husband and parent I am, than on any professional work I am called to do. My bonds to them hold me back from many sorts of opportunities. And yet *these do not feel like bonds. They are . . . my liberation.* They force me to be a different sort of human being, in a way in which I want and need to be forced."[2]

Abraham Lincoln captured the idea that we find our best selves—our liberation—in honoring the natural connection between our deepest human bonds and the higher elements of human nature: "Though passion may have strained, it must not break our bonds of affection. The mystic chords of memory . . . will yet swell . . . when again touched, as surely they will be, by the better angels of our nature."[3]

As time went on, Brian and Kathy began making their own discoveries about inner wellsprings and the bonds that liberate. After starting their family with a robust little guy who has Brian's head and Kathy's smile, they found they were expecting child number two. But this baby threatened to come too early to live.

Kathy began losing amniotic fluid at nineteen weeks, and the fluid loss continued. Their doctors urged them to encourage a miscarriage or induce an abortion. A hireling would have thought this was a reasonable approach—the statistical odds did not favor the baby's survival, and the parents needed to get on with their already demanding lives.

But Brian and Kathy consciously chose to "observe their covenants by sacrifice" (D&C 97:8). Active, energetic Kathy lay almost motionless at home for five weeks and then in a hospital bed for another five weeks. For a young mother whose every day was a study in perpetual motion, few things could have been harder than being confined to total bed rest.

Brian found ways to be with Kathy whenever he was not working or sleeping—and some hours when he tried to do both. They prayed their child to earth. After she was born, she required eleven more weeks in the hospital. Then they discovered that, apparently due to causes associated with her birth, she has severe cerebral palsy. But she is here, and she is theirs. They named her Melissa. They think of her as the "life" God gave them. Her physical life, despite her limitations, is a miracle. The spiritual life she has brought her parents is no less miraculous.

One night before Melissa's birth, as Kathy waited patiently upon the Lord in the hospital, she wondered why doing something so hard was in fact quite bearable—actually, more than bearable. As the growing strength of her baby drew steadily on the waning strength of her own body, she wondered aloud to Brian if perhaps her willingness to sacrifice herself were in some small way like the Good Shepherd's sacrifice for her. She said, "I had expected that trying to give so much would really be a burden, but somehow this feels more like a privilege."

Kathy and Brian gave their hearts to God by giving them to

their child. In the process, they learned that theirs is a covenant marriage, binding them in holy permanence to each other and to the Lord. They also discovered that these bonds were their spiritual liberation, because their giving ran deep enough to tap into the well of living water. They traded their lives of comfort for the bumps and bruises of their covenants and in doing so found a tie to the Savior that they would otherwise not have known. Central to that tie was that their covenants asked them, quite unexpectedly, to emulate Christ's sacrifice with their own.

One of the survivors of the Martin and Willie handcart company disaster said of his group's ordeal: "'Not one of that company ever apostatized or left the Church, because everyone of us came through with the absolute knowledge that God lives for we became acquainted with him in our extremities. . . . The price we paid to become acquainted with God was a privilege to pay.'"[4]

Brian, Kathy, and the handcart survivors all discovered the same doctrinal link between *burdens* and *privileges:* the burden is the price we pay for the privilege of coming to know God, a knowledge that yields eternal life: "And this is life eternal, that they might know thee the only true God, and Jesus Christ, whom thou hast sent" (John 17:3).

When Alma and his people were in bondage to the wicked Amulon, they prayed "mightily to God" for deliverance from their cruel burdens (Mosiah 24:10). "The voice of the Lord came to them in their afflictions, saying: Lift up your heads and be of good comfort, for I know of the *covenant* which ye have made unto me; and *I will covenant with my people and deliver them out of bondage.* And I will also ease the burdens which are put upon your shoulders, that even you cannot feel them . . . that ye may stand as witnesses . . . that ye may know of a surety that I . . . do visit my people in their afflictions." Then their "burdens . . . were made light; yea, the Lord did strengthen them that they could bear up their burdens with ease" (Mosiah 24:13–15; italics added).

For Alma's people, the burdens were physical, but the privilege was the spiritual one of coming to know of a surety, as witnesses, that the Lord *does* visit and bear up his people in their afflictions. Without the burden, there would have been no privilege; without the misery, no joy. And central to this process was a *covenant* relationship—the two-way covenants of the Atonement between Christ and His people, His "true followers" (Moroni 7:48).

Alma's son Alma taught that as we plant in our hearts the seed of desire to know Christ, the seed dies into becoming a tree of life, full of rich fruit. In its fulness, this tree springs up "in you unto everlasting life. And then may God grant unto you that your burdens may be light, through the joy of his Son" (Alma 33:23).

So is being a partner in a genuine covenant marriage a burden or a privilege? Yes. When they are afflicted in each other's afflictions, the covenant partners drill all the way down to the deep, living water of their personal covenants with Him who is afflicted in their afflictions.

This three-way, continuous sharing of afflictions and covenants turns burdens into privileges. By this process, the at-one-ness of marriage mirrors the At-one-ment of Him who said, "Holy Father, keep through thine own name those whom thou hast given me, that they may be one, as we are . . . ; as thou, Father, art in me, and I in thee, that they also may be one in us" (John 17:11, 21).

CHAPTER SIXTEEN

GLIMPSES OF COVENANT MARRIAGE

On a sunny Saturday in a corner of Australia, I take a short walk, listening to the colorful birds who squawk to each other across the treetops. I stroll past the large, glass windows of a high-ceilinged luxury hotel lobby—and find that a wedding is about to take place there. With other uninvited, curious guests, I stand at the crowd's edges to watch the sight.

The wedding party lines up in uncomfortably formal clothes, antiquated in a world that has mostly given up on social formalities. The bride's father, trying to appear in charge, ushers her forward to meet her groom. Her bare shoulders atop her elegant white dress seem oddly out of harmony with the dark tuxes in that row of freshly scrubbed Aussie groomsmen. The soul-song of recorded music croons, "From this moment on . . ."

Other onlookers crowd around the scene. Some are on stairways at the back of the massive room. Others peer through the tall glass from outside. A few children gaze in innocent wonder. Several complete strangers to the wedding lift up their cameras, impulsively wanting to treasure this moment of anonymous bliss.

Those most captivated in our self-appointed cheering section are the children and the old people. A wedding's magic is irresistible. I think of Wal Richards's wedding photographs in Maryborough.

How universal this experience is. Looks of vicarious excitement and hope are spread across every face, even the skeptical ones. Their hearts are telling them things their minds perhaps struggle to understand.

Their hearts tell them that real love should be eternal. Their sense of history should tell them that the difference between being married and unmarried is a difference in *kind,* not just a difference in *degree.* Either you're married, or you're not. We all understood that once, and our striving for what marriage expected of us made people try harder than most do now.

But their heads tell them that today's relationships are more matters of degree—degrees of commitment along the full spectrum from "sort of" living together to being fully married. Many people fear really giving their hearts in marriage any more. They often keep the lion's share of their hearts to themselves in a vaguely sensed "right" to remain free, unbounded. And in this loneliness by degrees, too many people become unhappy, each in his or her own free way. Mother Teresa once said, "In the West there is loneliness, which I call the leprosy of the West. In many ways it is worse than our poor in Calcutta."[1]

As the wedding concludes, I notice the birds again. Did they pause in their singing while the vows were spoken? Their chatter reminds me that certain kinds of birds mate for life. By just following their instincts, these birds may know more about covenant marriage than do many twenty-first-century humans. We need to tell our children this part when we tell them about the birds and the bees.

The naturalist Hudson wrote of his adventures among the birds, documenting their habits—including their mating for life. Brigham Young University's renowned Welsh poet, Leslie Norris, captured that instinct for permanence in "Hudson's Geese":

Hudson tells us of them,
the two migrating geese,
she hurt in the wing
indomitably walking
the length of a continent,
and he wheeling above,
calling his distress.
They could not have lived.
Already I see her wing
scraped past the bone
as she drags it through rubble.
A fox, maybe, took her
in his snap jaws. And what
would he do, the point
of his circling gone?
The wilderness of his cry
falling through an air
turned instantly to winter
would warn the guns of him.
If a fowler dropped him,
let it have been quick,
pellets hitting brain
and heart so his weight
came down senseless,
and nothing but his body
to enter the dog's mouth.[2]

"Nothing but his body?" Perhaps the two geese were soul mates—don't let the dog have his soul too. Let their souls somehow be together, always, undisturbed by dogs—or wolves. Leslie Norris would see that. His wife, Kitty, has nourished the soul of his poetry throughout their lifelong conversation. Kitty was very sick recently, and in her afflictions Leslie was afflicted. I saw it in his eyes when he spoke of her. She is the point of his circling; he, the point of hers.

And "he, wheeling above, calling his distress" loudly, draws too near the ground to search for his mate. Surely "the wilderness of his cry" will put his own life at risk from waiting hunters. What does "mating for life" mean about the way we give our lives?

The Good Shepherd said He gives His life for the sheep. He was referring to His own atoning sacrifice. But when our covenant relationships with each other emulate His covenants with us, we also commit our entire lives. That's true of citizens, who may give their lives to defend their country. President Spencer Kimball taught that a husband "is duty bound to protect [his wife] and defend her," just as Christ gave His life for the Church.[3]

I know a mission president who, with his wife, served in a very dangerous country. Robbery, rape, and even murder were daily occurrences in their city, a place riven with poverty and anarchy. They were careful to observe safety standards. But they knew the daily risks. Once he told me that it helped him come to peace with their conditions when he decided that he really was ready to defend his wife with his own life. He said it softly, his eyes moist with tears. His wife took his hand in hers. Their eyes met for a moment, and I caught just a glimpse of their covenant marriage.

Almost always we give our lives more gradually, in pieces the size of a day or an hour. But we do give our lives, to whatever causes or people matter most to us. In a noted play about Joan of Arc, Joan says that each of us gives his life for what he believes: "Sometimes people believe in little or nothing, nevertheless they give their lives to that little or nothing. One life is all we have, and we live it as we believe in living it, and then it's gone."[4] A shepherd gives his hours and his days for his sheep.

Sometimes we know true shepherds well enough to glimpse both the price of their burdens and the peace of their privileges. For example, a seasoned priesthood leader named Steve told me what he learned about observing his covenants by sacrifice. He was so preoccupied with his Church service that he didn't sense soon enough that he and his wife, Carol, were gradually drifting apart. Each began losing touch with the other's real needs and daily interests. Carol became so involved with some new friends that her emotional allegiance began shifting from the orbit of her marriage to the orbit of her friends. For a time her allegiance shared both orbits. Then it moved all the way to the friends.

On the day Steve learned that Carol had been involved with another man, in his shock he could think only of going home—even though he was home. But the home of his marriage felt shattered, and the home of his childhood beckoned nostalgically. What had happened wasn't supposed to happen. The wolf was inside his door, and he felt ashamed, embarrassed, betrayed. He could think only of fleeing. Early one morning Steve began driving alone toward his hometown. He made a plan to leave his job, get a divorce, and take his children to live with his parents until he could get reestablished.

When Steve's car reached a fork in the road, he scrambled to refocus his thoughts. He needed to turn right toward his hometown, but he had in more recent times grown accustomed to turning left at this fork. That was the route they always took on their trips from his stake to the temple. In a move that felt, and was, more like instinct than reason, he turned left toward the temple—and then began arguing with himself. He was in no mood to be in the temple. Or was he? He simply felt drawn there. As he kept driving, his memory began searching for the language of the marriage sealing ordinance.

When he reached the temple, Steve found an appropriate way to hear once more the words that had been spoken years earlier when he and his wife knelt at the temple altar. Then he turned around, literally and figuratively, and returned to the home of his wife and children. He had discovered that the road to the temple is the real road home.

Over time, Steve and Carol found their way through their joint affliction. At first it was an awful experience, he said, for both of them. It awakened them to the painful discovery that they had simply stopped paying honest *attention* to each other, taking too much for granted. As they started over, rebuilding their relationship, Steve listened to Carol and shared with her as never before. He discovered capacities he didn't know he had within himself, and he began seeing more in her. He concluded with words very similar to Meg's: The spiritual wakeup call of their trauma gave their relationship a new depth and renewed purpose (see chapter 3). He said the past few months had been the sweetest season they had known.

Steve's experience calls to mind the book of Hosea in the Old Testament. Some commentators regard Hosea's attitude as a turning point in Israel's ability to see Jehovah as a God of mercy, not simply a God of justice. It is possible that Hosea was able to comprehend Jehovah's capacity to forgive, not just to judge, because Hosea learned to replace harsh judgment with forgiving compassion toward his own wife. The merciful are the only ones who can obtain mercy.

Elder Ronald Poelman once told the Hosea story in a modern setting.[5] He described a man whose wife left him for a worldly life of adultery. One day the man unexpectedly saw the woman, whose life was by then a disaster. Feeling great compassion for her, he paid her debts and invited her home with him, where he worked to heal her. As he did this, the modern Hosea discovered all over again the love he had earlier felt for her. Elder Poelman compared this man's spirit of compassionate forgiveness with the mercy Hosea extended to the woman he had married, whom the book of Hosea describes, perhaps allegorically, as "a wife of whoredoms" (Hosea 1:2).

I was once in an intensely difficult interview with a priesthood leader named Jim, who had been accused of serious transgressions. Two female witnesses had already told me firsthand of their experiences with him. What they said rang true. Jim requested that his wife, Ann, be present when I met with him, even though he sensed what was coming. She listened incredulously as I told them what the witnesses had said. For more than an hour, he indignantly denied the accusations and offered other explanations. Ann shared his sense of injustice, supporting his claims and demanding to know why people would accuse her husband so unjustly.

We paused for a long time. I had no more evidence to present. The room was very quiet. I noticed a picture of the Savior on the office wall. With a prayer in my heart that they would feel His love, I gestured toward the picture. I began talking about the Atonement, about eternal life, and about the forgiveness that is possible for the repentant, the honest in heart. I bore witness of the Lord's cleansing power. I said I knew they both longed to be with Him, together. All was quiet again.

Then Ann began talking softly to Jim in their native language. She spoke in low, animated tones. The translator by my side became so absorbed in listening to her that he forgot to tell me what she was saying. She spoke intensely but was not harsh or angry. It was private husband-wife talk, as if no one else were in the room.

I whispered to the translator, "What is she saying?"

He whispered back, "Is it possible that these things are true? Is it possible? If they are, you must confess, you must repent, or we are unworthy of the Lord's presence. You must tell the truth, whatever it is. I will stand by you. Don't be afraid. If these things are true, I feel like dying inside from pain. But we must be truthful. I will not leave you alone."

Suddenly Jim put his hands over his face and began to sob. He shook his head. He took Ann's hand. Then he said, "It's all true. It's all true." They both cried and cried.

I was astounded at Ann's influence. He never would have faced that dreaded truth if she had not been present. He had been utterly unwilling to bear the shame of his guilt until he discovered that she was willing to bear it with him. Then he could face whatever other rejection might follow, public or private, as long as she did not reject him.

I also recall an experience with Mike and Jackie, which taught me something about the completeness of cleaving together. I had known both of them for some time but was unaware of strain in their marriage. When Mike came to talk, he was visibly shaken by the possibility that she no longer trusted him. He said she meant everything to him—he couldn't face a life without her. Yet the prospect of their losing each other loomed large that day. Among other things, he said they were really stuck over a difference of opinion about how he interacted with other women.

Mike had recently become reacquainted with a married woman he had known years earlier when both were single. They had lately exchanged a few phone calls, "just to talk." When he casually mentioned the calls to Jackie, she was deeply hurt and asked him not to call his old friend any more. He couldn't understand the problem. "Is it a sin to have a friend of the opposite sex?" he asked in genuine sincerity. I said no but added that in the complete context, the question probably wasn't that simple.

Then I said that except when they need urgent help, spouses should regard each other as their primary—in some ways their only—emotional confidant. Once you're married, of course you still have close friends, but not even your parents or those friends stand in the inner circle of your emotional confidence in each other. This idea is part of the pattern we find with Adam and Eve: "Therefore shall a man leave his father and his mother, and shall cleave unto his wife: and they shall be one flesh" (Genesis 2:24).

The day after talking with Mike, I recalled a distinctive, familiar voice from the past, which expressed more exactly what I was feeling. It was from President Spencer W. Kimball. He warned those "who think it is not improper to flirt a little, to share their hearts. [However] the Lord says in no uncertain terms: 'Thou shalt love thy wife with all thy heart, and shalt cleave unto her and none else.' (D&C 42:22) And when the Lord says all thy heart, it allows for no sharing nor depriving. The words *none else* eliminate everyone and everything. The spouse then becomes pre-eminent in the life of the husband or wife, and neither social life nor occupational life nor political life nor any other interest nor person nor thing shall ever take precedence over the companion spouse."[6]

Moreover, President Kimball taught, a husband and wife must be sure their "whole thoughts and desires and love are all centered in one being, their companion, and both are working together for the upbuilding of the kingdom of God, then happiness is at its pinnacle.

" . . . Frequently, people continue to cleave unto their mothers and their fathers and their friends. Sometimes mothers will not relinquish the hold they have had upon their children, and husbands as well as wives return to their mothers and fathers for advice and counsel and to confide; whereas cleaving should be to the wife or husband in most things, and all intimacies should be kept in great secrecy and privacy from others."[7]

I called Mike to share President Kimball's teachings. Mike listened carefully. He sensed that we were talking about a concept and an attitude, not a rule book. I later learned that following this counsel had set Mike and Jackie free to enjoy and appreciate each other with a refreshing fulness. They found that the exclusivity of emotional intimacy in wholehearted cleaving expands, it does not contract, the boundaries of our joy.

These stories are but impressionistic hints that reaffirm and clarify one fundamental doctrine—good shepherds stay with their flocks, no matter what wolves come. This major premise for all reasoning about the specifics of marital experience is at the heart of covenant marriage.

Before leaving that point, however, we should in fairness ask whether leaving the flock in the form of divorce is ever acceptable for a Latter-day Saint. President Gordon B. Hinckley began his response to this question by quoting the Savior: "What therefore God hath joined together, let not man put asunder" (Matthew 19:6). Then he added, "I am not one to say that [divorce] is never justified. But I say without hesitation that this plague among us, which seems to be growing everywhere, is not of God, but rather is the work of the adversary of righteousness and peace and truth."[8]

The reluctance of the Lord's prophets to offer a more precise standard flows from the reality that, as Elder David B. Haight put it, "divorce can never really be final. How can mothers and fathers really divorce themselves from their own flesh and blood children, or from the memories of days and years of shared experiences which have become part of their very lives."[9]

President Boyd K. Packer has said: "Some marriages have broken up in spite of all that one partner could do to hold the marriage together. While there may be faults on both sides, I do not condemn the innocent one who suffers in spite of all that was desired and done to save the marriage. And to you I say, do not lose faith in marriage itself."[10]

Thus the responsibility for divorce is a very personal one. President James E. Faust said that he did "not claim the wisdom nor authority to definitively state what is 'just cause' [for severing marriage covenants]. Only the parties to the marriage can determine this. They must bear the responsibility for the train of consequences which inevitably follow if these covenants are not honored. In my opinion, 'just cause' should be nothing less serious than a prolonged and apparently irredeemable relationship which is destructive of a person's dignity as a human being.

"At the same time, I have strong feelings about what is not provocation for breaking the sacred covenants of marriage. Surely it is not simply 'mental distress,' nor 'personality differences,' nor 'having grown apart,' nor having 'fallen out of love.' This is especially so where there are children."[11]

CHAPTER SEVENTEEN

EQUAL PARTNERS

Becoming a partner is a kind of nirvana for a young lawyer, because not all lawyers in a firm are equal. During my law practice days, I was in a Wall Street law office representing a Utah client. Needing a place to work, I was assigned the use of an associates' conference room. (Associates are young lawyers who as yet have no partnership or ownership interest in the firm.) I noticed that all the pencils at the work table were about half the length of regular pencils. Finding that a little odd, I joked to a secretary that these must be associates' pencils. It was no joke. She said the firm's partners used only new pencils and handed them down to the associates when they were half used up.

Some spouses feel like associates in their marriages, with no equity interest, no participation in partnership accounting meetings, and getting only leftover money, equipment, pencils, or otherwise. But the Proclamation on the Family teaches the doctrine of an "equal partner" marriage:

"Fathers are to preside over their families in love and righteousness and are responsible to provide the necessities of life and protection for their families. Mothers are primarily responsible for the nurture of their children. In these sacred responsibilities, fathers and mothers are obligated to help one another as equal partners. Disability, death, or other circumstances may necessitate individual adaptation."[1]

This understanding of marriage—equal partners with distinctive roles—differs from the approach of both traditional Christianity and modern secular liberation theory. The Victorian marriage of nineteenth-century England illustrates the traditional view: a marriage composed of a dominant husband and a subordinate wife. Some Christian churches still teach this concept. For example, one denomination's formal statement of faith still says that wives should "submit graciously" to their husbands.[2]

Much of this traditional understanding began a few hundred years after Christ. It drew on the false theological premise that the Fall of Adam and Eve was a tragic mistake and that Eve was the primary culprit. (I recently saw a bumper sticker that read, "Eve Was Framed.") Some who held this view taught that every woman was "an Eve" on whom "the sentence of God lives on . . . ; the guilt, of necessity, lives on too."[3] Women's submission to men was considered a fair punishment for Eve's sin when she first ate the forbidden fruit. All of this derived from an incorrect understanding of the Fall, an error that has led to the false belief that humans (including babies) have an inherently evil nature.

The restored gospel takes a totally different view of both the Fall and Mother Eve, which leads us to a different understanding about human nature, marriage, and the place of women. We reject the doctrine that mankind is stained by Adam and Eve's original sin, believing that "men will be punished for their own sins, and not for Adam's transgression" (Articles of Faith 1:2). The children of Adam and Eve were not born with an evil nature; rather, they were born "whole" (Moses 6:54) or "innocent" (D&C 93:38) into a world where they could experience temptation, misery, and joy. God sent them to earth precisely so that they could learn to understand the sweet by tasting the bitter (D&C 29:39).

The Fall was by no means a disaster. Quite the opposite. Elder John A. Widtsoe wrote that the Fall and the Atonement were "the most glorious events in the history of mankind."[4] After they left the Garden and an angel taught them about the Atonement and their mortal purpose, both Adam and Eve exulted in the joy of their redemption. Elder Widtsoe said these "were not the words of sinners" but the words of people who freely chose mortality— with all its hazards, after God had warned them that this choice would subject them to death, sorrow, and misery—as the price to know joy.[5]

As Lehi taught, "Adam fell that men might be [mortal]; and men are [mortal], that they might have joy" (2 Nephi 2:25). The Fall, and Eve's initial decision, were so essential in fulfilling the plan of salvation that President Joseph Fielding Smith said: "Adam and Eve could have remained in the Garden of Eden to this day, if Eve hadn't done [what she did].

"[W]hen I kneel in prayer, I feel to thank Mother Eve, for if she hadn't had that influence over Adam, . . . they would still be [there]. We wouldn't have come into this world. So the commentators made a great mistake when they put in the Bible at the top of page 3, as I think it is, . . . the statement, 'Man's shameful fall.'"[6]

Neither the traditional Victorian model of marriage nor the modern liberationist model is sound, theologically or psychologically. The contemporary view rejects the idea of male and female roles, either because people believe there are no innate differences between men and women or because they reject anybody's right to suggest gender-based roles. This mindset not only rejects the idea of gender roles but its extreme version also rejects society's right to define what marriage is, leaving that definition to each individual.

The Victorian model treated women as *dependent* on their husbands. Today's liberationist model treats women as *independent* of their husbands and husbands as *independent* of their wives. But the restored gospel teaches that husbands and wives are *interdependent* with each other. Equal. Partners.

In their life after the Fall, these interdependent partners worked together ("Adam began to till the earth, . . . And Eve, also, his wife, did labor with him"; Moses 5:1); they prayed and worshipped God together ("Adam and Eve . . . called upon the name of the Lord, and they heard the voice of the Lord"; Moses 5:4); and they taught their children together (Moses 5:12).

The Fall's promised consequences of "sorrow" in childbearing and "sweat" from tilling the earth were not punishments for disobedience but were simply the growing pains of progression through mortal experience.

Further, when we read that Eve was Adam's "help meet" (Genesis 2:18), the original Hebrew term for "meet" means Eve was adequate for, or equal to, Adam. She was not his servant, his subordinate, or his "associate" in the firm. And the Hebrew for "help" in "help meet" is *ezer*, suggesting divine rather than human help—Eve drew on heavenly powers when she supplied their marriage with the spiritual instincts available to women as a gender gift.[7] As Elder Boyd K. Packer said, men and women are by nature different, and while they share the basic human traits, the "virtues and attributes upon which perfection and exaltation depend come [more] naturally to a woman and are refined through marriage and motherhood."[8]

Some ancient Christian texts, written before Augustine stated his dark doctrine of the Fall, recount that when God took Eve from Adam's body and placed her before him, Adam saw in her "not a mere marital partner but a spiritual power." In these texts, Adam represents "ordinary consciousness," while Eve represents more of the spiritual element in our nature.

Therefore, Adam saw in Eve both the roots and the promise of his own inner spiritual nature. Another ancient text describes Eve as the "perfect primal intelligence" who "calls out to Adam" to "wake up, recognize her, and so receive spiritual illumination." Eve thus calls to Adam, "I am the intelligence of the pure life. . . . Arise and remember . . . and follow your root, which is I . . . and beware of the deep sleep."[9] If Adam will "arise and remember" by listening to Eve, he will be blessed by paying attention to her instincts and counsel.

Another writer from this early era said that death began when "Eve . . . became separated from [the body of] Adam." And only when Adam and Eve were reunited in marriage were they both "capable of withstanding physical and emotional impulses that, unchecked, could drive him or her toward self-destruction and evil."[10]

This insight echoes Joseph Campbell's comment on the hidden instinct in our innate longing to marry. Marriage, he said, "is the reunion of the separated duad. Originally you were one. You are now two in the world, but the recognition of the spiritual identity is what marriage is. It's different from [only] a love affair." This "reunion of the self with the self, with the male or female grounding of ourselves," reflects "the Chinese image of the Tao, with the dark and light interacting," the "relationship of yang and yin, male and female." In this relationship, "the one isn't just you, it's the two together as one."[11]

So marriage is what lawyers call an "entity," a legal institution to which each partner owes real allegiance. And because of the enhancing effect of each partner on the other, the whole entity is greater than the sum of its two parts.

Although not scripture, these sources are consistent with the scriptural description of Adam and Eve's unity. After Eve's creation, Adam said: "This I know now is bone of my bones, and flesh of my flesh; she shall be called Woman, because she was taken out of man. Therefore shall a man leave his father and his mother, and shall cleave unto his wife; and they shall be one flesh" (Moses 3:23–24). Paul wrote of this male-female interdependence: "Neither is the man without the woman, neither the woman without the man, in the Lord. For as the woman is of the man, even so is the man also by the woman" (1 Corinthians 11:11–12). The woman, Eve, was taken out of the man, Adam; and each man is born of a woman, his mother.

Of course, just as the three members of the Godhead are distinct personages who retain their individual identity, the male and female—Adam and Eve—are distinct beings with their own personalities. Their eternal partnership in marriage unites its partners in purpose, just as the members of the Godhead are united in their purpose.

What is Adam's "presiding" role in this relationship? After they had partaken of the forbidden fruit, God told Eve that Adam "shall rule over thee" (Genesis 3:16). The original Hebrew for this phrase uses "rule" in a way that suggests leadership but has less authoritarian connotations than the Hebrew verb used to describe Adam's "having dominion over" the animals of the earth.

A "ruler" could also suggest a standard-setting example for others, which imposes upon Adam the duty to live so that others may measure the rightness of their conduct by watching his. This aspirational sense of "ruler" is not so much a privilege of power as an obligation to practice what he preaches, because others are entitled to look to him to model how they should live. Further, the word "over" as used with "rule over" here uses the Hebrew preposition "bet," which usually means to rule "with" more than to rule "over."

Doctrine and Covenants 121 makes clear that any husband's presiding priesthood authority is explicitly conditioned on "the principles of righteousness" and that heaven simply terminates a man's authority when he exercises "dominion" in any degree of unrighteousness (vv. 36, 37).

Perhaps for such reasons, President Kimball preferred the term "preside" rather than the term "rule." Moreover, he said, "No woman has ever been asked by the Church authorities to follow her husband into an evil pit. She is to follow him [only] as he follows and obeys the Savior of the world, but in deciding [whether he *is* obeying Christ], she should always be sure she is fair."[12] President Kimball's language gives each wife enough responsibility to create a partnership full of checks and balances. No wonder he also said, "Let us speak of marriage as a *full* partnership. We do not want our LDS women to be *silent* partners or *limited* partners [but, rather,] a *contributing* and *full* partner."[13]

LDS historian Richard Bushman has noted that ever since Joseph Smith established the revealed temple ordinances in Nauvoo, women have "received and administered temple ordinances along with men." Moreover, the temple narrative centers on Adam and Eve as "a representative couple" rather than on any individual. Thus, "women were given a place in the ritual life of the Church beyond anything Freemasonry or the fraternal lodges ever imagined."[14]

Elder Dallin H. Oaks once explained the difference between presiding in the Church's organizations, such as in a stake or a ward, and presiding in the home. He quoted the "equal partners" principle from the Family Proclamation and then said this concept does *not* apply to a ward organization. The Relief Society president and her ward bishop, for example, are not equal partners in administering the affairs of the ward; however, that same Relief Society president *is* an equal partner with her husband in administering the affairs of their home.

He mentioned one priesthood leader who directs the activities of many Church members. When this man lets his "gentle-but-firm style of unilateral decision-making spill over into a communication with his wife, she appropriately gives him this three-word reminder: 'You're home, now!'" Elder Oaks also compared Adam and Eve's relationship to each other with their relationship to the Lord. He said that "the word *obey* is used in describing our covenants with the Lord and [the word] *counsel* is used in expressing [a married couple's] relationship with one another."[15]

Like partners in other ventures, each marriage partner brings distinctive gifts and assets to the partnership, creating a stronger entity than if their talents were the same. They need not perform the same functions to be equal partners. And, as the Family Proclamation states, they are to help one another in performing their tasks. The woman's innate spiritual instincts are like a moral magnet, pointing toward spiritual north, except when its magnetic particles are unnaturally traumatized. In addition to his own spiritual instincts, the man's presiding gift is the holy priesthood, except when he is not living the principles of righteousness. And their "counseling" is reciprocal: If he is wise, he will listen to the promptings of her inner spiritual compass, just as she hearkens to his righteous counsel.

The doctrines of justice and mercy offer an analogy for this coming together of the masculine and the feminine. In his great discourse on justice and mercy, Alma describes justice as masculine and mercy as feminine: "Justice exerciseth all *his* demands, and also mercy claimeth all which is *her* own; and thus, none but the truly penitent are saved" (Alma 42:24; italics added). This does not mean that women are not just nor that men are not merciful. But in the masculine sense of justice and the feminine sense of mercy, we see interdependent principles that are reconciled by the higher unifying power of the Atonement. Here is perhaps a type of the way a husband and wife are unified by the combined male and female elements of a higher divine nature.

This is not to suggest rigid role differentiations for all times and seasons in either a man's or a woman's life. Men as well as women have both a conscience and the Holy Ghost to prompt them. The modern prophets have always taught that men as well as women should see family life as their most important work. They have also always placed high value on women's education and their participation in society.

The point is a simple one: Marriage is a partnership of equals whose most essential roles both revolve around their families. Each of them also strives individually to become a fully rounded disciple of Christ, developing Christian attributes as a complete spiritual being. In that quest, both husband and wife have strong reasons to listen to each other, to follow each other, to discipline themselves so that the voice of each deserves to be heard by the other.

Elder Neal A. Maxwell once said that for too long in the Church, men have been the theologians while women have been the Christians. Really, each one should be both a theologian and a Christian. An incident from Elder Maxwell's life illustrates this point.

When he and his wife, Colleen, first learned that he had leukemia in 1996, his prospects for recovery were very bleak. He had worked for years on making himself "willing to submit" (Mosiah 3:19) to the Lord's will. So in his desire to accept whatever the Lord allotted him, Elder Maxwell felt he had no claim to a special miracle. If it was time for him to face death, he didn't want to shrink from drinking whatever bitter cup was his.

But Colleen thought he was too resigned and ready to yield. Speaking directly, she told her husband that Christ Himself earnestly pleaded first, "If it be possible, let this cup pass from me." Only then did He submit himself with, "Nevertheless not as I will, but as thou wilt" (Matthew 26:39). Elder Maxwell saw her doctrinal insight and agreed. As a result, they energetically looked for and willingly accepted a new cancer treatment therapy. They continued pleading together for his life, as divine intervention spared him for several more years. He gladly acknowledged that he was not the only theologian in their marriage.[16]

In an equal-partner marriage, "love is not possession, but participation, . . . part of that co-creation which is our human calling."[17] Here the husband and wife are merged into the synergistic oneness of an "everlasting dominion" which, "without compulsory means" shall flow with love and spiritual life unto them and their posterity, "forever and ever" (D&C 121:46). That dominion, the little kingdom called their family, can flow forever only by non-compulsory means. Each partner gives the other something he or she does not have and without which neither can be complete and return to God's presence.

CHAPTER EIGHTEEN

THE MORAL INFLUENCE
OF WOMEN

The Proclamation on the Family states that "marriage between a man and a woman is ordained of God."[1] Each partner makes a unique and crucial contribution. Yet they are not two solos but the interdependent parts of a duet. Both they and the larger society must assign equal value to each part. Let us consider the moral influence of women and then of men.

Large-scale cultural forces are eroding our foundations of personal peace, love, and human attachments. Whatever held family relationships together suddenly feels weaker now. At times this feels like an ecological disaster, as if a vital organism in the environment is disappearing.

Patricia Holland, the wife of Elder Jeffrey R. Holland, has said, "If I were Satan and wanted to destroy a society, I think I would stage a full-blown blitz on women."[2] What did she mean? Men and women share the traits of human nature and often perform the same tasks. But some strengths are gender-specific. And we are losing what women have traditionally contributed to cultural cohesion. Like the mortar that keeps a brick wall from toppling over, women have held together our most precious relationships—our marriages and child-parent ties. But now we're seeing cracks in that mortar, which reveals some things we have too long taken for granted.

A salesman walked down a street past a group of boys playing baseball. No one answered the door at the house where he was to call. Through a side door, he saw a boy the age of those playing in the street, dutifully practicing the piano, baseball gear leaning against the wall. He called, "Excuse me, sonny, is your mother home?" The boy glanced at his baseball gear and said glumly from the keyboard, "What do you think?"

Studies of third-world development show that of all the factors that affect a culture's social and economic growth, perhaps the most significant one is the literacy of their women.[3] Women have always lifted entire cultures. Their influence begins in each society's very core—the home. Here women have always taught and modeled what Alexis de Tocqueville called "the habits of the heart," the civilizing mores or attitudes that create a sense of personal virtue and duty to the community, without which free societies cannot exist.[4]

Shakespeare's *Macbeth* teaches powerfully about the moral influence of women. He first uses his phrase "the milk of human kindness" when Lady Macbeth is persuading her husband to murder the king and take his throne. As Macbeth hesitates, his wife sneers: "Thy nature . . . is too full o' th' milk of human kindness." Then, in a haunting passage, from her balcony she taunts the evil forces of the universe to "unsex me here, and fill me . . . with direst cruelty. . . . And take my [woman's] milk for gall. . . . Come, thick night."[5]

Lady Macbeth's womanly heart makes her incapable of taking a life unless she renounces her female instinct to give and nurture life. Later, after they have killed the king, she slowly goes insane and then dies—not just from guilt but perhaps also from symbolically renouncing her nature.

"The milk of human kindness" is a symbol of female nurturing at many levels. Especially it means the moral influence of women, an influence that begins with a woman's personal gifts as well as her gender-based gifts. As Lady Macbeth shows, a woman can reject her gifts. More typical, however, are women who nourish their own growth in a demanding process that teaches them how to become moral beings who can then influence others to follow them. Although some male and female gifts may differ, both genders share the human need to learn in developmental stages, such as those discussed in chapter 19.

In at least four major ways, modern society has devalued female nurturing, through cultural changes that undermine a woman's incentive to grow and to give. Seeing more clearly what we're losing can help us regain it.

First, motherhood has been devalued. For most of our history, the word *motherhood* meant honor, endearment, and sacrifice. Victor Hugo wrote, "She broke the bread into two fragments and gave them to her children, who ate with eagerness. 'She hath kept none for herself,' grumbled the sergeant.

"'Because she is not hungry,' said a soldier.

"'No,' said the sergeant, 'because she is a mother.'"[6]

Yet this spirit of self-sacrifice has become a contentious issue in recent years, making contentious the very idea of motherhood. An essay called "The Problem of Mothering," for example, tells us that "explorations of women's oppression [challenge] the social assignment of mothering to women [because] women's oppression is in some way connected to mothering."[7] Other critics have attacked the sacrificing mother whose selflessness has allowed and encouraged male domination. They argue that stereotyping the motherly role forces women to accept a sexist "division of labour" everywhere, "most especially in family relationships."[8]

These social critics do have a point. Some people have exploited mothers' willingness to accept relentless demands. And some women have felt undue pressure to conform to rigid roles that deny a woman's sense of self. But the critics have swung the pendulum too far. As *Newsweek* put it, they "sometimes crossed the line into outright contempt for motherhood."[9]

One woman I know is disturbed at the degree to which radical feminist attitudes have recently taught some young LDS wives to place their own needs and agendas ahead of those of husband and family. Some of them draw strict lines around how much they will give and how much they will support their families, feeling that looking out for themselves and their personal priorities is their primary allegiance, even their entitlement in this day of liberation from past shackles.

If being selfless means a woman must give up her own identity and personal growth, that understanding of selflessness is wrong. That was a weakness in some versions of the Victorian model of motherhood, which viewed women as excessively *dependent* on their husbands. But, as we have seen, today's liberationist model goes too far the other way, stereotyping women as excessively *independent* of their families—which is the problem my friend sees.

The more sensible view is that of the Family Proclamation, which describes husbands and wives as *interdependent,* with each other as "equal partners" who "help one another" in fulfilling their individual roles.[10]

The critics who thrust mothers from dependence to independence skipped the fertile middle ground of interdependence. Those who moved mothers from selflessness to selfishness skipped the fertile middle ground of self-chosen sacrifice that contributes to a woman's personal growth. Because of these excesses, debates about the value of motherhood have, ironically, caused the general society to discount not only mothers but women in general.

One woman's essay, "Despising Our Mothers, Despising Ourselves," reported that despite many victories for women since the 1960s, the self-respect of American women is at an all-time low. Why? Because we've experienced not just a revolt against men's oppression but also a revolt against women: "Heroic women who dedicated their lives to children as mothers, teachers, nurses, social workers, have been made to feel stupid and second rate because they [took] seriously the Judeao-Christian precept that it was better to do for others than for oneself." Devaluing motherhood devalues "the primary work of most women throughout history," which tells women that they "aren't worth serious consideration."[11]

Then what happens? Society's bricks begin to collapse. Consider the unprecedented example of child brutality. American schools have now witnessed several cases of children shooting other children, something the world had never seen before. The forerunner to these events was the world-shocking 1993 case of James Bulger, in which two ten-year-old boys murdered a two-year-old child in England. This crime prompted some British researchers to probe how children learn the difference between right and wrong. They found that a child's understanding of the difference between good and evil emerges emotionally long before it emerges rationally, so that the orientation of a child's conscience begins with its earliest relationship with its mother.

A child is an echo chamber. If he hears the sounds of love from his mother, he will later echo those sounds to others. But if the mother's signals are confusing and hateful, the child is more likely later to sound confused and hateful.[12] Whether a mother feels support from her husband, her family, and her society profoundly influences whether she feels like a mother of hope, who values herself enough to nurture a child of hope with the milk of human kindness. And children of hope create a society of hope.

Even though only about half of today's United States mothers feel valued in that role by the surrounding society, mothers' own sense of satisfaction is amazingly resilient. A 2005 study found that 81 percent of American mothers consider their mothering the most important thing they do, and 97 percent feel very or somewhat satisfied with their overall lives as mothers. Yet nearly all (95 percent) wish that American culture made it easier to instill positive values in their children.[13]

A second area in which society is devaluing the gender-specific gifts of women is sexual behavior. Historically, the keystone of the archway to sexual fidelity was the intuitive sexual self-control of women. Most women reflect in the expression of their sexuality an inner moral compass that can point true north, like a natural magnet. Of course, just as a natural magnet can lose its power through damage or trauma, women can also lose their natural moral magnetism. And many men have demonstrated the capacity for moral self-direction. But throughout history, women have tended to be society's primary teachers of acceptable sexual mores.

Perhaps this is one reason why the Lord said through the prophet Jacob that He "delight[s] in the chastity of women." Thus He grieves over "the fair daughters of this people" when actions by men "lead away captive the daughters of my people because of their tenderness" (Jacob 2:28, 32–33).

Writer Leon Kass says of this tenderness in women: "A fine woman understood that giving her body (in earlier times, even her kiss), meant giving her heart, which was too precious to be bestowed on anyone who would not prove worthy, at the very least by pledging himself in marriage to be her defender and her lover forever." Thus, "it is largely through the purity of her morals, self-regulated, that woman wields her influence, both before and after marriage. Men . . . will always do what is pleasing to women, but only if women suitably control and channel their own considerable sexual power."[14]

This view of female sexuality deplores any abuse of women. It also celebrates the spiritual and emotional fulfillment of marriage for both women and men. Yet women have too long endured the unfairness of a cultural "double standard" that tolerated promiscuity in men while condemning it in women. Sociologist David Popenoe writes that "men the world over are more sexually driven and 'promiscuous,' while women are more concerned with lasting relationships." Thus women have been "expected to set limits on the extent of sexual intimacy."[15]

A double standard that winks at this male laxness enough to excuse it is unequal and unfair. Society might have responded to such inequality by demanding fidelity of men. It is as if our culture had two hands: a female hand that was healthy and a male hand that was withered. In the name of equality, however, we held up both hands and asked, "Please make both of my hands the same"—and both hands became withered. Thus has our generation romped into history's most staggering sexual revolution, seeking male-female equality by encouraging women to imitate the habitual promiscuity of men.

This odd combination of sexual liberation and women's liberation has, with great irony, now liberated men—not only from a sexual conscience but also from the sense of family responsibility that women's higher sexual standards once demanded of men. And the biggest losers in this process are, sadly, children and women, the very women who have lost their former power to demand lasting commitments from the fathers of their children.

Despite the unfairness of the double standard, our traditional concept of marriage made serious demands of men. As discussed more fully in chapter 19, the pattern and power of the priesthood bless LDS men with a greater sense of family commitment than is found anywhere in society. But most men, says Popenoe, are not as "biologically attuned to being committed fathers as women are to being committed mothers."[16] So marriage was our culture's way of teaching men to provide for and protect their families. Yet our current culture of divorce shows us that because male commitment is often a learned behavior, it "is fragile and can disappear" when the culture no longer expects or teaches it.[17] Many men won't stay married unless their culture requires it of them.[18]

By expecting men to marry, our culture sent men a message that controlled the damage of the double standard. But in the rush toward women's sexual liberation, society seems less willing to expect men to marry. This gives up not only the double standard for sexual behavior but also the power of marriage to tame the male wanderlust. And the losers in this hasty bargaining are not men but women—and, even more so, children.

Third, our culture has begun to devalue women's innate yearning for permanent marriage bonds, throwing out our babies with the bathwater of resentment toward the very idea of marital commitment. After surveying the gale-force damage to children from years of runaway divorce and illegitimacy rates, Popenoe concludes that our only hope today is what he calls "the female predisposition toward permanent pair bonding." What does he mean? He means women prefer permanent marriage. For instance, most young women once would have answered the sexual propositioning of a young man with forceful authority: "Not until you marry me."

And why is this a "female predisposition"? Popenoe writes that women have certain innate qualities that differ from men's, including a stronger desire for long-term marriage. "Women, who can bear only a limited number of children" and who must nurture them through years of dependency, "have a great [inner] incentive to invest their energy in rearing [their] children, while men, who can father innumerable offspring, do not."[19] Because childrearing is so demanding, women have found ways to keep their children's fathers close at hand.

Women's desire for long-term mates has also made them more selective about whom they marry.[20] This desire, with the social benefits that flow from raising secure, healthy children in a stable home, has led women and civilized cultures to entice fathers to share the yoke of family responsibility through marriage bonds.

The chain of being that moves from a mother of hope to a child of hope to a society of hope gives our culture an enormous interest in permanent marriage. Thus the woman's greater desire for permanence is the mortar holding together the bricks of social stability.

When the marriage bond is secure, a wife stands at the center of moral gravity for her family's universe, holding her husband close with her gravitational pull. When he moves outward to the perimeter of the home and community to protect and provide for his family, as the Family Proclamation directs, he is like a falcon and she is his falconer. If he strays too far, he will no longer hear her voice, ever calling him home. William Butler Yeats tells us what happens then:

> *Turning and turning in the widening gyre*
> *The falcon cannot hear the falconer;*

Things fall apart; the centre cannot hold;
Mere anarchy is loosed upon the world.[21]

Society's recent devaluation of the female center of moral gravity leads to that disintegration.

Fourth, society undervalues the moral influence that lies in women's gifts for nurturing human relationships. Research shows that women will often sacrifice an achievement for the sake of a relationship, whereas men will more likely sacrifice a relationship for the sake of an achievement. And strong relationships hold both families and societies together.

Other studies tell us that the women's nurturing gifts sustain personal relationships in ways that bless all intersections of community activity. Economists praise this female strength as an asset in the economy of the future, with its emphasis on personal networks.[22]

The Church has long involved women in decision-making processes and personal ministering to local congregations. The Relief Society is a sisterhood for all adult women. Through this sisterhood, women learn to strengthen not only family bonds but a multitude of other relationships that are nourished—sometimes kept alive—by the milk of human kindness. Women's perspectives can profoundly enrich many fields of human endeavor without compromising the primary value of home and family.

The biblical story of Mary's relationship with her cousin Elisabeth, to whom she went to share, to talk, and to receive support, illustrates the influence of women's bonding. Because women can give so much to each other, one possible result of devaluing relationships is to isolate women from one another—perhaps by making them more competitive, like men. Once again, we need two healthy hands for both genders, in gestures of compassion, not competition.

If the adversary can convince LDS women to criticize each other rather than connecting with and supporting each other, he wins the day by driving wedges into natural relationships of strength. Some of these wedges come from rigid women, who are too narrow in the degree of personal choice and diversity they will tolerate in other LDS women. At the other extreme, some wedges come from LDS women who dangle one foot in Zion and the other in Babylon, wanting not to be thought weird by their non-LDS friends. Women in these two groups can really have at each other, turning the power of relationships from peace to war. They so much need to love and support each other without judging harshly—especially now that the surrounding culture is providing little support for family priorities.

In summary, consider a true story from Australian history that illustrates the power of women as mothers of hope, women of fidelity, wives of commitment, and nurturers of human ties. When first a British colony, Australia was a vast wilderness jail for exiled convicts. Until 1850, six of every seven Britons who went "down under" were men. And the few women were themselves often convicts or social outcasts. The men ruthlessly exploited them, rendering most of them as women without hope, powerless to change their conditions.

In 1840, a reformer named Caroline Chisholm urged that more women would stabilize the culture. She told the British government the best way to establish a "good and great" community in Australia: "For all the clergy you can despatch, all the schoolmasters you can appoint, all the churches you can build, and all the books you can export, will never do much good without . . . 'God's police'—wives and little children—good and virtuous women."[23]

Chisholm searched for women to raise the moral standard of

the people. For twenty years she traveled to England, recruiting young women and couples who shared the common-sense principles of family life. Over time, these women tamed the men who tamed the wild land, and civil society gradually emerged, aided by new state policies that raised women's status and reinforced family life.[24] As one historian said, "The initial reluctance of the wild colonial boys to marry was eroded fairly quickly." Eventually, thousands of new immigrants who shared the vision of these "good and virtuous women" established stable families as the basic unit of Australian society more quickly than had occurred in any other Western country.[25]

This striking story of women's moral influence grew from a deliberate plan to replace a "rough and wild" penal colony with "a more moral civilization" that capitalized on women's innate civilizing capacity.[26] Thus Australia became a land flowing with a healthy environment of milk and honey—the woman's touch, which nurtures those habits of the heart without which no civil society can exist.

Some branches of feminism, like the "equity feminists" who emphasize the need for fairness and equal dignity, support and honor this role of women as mothers and civilizing agents. The more extreme "radical" feminists reject that role, because they fear that emphasizing inherent differences between men and women will cause gender discrimination that places women in subordinate roles. However, despite many similarities, men and women do differ innately in some crucial ways.

For example, psychologist Carol Gilligan's 1982 book *In a Different Voice* shows how women and men perceive the same things in different ways and speak "in a different voice" from one another. Gilligan found that women have a stronger commitment to caregiving than men do. If society can value this gender gift without creating discrimination against women, we just might experience, as Australian writer Anne Summers put it, "a genuine breakthrough in our thinking about the qualities contemporary society now has the greatest need for."[27]

The recent women's movements opened many doors to women and awakened many men who had taken advantage of women's willingness to give their bread to others and keep none for themselves. But that pendulum has moved some attitudes too far, devaluing and damaging our culture's support for motherhood, sexual fidelity, marriage, and women's distinctive voices.

It is now time to pull the pendulum back to the center, to true north, the moral compass point that will nurture our children and communities with the milk of human kindness. Surely society can restore the confidence of today's women in their own instincts without coercing them into being nonentities. Surely we can invite men to follow the examples of compassion they see in their mothers, wives, and daughters. We have already learned the hard way that women, children, and the entire culture are worse off when we seek equality between men and women by encouraging women to adopt permissive male lifestyles.

We need a more responsible form of equality that celebrates and preserves the natural moral influence of women, thereby encouraging both men and women to honor the equal yoke and lifelong commitments of marriage. That kind of progress will make the civilization of the twenty-first century not only more equal but infinitely more civilized.

CHAPTER NINETEEN

THE MORAL INFLUENCE
OF MEN

Elder M. Russell Ballard's book *Counseling with Our Councils* encouraged priesthood leaders and fathers to listen to women with greater attention and sensitivity. President Boyd K. Packer also taught:

"However much priesthood power and authority the men may possess—however much wisdom and experience they may accumulate—the safety of the family, the integrity of the doctrine, the ordinances, the covenants, indeed the future of the Church, rests equally upon the women. . . .

"The leaders of Relief Society, Young Women, and Primary are all members of the ward and stake councils, and they have a unity which comes from their membership in Relief Society."

Regarding this unity of sisterhood, he compared Relief Society to a priesthood quorum. Then he said, "To the degree that [priesthood] leaders ignore the contribution and influence of these sisters, in [ward and stake] councils and in the home, the work of the priesthood itself is limited and weakened."[1]

At about the same time President Packer and Elder Ballard

gave this counsel, the Church was emphasizing the role of women and ward councils in its leadership training. Curious to see how our teaching on this subject was being understood, I talked with the three stake auxiliary presidents in an Australian stake. I asked them, "Do the men in your lives listen to you?"

One of them asked, "Do you mean our husbands or our priesthood leaders?"

I replied, "Is there a difference?" They looked at each other and nodded yes.

So I asked them what proportion of the active women in their stake would say that (a) their husbands and (b) their priesthood leaders really do listen to them, taking their opinions seriously. After a brief conversation, the three women returned with their estimates, which showed the priesthood leaders a little more responsive than the husbands. I had hoped both estimates might be higher, but they weren't bad.

Then one of the women spoke with kind directness. "Elder Hafen, I know you're a bit disappointed. But the situation is improving. And I want to tell you something more important. No organization in the world teaches men to value women and children as much as does the priesthood of God. The men in my life listen to me because that is what holding the priesthood means to them. The priesthood teaches them to be servants, not masters. I thank the Lord for the influence of the priesthood."

The Preface to the Restoration (D&C 1) gives doctrinal meaning to the priesthood's being not only in the Church but also in a family. After speaking boldly about the apostasy and wickedness of "Babylon the great, which shall fall," the Lord declared that because of the "calamity which should come upon the inhabitants of the earth," He had restored His gospel through Joseph Smith. This would allow "the weak things of the world" to proclaim the restored gospel—why?—so that *"every man might speak in the name of God the Lord"* (D&C 1:16–20; italics added).

The thought of "every man" speaking with divine authority may sound strange to a world in which only trained, professional priests act as religious ministers. But that idea is familiar to those who know Christ's original pattern of a lay priesthood. He called ordinary fishermen as His first apostles, and then the Master taught His apprentices, by experience, how to follow Him as His disciples.

What does "every man [speaking] in the name of God" make possible? The Lord continues, "That faith also might increase in the earth; that mine everlasting covenant might be established; that the fulness of my gospel might be proclaimed by the weak and the simple unto the ends of the world" (D&C 1:20–23). In other words, those who do speak in God's name learn by qualifying for that experience how to increase their own faith and the faith of others, helping to establish the everlasting covenant in all the earth.

Faithful priesthood holders soon learn that "the powers of heaven" can "be controlled . . . only upon the principles of righteousness"—"by persuasion, by long-suffering, by gentleness and meekness, and by love unfeigned; by kindness, and pure knowledge, which shall greatly enlarge the soul without hypocrisy, and without guile" (D&C 121:36, 41–42). When that happens, they listen to women, children, and other men with the ears of servants, not masters.

As an example of this process, more than forty years ago I helped teach the gospel to a recently married young German couple. The husband, Helmut, sensed the truth of our message before his wife, Elise, did, and he patiently nourished her growing testimony until her baptism. From then on, they nourished each other and their family, raising four children in the Church. They served in many callings, including her years as a Relief Society president and his as a bishop. Three of their children served missions.

While assigned to Germany in 2003, Marie and I received an invitation to the temple marriage of their youngest child. I thought that perhaps because of our long association and because I hold the sealing power, I should volunteer to perform the marriage. Somewhat gingerly, I asked Helmut, "Who is performing the sealing?"

He replied matter-of-factly, "I am."

Surprised, I said, "How can you do that?"

He responded, "I've been a sealer in the temple for several years."

A few days later Marie and I were in the sacred sealing room with Helmut, Elise, and all four of their children and their respective spouses, all of them Europeans. I learned then that as sweet as it is to perform a temple sealing, it was far sweeter to watch Helmut perform this one. My mind won't forget this picture of our once-young investigator, his mature and kindly face now full of light, his hair a little silver at the edges, his wife and all of his family looking to him as he said those sacred, eternal words with full authority. I thought to myself, "That every man might speak in the name of God . . . ; that faith also might increase in the earth; that mine everlasting covenant might be established" (D&C 1:20–22).

Through four decades of exercising the priesthood, Helmut had learned to speak in the name of the Lord, not only with the appearance of authority but with the authentic authority that comes from living the conditions of meek and gentle righteousness on which true priesthood power is predicated. Helmut learned about this process the way all who know it have learned it—by following a pattern taught by Adam, Enoch, Abraham, and all other followers of righteousness down to the present day.

I want to describe how that ancient pattern helps boys become men. I will use terms that apply not only today but also in the village of an ancient society. I do this partly to seek for clarity but also because so many traditional societies have handed down remnants of this pattern. I have seen bits and pieces of these ancient ideas among indigenous peoples in the islands of the Pacific and among the Aborigines of Australia. Certain elements in this pattern of male development are so common among subsistence-level societies that historians tell us that much of the pattern belongs to "the language of human universals."[2]

I look at these fragments the way Hugh Nibley looked at recorded hints of temple worship among the societies of antiquity. Through his years of research in ancient languages and records, Brother Nibley learned that the "complex of Mormon temple architecture, symbolism, and ritual process" are "found in abundance in the ancient world." He discovered that temple worship has many more parallels in ancient cultures than it does in the culture Joseph Smith inhabited. "The Hopi Indians, for example, come closest of all . . . and where did they get [their understanding of temple-like ritual]?" The source of such knowledge among these peoples is, of course, that "ancient cultures had these [temple] ordinances and lost them," while retaining some scattered pieces of the original whole.[3]

The Proclamation on the Family states: "By divine design, fathers are to *preside* over their families in love and righteousness and are responsible to *provide* the necessities of life and *protection* for their families. Mothers are primarily responsible for the nurture of their children. In these sacred responsibilities, fathers and mothers are obligated to help one another as equal partners."[4] Regarding the male role, consider an example that compares these prophetic teachings with that found in anciently established patterns.

In describing what he called the "paternal imperative," the eminent psychiatrist David Gutmann wrote that universally, "across our species," based on "the cross-cultural record," men have carried out the duty of "physical security on the perimeter" of human settlements, along with other activities that must be done at a distance, often requiring long absences from home—"hunting, trapping, herding, deep-sea fishing, offensive warfare." Women, meanwhile, are "generally assigned to secure areas, there to supply the formative experiences that give rise to emotional security in children." Men and women share activities that take place closer to home, like farming and building shelters, but "hearth-side activities, particularly those having to do with preserving and preparing food and with the care of young children, are almost exclusively the province of women."[5]

Gutman adds that "sociologists cannot explain these findings." They are simply part of "a species regularity, an expression of our bio-psychological nature, and not to some pan-social masculine conspiracy to keep women barefoot and pregnant in their domestic prisons. Incontestably, men are creatures of the perimeter; and while they start out swaddled to their mothers in the home, they must eventually leave it for the extra-domestic world. Later, as fathers, they must re-enter that domain and eventually work out a schedule of movement . . . between . . . the perimeter and the intimacies of the domestic zone [of real fatherhood]."[6]

I see this pattern of male development in the life experience of a young man who grows to maturity in a Latter-day Saint home. Because my purpose is very general, some of what follows is quite simple and abstract. I have arbitrarily chosen the age ranges, and there is much overlap between the stages of growth. The roles of each successive "new authority figure" also overlap, some of them continuously. For instance, good fathers are involved in nurturing their babies from the day they are born, even though we will see how the father's role may become more distinct with time.

I mean only to suggest that at some time in each developmental stage a new authority figure enters the young man's life, teaching him a new level of divine "law" and offering a new ordinance or "rite of passage" that is both a developmental symbol and an additional source of power. Just as some of what we saw in the chapter on women also applies to men, the general process of the following growth stages clearly applies to women. I also realize that this is an idealized framework that does not fit every individual case. For example, a male convert to the Church may come late to this process yet still fulfill its end goals successfully.

Age	Place	New Authority Figure	Law	Rite of Passage
0–5	Hearth	Mother	Feelings about Right v. Wrong	Baby's blessing
6–11	Home, Family	Father	Knowledge of Right v. Wrong	Baptism
12–17	Ward, Village	Bishop, Village Fathers	Ten Commandments	Aaronic Priesthood
18–21	Church, Country	Prophet, Scriptural Fathers	Law of Christ	Melchizedek Priesthood
19+	Universe	The Lord	Divine Tutorial	Temple, Mission, Eternal Marriage

The male child begins life at the "hearth," a symbol for home, securely in his mother's arms. As we saw in Chapter 18, the deep emotional attachments of the hearth let the mother transmit to the baby a *feeling* about what to her seems right and wrong in the universe. The "rite of passage" in this beginning stage is when the baby receives a name through a priesthood blessing, launching both child and parents on the lifelong path of "lead me, guide me, walk beside me, / Help me find the way."[7] Of the roles of father and mother in these earliest years, President James E. Faust said:

"A mother's influence is paramount with newborns and in the first years of a child's life. The father's influence increases as the child grows older. However, each parent is necessary at various times in a child's development. Both fathers and mothers . . . are equipped to nurture children, but their approaches are different. Mothers seem to take a dominant role in preparing children to live within their families, present and future. Fathers seem best equipped to prepare children to function in the environment outside the family."[8]

In stage two, then, the father becomes ever larger in his son's world, teaching him about God's laws of right and wrong, adding to the first stirrings of conscience nourished by the mother. The father's role mixes love and discipline. "Sometimes he has to be a buddy; sometimes he has to set an example; sometimes he has to be the disciplinarian, the adversary." He "must judiciously mingle conflict and attachment." He is "not afraid of his legitimate power and authority." He will participate in nurturing and household tasks but still has "a unique role, often disciplinary or confrontational in nature," which earns the respect he needs so he can help his son gradually separate from dependence on his mother and look outward to assume membership in the family and community.[9]

The father must live the laws that purport to guide his own life, for his priesthood is conditioned on the principles of righteousness.

Like King Arthur, he rules by conviction, not force. Ruling by force alone undercuts the entire process of his son's growth, teaching him the false principle that might is right.

In this early stage, both parents teach their children that law is more than a feeling, helping them to "understand the doctrine of repentance" and "faith in Christ" (D&C 68:25)—in the child's terms, "I'm sorry" and "trust Jesus." This preparation readies the child for baptism and membership in the Church at age eight. As he now begins to focus on preparing to receive the priesthood, his interests extend beyond the hearth and family. At age twelve he becomes a deacon, and his first use of priesthood power is to serve the people of his ward.

I first saw fathers and young men as symbols of law in a Samoan village, where the men would take their places each evening at dusk, standing like sentinels around the perimeter road of the village, silently sending the message that it was time for all the villagers to come home. Seeing this mentoring association of older men with younger men, I thought of how the priesthood gives young men an association with other male authority figures outside the family. Such associations encourage allegiance to a community's laws, a larger, more objective moral framework than a father's personal set of rules. A deacon also joins a quorum of boys his own age—a team of righteousness—whose peer influence will reinforce parental teaching rather than tear him away from it.

As a priesthood holder, the boy also learns the twin principles of service and sacrifice. I remember a Tongan boy who preferred playing soccer to attending Church. Then he became a deacon, and passing the sacrament in a white shirt gave him a satisfying sense of service and privilege he hadn't known before. Now he looked forward to being in Church meetings on Sunday rather than on the soccer field.

I recall another story of a Samoan boy who had just become a deacon. The village chiefs who were not Church members told him that he was of the lineage that could one day qualify him to be his country's king but he would need to renounce his priesthood. Showing that he understood the principle of sacrifice, he replied, "I would rather be a deacon in the Aaronic Priesthood than the king of Samoa."

When a young man is ready to receive the Melchizedek Priesthood at age eighteen, his span of allegiance moves beyond the village to his country, beyond his ward to his stake. Soon he may receive a letter from the Lord's prophet, calling him as a full-time missionary to represent the entire Church, anywhere in the world. Now, guided by a mission president, who is also called by the prophet, he begins to identify with universal principles of manhood, for he is also old enough to become a soldier, defending his country, if necessary with his own life. He is both protector and provider.

During his adolescence, the son must also come to terms with his father's authority. With his father as his shelter during his move toward independent identity, ideally he will, as Gutmann says, "give up infantile . . . fantasies of acquiring the father's powers by violence in favor of a disciplined filial apprenticeship built on identification with him and his powers."[10] As he resolves natural conflicts with his father and other authority figures, he becomes willing to accept their counsel, as from coaches, teachers, and quorum leaders. He takes his place in a world beyond the family, sensing that his strength should be a resource, not a threat, to that world.

Internally, he then begins to feel the authority of his own conscience, which "converts his outward-directed aggression back against himself" so that he "will not . . . hurt . . . those that he either loves or should love." By the discipline of fasting, accepting calls, living by the rules, and serving others, he can sense his value to the community as a defender against its moral enemies. Now he learns about sacrificing for interests larger than self-interest, and his "moral suffering pays the dues for moral strength."[11]

Social historian Christopher Lasch eloquently captured this point: "The best argument for the indispensability of the family [is] that children grow up best under conditions of 'intense emotional involvement with their parents.'" "Without struggling with the ambivalent emotions aroused by the union of love and discipline in his parents, the child never masters his inner rage or his fear of authority. It is for this reason that children need parents, not professional nurses and counselors."[12]

This process, whereby the child brings his self-oriented impulses into some kind of harmony with loving yet inevitably demanding parental authority explains how the cultural heritage is acquired and internalized by each generation. A child who moves successfully through this process learns to deal with his father figure in ways that enable him to succeed his father rather than to eliminate him. Thus the child productively comes to terms with the whole concept of authority. As a result, the child is able to "internalize moral standards in the form of a conscience." Without such experience, the child never does grow up. "Psychologically he remains in important ways a child, surrounded by authorities with whom he does not identify and whose authority he does not regard as legitimate."[13]

The process of internalizing moral standards is best illustrated by the doctrinal concept of the law of Christ, the new law that replaced the law of Moses.[14] This law of the higher priesthood is written not on tablets of stone but in the heart. It is no longer an external coercion but is now an inward passion. For, said the Lord,

"I will put my laws into their mind, and write them in their hearts . . . : and they shall not teach every man his neighbour . . . saying, Know the Lord: for all shall know me" (Hebrews 8:10–11).

I once read the missionary application of a young man who had written the Lord's teachings "in [the] fleshy tables of [his] heart" (2 Corinthians 3:3). His bishop, who was also his father, recommended his service in words that portray the priesthood's process of spiritual and moral development:

"It is a privilege to recommend my son for a mission. He has been groomed for this calling all his life. He is our National Junior 800 Meter Athletics Champion, so he is eligible to represent his country at the Sydney 2000 Olympic games. He has given up that dream to fulfill another dream of representing the Lord on a mission. He is athletic and strong in body, mind, and spirit. He knows how to focus and succeed and is now very focused on serving Heavenly Father with all his might. He has a deep love of the scriptures, the prophets, the Church, and missionary work. He loves to share with others the principles that have unlocked success in his own life. He has been tried in the furnace of affliction and has come through with physical and spiritual stamina. He has a healthy sense of destiny, knowing that if he puts the Lord first, all else will fall into place."

This young man was ready to serve a mission, not just because his family and friends thought he should but because he desired for himself to say, "I am a disciple of Jesus Christ. . . . I have been called of him to declare his word among his people" (3 Nephi 5:13).

When a young man has been ordained an elder, endowed in the temple, and called on a mission, he is then ready for the fifth, fully mature stage in which he finds his place in the universe through his personal relationship with God. That relationship—

which good missionaries always discover—becomes a personal
tutorial between a young apprentice and the Master himself. As
that process unfolds, he will discover that God expects him to sacrifice all worldly interests. If he can make that sacrifice with full
purpose of heart, eventually he will receive "an unction from the
Holy One." Then this "anointing which ye have received of him
abideth in you, and ye need not that any man teach you" (1 John
2:20, 27).

Recent changes in the Church's missionary program seek to
have every missionary catch and live this vision—raising the bar
of both their worthiness and their gospel understanding until they
know the Lord and His doctrines well enough truly to "teach by
the Spirit."

Tribal societies seek for such an analogous stage through a sac-
rificial experience in which the young man is expected to leave or
otherwise transcend the tribal elders and establish his own connection with the Infinite. The ritual may be a risky ordeal, in
which the young man, in imitation of a founding story of his
people, shows he can connect with and be guided by a Greater
Power.[15] It may be a quest to find and bring back an eagle's feather,
symbolic and literal proof of having scaled, alone, whatever
heights are required to commune with the power of Nature. "Go,
my son, go and earn your feather . . . make your people proud of
you."[16]

Then he becomes not just his father's son or the son of the village fathers but a protégé of Deity, whose acceptance and "whose
'medicine' or mana" will protect and empower him. Now he must
make actual contact with God, until he captures "some of the . . .
'father's' substance," which helps him visualize his own marriage
and fatherhood with divine perspective. Then, "knowing that he
can leave the home, the community, and its women, that he can

live on his own," he "can look towards mating, marriage, and fatherhood for himself,"[17] not seeing marriage as the child returning to the mother but as his opportunity to protect, provide, and preside righteously in his own home. Having allied himself with the extended earthly fathers and then with the Father of the Universe, he will be the kind of father they were to him—protecting, civilizing, and preserving divinely given values.

Because his moral development has succeeded, the son can then return with the symbolic fire he has obtained by his contact with God and, as a father himself, light the spiritual and moral fire of the hearth in his own home—and the process begins again for him, his wife, and their family.

The fully authentic version of this internalizing process is best taught in the doctrine and ordinances of the Melchizedek Priesthood and the temple endowment. We see this at work in the individual quest for spiritual development by prophets like Nephi, who desired to see the things his father saw. His faithfulness allowed him to see not only his father's vision of the tree of life but a prophetic vision of the future that helped prepare him to lead his people.

Moses also learned directly from God who he was and what he should become. In a high mountain, God taught Moses, "Behold, thou art my son; wherefore look. . . . I have a work for thee, Moses, my son" (Moses 1:4–6). Once he had seen this vision, Moses had the power to resist satanic temptation. So when "Satan came tempting him," Moses said to him, "Who art thou? For behold, I am a son of God. . . . Get thee hence, Satan; deceive me not; for God said unto me: Thou art after the similitude of mine Only Begotten" (Moses 1:12–16).

Joseph Smith experienced the same progressive pattern of development. In Joseph's early years, God called him "my servant"

(D&C 1:17). After Joseph grew through years of experience, God spoke to Joseph and his associates not as servants but as "my friends" (D&C 88:62). Then finally, in the fiery furnace of Liberty Jail, God spoke to Joseph as "*my son*" (D&C 121:7; italics added). Unlike a servant or a friend, a son inherits his father's all.

The parents who teach their sons this doctrine, the Church leaders who teach it to their youth, the mission presidents who teach it to their missionaries, will help a young man progress from being a child to being God's *servant,* then to being God's *friend,* and finally to the divine acceptance of being God's *son*—one who fulfills the oath and covenant of the Melchizedek Priesthood until he qualifies to inherit "all that my Father hath" (D&C 84:38).

A wife's moral gravity helps her husband stay in tune with the values of the hearth through the gravitational pull of her inner compass. Meanwhile, as this chapter has described, her husband makes his own contribution to those domestic values, not only at home but also at the community perimeter. The husband of the virtuous woman "is known in the gates, when he sitteth among the elders of the land" (Proverbs 31:23). But like the falcon to the falconer, he always returns to the hearth, guided not only by her calling him home but also by being attuned himself to "the song of redeeming love" (Alma 5:26).

The image of the falcon and the falconer suggests some distinction between the roles of fathers and mothers. In Gutmann's terms, "strong mothers build secure homes; strong fathers and fathers' sons maintain secure neighborhoods."[18] The Family Proclamation makes those equal but distinctive roles very clear.

Some modern critics apparently seek to eliminate the distinction between male and female roles in the domestic realm. However, one consequence of eliminating the male role is the relegation of fathers to being "second fiddle" mothers or being absent altogether. Without a valued place at home, men can be driven from marriage into what Gutmann calls the "masculine default habitats" of "the barroom, the battlefield, the adulterous bed," where they "feel like men, rather than failed mothers."[19] Then, men too often tragically turn their aggression against women, family, and community, ironically becoming the family's worst enemy instead of its foremost protector and provider.

I share Gutmann's concern about those today who would challenge the very idea of male authority. When male authority is in fact misused, that conduct deserves strong, clear correction—of the kind given in Doctrine and Covenants 121. But when men exercise authority through "the principles of righteousness" (D&C 121:36), they help preserve and perpetuate the future moral development of children, which makes possible a community life based on moral order.

I am thankful for the doctrine and pattern of the priesthood, which restores a full understanding of the way a boy can become a man, as he grows from being God's servant to God's friend to God's son. When he achieves that kind of spiritual and emotional maturity, a man who carries his priesthood in his heart will protect and provide for his little flock, even—like the Good Shepherd—with his life.

PART III

SOCIAL COVENANTS

CHAPTER TWENTY

THE CLADDAUGH RING: JOINING THE PAST WITH THE FUTURE

Having explored the personal covenants between wives and husbands, we now look at "social covenants," the interests other people have in our marriages. Covenant marriage especially includes our ties to that sacred circle we call our posterity—our children and their children. It also includes our ties to ancestors, extended families, and the larger community.

The doctrine of baptism illustrates how our covenants with God also create covenants with other people. Alma said, "As ye are desirous to come into the fold of God, and to be called his people, and are willing to bear one another's burdens, that they may be light; yea, and are willing to mourn with those that mourn; yea, and comfort those that stand in need of comfort, . . . if this be the desire of your hearts, what have you against being baptized in the name of the Lord, as a witness before him that ye have entered into a covenant with him" (Mosiah 18:8–10).

One new convert felt lonely and discouraged because the members of her branch did not help bear her burdens and comfort her. Then when she read Alma's words more carefully with the sister missionaries, they discovered together that he had not promised that her membership in the Church guaranteed that other members would comfort her; rather, her membership covenants asked her to comfort them! Once she saw that, she began reaching out to her branch members, and as she served them, her loneliness gradually disappeared.

We also see the idea that personal covenants lead to community covenants in the doctrine of building Zion. We come unto Christ individually, we work to become pure in heart personally, but as we do, we and others who share those desires join together to build Zion—the *community* where the pure in heart dwell (D&C 97:21) and where the people are "of one heart and one mind" and dwell "in righteousness" together (Moses 7:18).

Marie and I were once in the grey-green beauty of Belfast, Ireland. We noticed that many Irish women wore an unusually styled and attractive wedding ring. They called it the Claddaugh Ring, named for a region near Galway where, at some moment in unrecorded antiquity, the Claddaugh wedding tradition began. At the ring's center is a heart with two hands holding it, one on each side. A small crown rests on top of the heart.

We asked merchants in Belfast's jewelry stores about the meaning of the symbols. They weren't much help, saying such things as, "Oh, the heart is about love, romance—that sort of thing." Then we discovered in a book on Irish wedding traditions that each part of the Claddaugh design was symbolic to those who created it. Originally the ring was made of three parts, and it involved three people. The bride carried her part to the altar on her ring finger—a thin ring supporting a central element, a heart, with a small hand holding one side of the heart. This represented her hand in the gesture of offering of her heart.

At the ceremony, the groom would place on her finger a

second ring strand, which carried another tiny hand cupped to hold the other side of the heart. This represented the joining of their two hearts, held now by two thin rings cupping the heart on either side, one from each marriage partner.

Then a priest or state official would complete the wedding by adding a third thin strand to the ring on the bride's finger. This strand placed a small crown on the top of the heart—a symbol that God, the church, and the community were parties to the wedding and had a stake in its future. Thus the Claddaugh Ring depicted marriage not just as a two-way promise but as multiple covenants: those between the husband and wife, both of them with God, and both of them with the community.

"Marriage," said Wendell Berry, is "not just a bond between two people but . . . a bond between those two people and their forebears, their children, and their neighbors."[1] Weddings are community events. People don't wait in line and bring gifts when people sign a business contract. But the world over, people collectively celebrate weddings—kinfolk, neighbors, and friends who often feel real emotion about the event, because they sense that they somehow have a stake in what the marriage means and how it goes.

This understanding of wedding bonds suggests two themes

about covenant marriage. One theme, which we saw in discussing individualism, is that marriage "joins"—it is a "welding together," to use Joseph Smith's term (D&C 128:18)—a single man and a single woman in a way that is too personal and too permanent for a mere contract to accomplish. Only a sacred covenant can create this awesome "joining." Thus do these two single souls "die" into their new life, their new "union with one another as a soul 'dies' into its union with God."[2] But from this dying, as through a resurrection, a new sense of joined souls comes forth in the fruit and the freedom of new family life, posterity, and spiritual development.

The second theme is that the couple speak their sacred vows not only to each other but in front of their extended family and their community. Their bonds of belonging thus commit them outwardly to society, forward to their future children, and backward to their ancestors.

President Gordon B. Hinckley has felt this joining of the generations in both his past and his future. He told the students at BYU–Idaho:

"As I sat in the temple the other day looking at my great-grandchildren, a peculiar thing happened. . . . I suddenly realized that I stood midway, with three generations with which I am familiar behind me and three generations ahead of me.

"My heart literally turned to my fathers. My heart also turned to my posterity. I envisioned a chain of the generations [that] goes back . . . into the distant past. . . . It now reaches for three generations beyond me. I pictured that chain in my mind's eye, to date unbroken and shining and strong."

He thought of a time when, as a boy on his family farm, he tried to repair a chain that had snapped when he attempted to remove a tree with a tractor. He installed a repair link, "but it was never the same." The repair link "never quite fit. . . . It was always a misfit. It never looked right." So President Hinckley urged the students to "never do anything that would weaken the [generational] chain of which you are a fundamental part."

Reflecting on being in the temple, he added, "All that I have of mind and body, of tissue and limb and joint and brain, have come as an inheritance from those who were before me. And all that my posterity have has passed through me to them. I cannot afford to break that chain. My posterity cannot afford to break that chain." Then he recalled the tragedy of King David's son Absalom, whose mistakes had "broken the link of the chain of his generations." Upon hearing of Absalom's death, his father uttered words that evoke how parents feel when turning their hearts to their children: "O my son Absalom, my son, my son Absalom! would God I had died for thee, O Absalom, my son, my son!" (2 Samuel 18:33).[3]

What is this deeply ingrained sense of belonging that we feel for our ancestors and our posterity? It is clearly at the very heart of our theology, our sense of who we are and where we belong in eternity as well as time. This "welding link" eternally draws the hearts of the children and the fathers together. And the joining we call marriage is the indispensable bond that lets the present weld together the past and the future.

Joseph said that Elijah "shall turn the heart of the fathers to the children, and the heart of the children to their fathers, lest I come and smite the earth with a curse" (D&C 128:17, quoting Malachi 4:5–6). He also said "the earth will be smitten with a curse unless there is a welding link . . . between the fathers and the children." How important is this welding link? So crucial that "we without them cannot be made perfect; neither can they without us be made perfect." Indeed, it is "necessary in the ushering in of the dispensation of the fulness of times . . . that a whole and complete and perfect union, and welding together of dispensations . . . take place" (D&C 128:18).

Welding links and weddings—links in a great human chain that tie the generations endlessly together. Our understanding of this eternal chain of being gives Latter-day Saints a timeless *doctrinal* perspective on our own family's past and future—and therefore a perspective on our marriages—that modern minds simply can't seem to comprehend.

Because we cherish our posterity, we have a unique stake in the future. Many LDS parents have endured the jibes of people who believe they're overpopulating the earth when they have more than one or two children. One LDS mother was shopping one day with her five young sons trailing her grocery cart like little ducklings behind a mother duck. A woman approached her and asked, "Excuse me, are all those kids yours, or is this a picnic?" The mother replied, "Yes, they're all mine. And it's no picnic." The woman looked over those five bright little faces once more, shook her head, and said, "Give it up, honey. Give it up."

Yet many developed countries today face quite the opposite problem—an alarming "birth dearth." Women need to maintain a lifetime average of 2.1 births total fertility rate (TFR) to sustain a nation's population. The global TFR was 6.0 in 1972 but had plunged to 2.9 by 2004.[4] The United Nations projects a growth in world population from the current 5.1 billion people to about 7.7 billion by 2050; however, all of that growth will occur in the nonindustrialized, developing nations. Until then the developed world is likely to remain at its current level of 1.2 billion people.[5] Then, some estimates predict a swift worldwide decline after the global population peaks in 2050.[6]

Many developed nations, especially those in Europe and Asia, and even some still-developing countries (including China) will suffer major population declines in the next several decades.[7] In Germany, to take a typical European example, if the current TFR of 1.4 per woman continues, the national population will "wither from 82 million [in 2004] to an astonishing 24 million by 2100."[8] Japan predicts that its population will peak at 127 million in 2006 and then drop to 64 million by the century's end.[9]

This unprecedented tailspin is one of Europe's hottest current political issues, because it means that future generations won't have enough workers to fund existing retirement and social care obligations. As one sociologist put it, "Never in the last 650 years, since the time of the Black Plague, have birth and fertility rates fallen so far, so fast, so low, for so long, in so many places."[10]

The trend appears to have multiple causes—increased migration toward cities, divorce, abortion, later average age of marriage, and contraception.[11] Whatever the specific factors, one German interior minister spoke more generally: "To reject children is to reject life."[12] Former German political leader Kurt Biedenkopf calls the demographic downturn a "migration away from the future" caused by a self-oriented hostility toward children. Because of it, "our grandchildren's generation" will say, "you should have made provision for [your future], but you preferred to be consumers rather than bring children into the world."[13] A *New York Times* writer added, "Unless it can face up to and reverse its neglect of parenting, Europe's economic future is grim."[14]

As one friend put it, "Our houses are getting larger, while our families are getting smaller."[15] This pattern is especially ironic in Europe, where concern for preserving the environment enjoys high cultural priority. Many Europeans seem more concerned about their future trees than about their future children—who are the only ones who can take care of the future trees.

In a related trend, one Australian official sees an increasing proportion of the population who need care, such as the elderly, but a decreasing proportion who are willing to provide that care. His research found that married people are far more likely to care for the elderly than are unmarried cohabitants. Something about being married turns one's heart to an elderly parent.[16] I think of the Claddaugh Ring. Children to fathers. Welding links.

The LDS Church is not immune from today's population decline. Because of fewer children per family, the number of LDS high school graduates and potential missionaries from North America has recently begun to decline. Moreover, in a comparison of active Scandinavian and Germanic Latter-day Saints between 1996 and 2003, the number of adults remained about the same, but the number of Primary children declined in only seven years by nearly 30 percent.[17]

Today's erosion of "intergenerational solidarity" through depopulation reflects a shift in Western society from a child-centered culture that values marriage toward an adult-centered culture that gives priority to personal freedom.[18] This creates a global culture of "the diminished child," in which adults feel less obligation to their posterity and the future society. In return, young people feel less concerned about what they may owe or want to give older generations.

Historian Allan Carlson believe such factors as more working mothers, divorces, and illegitimate births are symptoms, not causes, of the recent change in attitudes—a "contest between vital faith that welcomes children and a secular individualism that does not want them." For him, "the 'population control campaign' [like someone with anorexia, probably] cannot stop, even though it has already gained [its] original 'zero-growth' ambitions." When adults devalue children and family life, "even a stable world population contains too many children."[19] Carlson concludes that "too many educated people [today] really don't care that much any more about the future."[20]

I heard that attitude expressed in a recent conversation on a train in Europe, when an elderly but able German businessman responded to the question, "What should your country do about the current population decline?" Said he, "I'll be dead in a few years. That's not my problem."

Not caring about the future touches a doctrinal and personal nerve for me. I had believed modern culture was losing its way about families, marriage, sex, and children primarily because so many people no longer care about the past. They have walked away from centuries of tradition and social taboos, casually uprooting deeply planted moral fences without seriously asking why those fences were put up in the first place. And I knew that the doctrines of the Restoration gave us the world's best understanding of why those boundaries exist.

Now I see another dimension of our doctrinal uniqueness. We understand, as no one else really does, both the history and also the future about being married and having children. Through the Restoration we know not only where family life came from but where it has the potential—even the destiny—to go. The spirit of family present that links our sense of family past to our sense of family future is a *marriage*—one in which the partners feel in their very bones the natural commitments that run both up and down the eternal chain of ancestry and posterity and also extend outward to their community.

Latter-day Saints care about the multigenerational family because our doctrine so fully comprehends both the past and the future, in which marriage is the knot that holds all our human intersections together. Conversely, there is a clear connection between not caring about the past and not caring about the future. The same spirit that thoughtlessly rejects traditional standards of marriage and sexual expression will just as uncritically reject cultural standards of loyalty to future generations. Those without the gospel don't feel "wedded" to either side of the intergenerational chain of which President Hinckley and Joseph Smith taught. The "me generation" has no idea about the eternal plan that gives the "we generation" its perspective and its meaning.

Nearly two centuries ago, Alexis de Tocqueville foresaw these risks in societies that focus so much on the me and the now that they lose their sense of connection to the past and the future: "They owe nothing to any man, they expect nothing from any man; they acquire the habit of always considering themselves as standing alone, and they are apt to imagine that their whole destiny is in their own hands.

"[This makes] every man forget his ancestors, [and] it hides his descendants and separates his contemporaries from him; it throws him back forever upon himself alone, and threatens in the end to confine him entirely within the solitude of his own heart."[21]

In contrast, the Family Proclamation states, "Children are an heritage of the Lord," and "God's commandment . . . to multiply and replenish the earth remains in force."[22] As President Boyd K. Packer said, "Do not be afraid to bring children into the world. We are under covenant to provide physical bodies so that spirits may enter mortality (see Genesis 1:28; Moses 2:28). Children are the future of the restored Church."[23] And in his classic tribute to the Mormon pioneers, President J. Reuben Clark Jr. reserved his greatest admiration for mothers who bore children on the trail: "Who will dare to say that angels did not cluster round and guard her and ease her rude bed, for she had given another choice spirit its mortal body, that it might work out its God-given destiny?"[24]

Latter-day Saints know more about family history than does any other group. We also understand that the tie between parents and children is the key to a future with meaning. As long ago as Moses, the Lord said, "Honour thy father and thy mother: *that thy days may be long upon the land* which the Lord thy God giveth thee" (Exodus 20:12; italics added). So He asks that we "seek diligently to turn the hearts of the children to their fathers, and the hearts of the fathers to the children" (D&C 98:16).

We stand clasping the past with one hand and the future with the other. That perspective helps us desire a marriage that succeeds "for the sake of the children"—not only for the sake of the immediate children but as part of building a multigenerational Zion wherever we live. Without such an eternal, intergenerational "welding link," neither we nor our ancestors nor our posterity can be made perfect.

Nothing brings more light to a child's face than the sacred assurance that he can be together, forever, with his family. Conversely, nothing tears at his heart more than sensing that the much-promised family belonging may be slipping from his grasp. We do not marry for ourselves alone. Our children are entitled to expect that we live not only for our future but for theirs.

CHAPTER TWENTY-ONE

CHILDREN AND THE SOCIAL INTEREST IN MARRIAGE

O ne of my first divorce cases as a young lawyer involved a family with several children. In those days, courts usually assigned custody of younger children to the mother, unless she was simply unfit. But for older children, the judge was supposed to consider, among other things, with which parent the child preferred to live. In our case, the divorcing couple had a daughter about twelve years old.

I don't remember much else about the case, but I cannot forget the moment in the judge's chambers when I sat with the other lawyer, the judge, and the twelve-year-old. When the judge asked whether she would rather live with her father or her mother, she began to cry and couldn't talk. Then she looked at us with anguished eyes and asked, "Why can't I live with both my mom and my dad? I love them both. Why is this happening? Who is doing this to our family?"

The image of this child feeling so torn apart expresses some of what it means that marriage is a bond not only between a husband and wife but between those two people, their children, their families, and the larger society. The rupture in her parents' marriage was rupturing her heart—just as, at the other end of the emotional spectrum, the healing and nourishing of a strong marriage feeds a child's soul.

Divorce can inflict such psychic damage on children that its long-term consequences are in some ways similar to the damage of child abuse, which can last a lifetime. Divorce seldom causes childhood trauma that runs as deep as the trauma inflicted by sexual abuse, and in a few cases, the children are better off with divorced parents than they are living in a family of high conflict. But the chances are that many adults who divorce do not realize the damage their decision can cause their children, just as many sexually abusive parents are woefully unaware of the damage they do. What to them may seem trivial can shatter a child's emotional life, imposing a trauma that will unfold for years, hindering the child's own later marriage and life experience.

Only in the last few years have we begun to see the aggregate personal and social consequences of doubling the divorce rate and quintupling the illegitimacy rate over a period of thirty years. During the 1970s and 80s it was difficult to find a consensus among researchers on these issues, mostly because it takes a generation to demonstrate what happens to children who grow up in single-parent families. Also, the public had so willingly embraced greater tolerance for alternative family lifestyles that prevailing "politically correct" attitudes created a conflict of interest for many researchers.

For example, in the United States presidential election of 1992, Dan Quayle was essentially laughed off the national stage for taking a stand against the deliberate decision of a popular TV character, Murphy Brown, to have a child out of wedlock. Quayle wanted to underscore his belief that children in single-parent homes are at much greater risk than children with two parents, and he thought society should have something to say about what family structure was best for children. The public's initially negative reaction to Quayle reflected the combination of tolerance and ambivalence about personal lifestyle choices that had characterized the 1980s.

Then in 1993, a scholar named Barbara Whitehead published an article called "Dan Quayle Was Right" in the prestigious *Atlantic* magazine. She said that the Murphy Brown show, and the media's reactions to it, depicted "unwed parenthood . . . not only as a way to find happiness but also as a way to exhibit such virtues as honesty and courage." She thought the media's reaction illustrated broader efforts to depict "the married two-parent family as a source of pathology." All of this, she explained, is part of an attempt to "normalize what was once considered deviant behavior," such as divorce and out-of-wedlock birth.[1]

She then shared extensive research describing the harmful effects of single-parent households on children, at both the individual and the social levels. In general, despite some admirable exceptions by single parents who succeed valiantly despite the risks, children in single-parent or step-parent families are more likely than children in intact families to be poor, to drop out of school, to have trouble with the law—to do worse, in short, by most definitions of well-being than children in two-parent families. These children are also more likely to be abused physically or sexually. More have emotional problems, require professional counseling, and suffer from drug abuse. And, contrary to some popular assumptions, they don't just "bounce back" after divorce or their parents' remarriage; instead, many of their problems continue for years, enough years that they are much more likely to have troubled marriages themselves.[2]

This is not to say that the children of divorced parents cannot recover from the effects of their experience. Many do, especially when blessed with an understanding of the gospel and the Atonement's power to repair the breach (Isaiah 58:12). Many establish very secure homes, in which their early life experience actually increases their sensitivity to the factors that maintain a strong marriage. These cases are a tribute to those who succeed against the odds.

Two years later, in 1995, a group of scholars, including Barbara Whitehead, published a document called *Marriage in America,* which called on the nation to "rebuild a family culture based on enduring marital relationships." They summarized a large body of research to conclude that the no-fault "divorce revolution" of 1968 had failed to reach its "goals of fairness and economic equality." Morever, society is sending American children cultural messages that are "either indifferent or hostile to marriage," thereby "failing to teach the next generation about the meaning, purposes, and responsibilities of marriage. If this trend continues, it will constitute nothing less than an act of cultural suicide."[3] This group's work helped to create the national "marriage movement" of 2000.

The data behind these conclusions showed that despite society's having spent more on children in recent years in public schools, welfare programs, and other places, child well-being "has not improved. It has gotten worse—much worse."[4]

For example:

- Juvenile violent crime increased sixfold between 1960 and 1992.[5]
- Reports of child neglect and abuse have quintupled since 1976.[6]
- Children's psychological disorders have all worsened—from

eating disorders to drug abuse. Depression among children has increased 1,000 percent since the 1950s.[7]
- Suicide among teenagers has increased 300 percent since the 1960s.[8]
- Children spend eleven fewer hours per week with their parents than in the 1960s.[9]
- Poverty has shifted increasingly to children.[10]

The number of couples living together increased nearly tenfold between 1960 and 1998. More than half of all first marriages are now preceded by couples living together.[11]

David Blankenhorn drew on these trends to write *Fatherless America: Confronting Our Most Urgent Social Problem.* His findings describe the products of divorce and births outside wedlock, dealing primarily with youth violence, domestic violence against women, child sexual abuse, and child poverty. While such complex social ills have many causes, Blankenhorn and his associates concluded that "the decline of marriage" is their common denominator: "The most important causal factor of declining child well-being is the remarkable collapse of marriage, leading to growing family instability and decreasing parental investment in children."[12]

President Gordon B. Hinckley quoted a similar study in 2003: "Boys raised out of intact marriages are, on average, more than twice as likely as other boys to end up jailed. . . . A child born to an unwed mother is about 2½ times as likely to end up imprisoned, while a boy whose parents split during his teen years is about 2½ times as likely to be imprisoned."[13]

By 2001, data from the 2000 United States Census showed that the thirty-year trend toward more unwed childbearing and more divorce has remained fairly stable since 1995. Now scholars who have been urging a return to pro-marriage attitudes hope they may "soon be able to say, for the first time in decades, that our national priority is to *sustain*" the slight but apparent trend toward more family stability.[14]

Still, a group of thirteen recognized family scholars in 2002 published a report that summarized years of data with such findings as the following:

- Children of divorced or unwed parents are more likely than other children to become divorced themselves or have children outside marriage.
- Divorce and unmarried childbearing increase poverty for both children and mothers.
- Children of divorced or unwed parents have higher rates of psychological distress, mental illness, suicide, and educational failure.
- Boys raised in single-parent families are twice as likely to engage in criminal behavior.
- Children living with single mothers, stepfathers, or mother's boyfriends are at greater risk of abuse.[15]

Church members are not immune to these national trends. For example, the proportion of LDS young people who suffer from emotional and mental disorders seems to have increased substantially in recent years. Dr. W. Dean Belnap, an LDS psychiatrist who has spent many years working with troubled adolescents, told me he has found that family breakdown is the most significant cause of such problems among LDS youth, because these breakdowns disturb a child's normal psychological development and identity formation.[16]

A study in 2003 by the Commission on Children at Risk, *Hardwired to Connect,* validates Dr. Belnap's conclusion. It reports "the deteriorating mental and behavioral health of U.S. children," a national "crisis" caused primarily by a lack of "close connections to other people, and deep connections to moral and spiritual meaning."[17] And the family, which "is usually the source of the most enduring and formative relationships in a child's life," has grown "steadily weaker" since the mid 1960s.[18]

It was precisely to guard against such harm that the state has honored and upheld marriage as a social institution, not just as a private, affectionate partnership but as the very best place—with two parents whenever possible—to raise children.

That's why the Irish in Galway placed that little crown on top of the heart held by the two cupped hands in the Claddaugh Ring. That's why people in all nations have required a marriage license to start a family and a judge's decree to get a divorce. That's why legislatures and parliaments have retained the right to say which relationships, which privileges, and which duties will create and sustain marriages that promote society's welfare.

All societies, until now, have been unwilling to leave the creation and dissolution of marriages to mere individual preferences, because the way children are reared affects entire cultures. England's Patrick Devlin once described the traditional understanding:

"The association of man and woman in wedlock has from time immemorial been of such importance in every society that its regulation has always been a matter of morals. Whether the union . . . should be dissoluble or not, and what obligations the spouses should undertake towards each other are not questions which any society has ever left to individuals to settle for themselves. They must be settled according to ideas of right and wrong which prevail in that society, that is, according to its moral law; and because the institution of marriage is fundamental to society the moral law regulates it very closely—much more closely than in most other subjects in which the moral and secular law both operate."[19]

Until the last three decades, our laws and social attitudes reflected this understanding. But today's environment reinforces the idea that marriage is a private choice, not a public commitment.

Meanwhile, the doctrine of the restored gospel about what parents owe children and society remains clear:

"Husband and wife have a solemn responsibility to love and care for each other and for their children. . . . Parents have a sacred duty to rear their children in love and righteousness, to provide for their physical and spiritual needs, to teach them to love and serve one another, to observe the commandments of God and to be law-abiding citizens wherever they live. Husbands and wives . . . will be held accountable before God for the discharge of these obligations. . . .

"We warn that individuals who violate covenants of chastity, who abuse spouse or offspring, or who fail to fulfill family responsibilities will one day stand accountable before God."[20]

Yet recent social and cultural changes have moved so far and so fast that young Latter-day Saints these days are often surprised to discover how different the Church's teachings are from society's norms—and, therefore, from what may seem "normal" to them. Here are a few examples of the disconnect between gospel teachings and society's changing family mores:

It is now far more common than it once was for a single LDS girl to keep a child she has borne out of wedlock, despite the Church's counsel in such cases to marry or, if that is not feasible, to place the child for adoption. More than a few Laurel advisers have wondered whether to allow a seventeen-year old single girl to bring her baby to class; however, a Church directive states that an unwed mother should not bring her baby to Young Women classes.

Missionaries all over the world find themselves teaching the gospel to unmarried couples who live together. These couples are sometimes mystified by the requirement that they must marry before they can be baptized.

Some LDS young women, who nearly always want to have children, now say they are frightened by the very concept of marriage, having picked up the message from the current environment that marriage can trap them or tie them down. The connection between a mature marriage and raising spiritually healthy children is not as obvious to our young people as it is to older generations.

These trends have deprived many of the rising generation of a once-instinctive understanding about the influence of family lifestyle and divorce patterns on the character and behavior of children and, hence, society. The entertainment media continually reinforce the assumption that "personal lifestyle" issues about living together, making love, and having children are all matters of strictly personal choice—victimless acts to be decided by consenting partners. As such attitudes ripple through the culture, it is no surprise that we are losing our collective grasp of what marriage and parenting are about. People all around us are giving up, getting out, and stepping out as if there were no tomorrow—and no children.

A few divorces may actually be necessary to protect children in "high-conflict families" who are "at great psychological risk." But such cases are rare. In fact, "only a minority of divorces grow out of pathological situations; much more common are divorces in families unscarred by physical assault." And divorcing families that have lived with, and perhaps worked on, manageable conflict typically discover that the inevitable messiness of divorce makes things worse for everyone—because "family breakup [itself] generates its own conflict."[21] The benefits of divorce seldom outweigh the costs, especially if one counts the costs to children.

Amid this confusion, adults who seek to be free from the constraints of traditional family attitudes simply have a conflict of interest in evaluating the effect of their own behavior on children. Barbara Whitehead illuminated this conflict in her 1993 article, when she compared Hallmark cards for divorced adults with Hallmark cards for their children: "For grown-ups, divorce heralds new beginnings (A HOT NEW SINGLE). For children, divorce brings separation and loss. ('I'm sorry I'm not always there when you need me.'). . . .

"These cards . . . point to an uncomfortable . . . fact: *what contributes to a parent's happiness may detract from a child's happiness.* . . . In short, family disruption creates a deep division between parents' interests and the interests of children."[22]

After describing the damage done by today's increased family disintegration, Whitehead reported that the nation is not as alarmed about all of this as one might expect, primarily because the American people (like those in many other developed nations) have simply changed their minds about whether family disruption is bad:

"What had once been regarded as hostile to children's best interests [is] now considered essential to adults' happiness. . . .

"Once the social metric shifts from child well-being to adult well-being, it is hard to see divorce and nonmarital birth in anything but a positive light. . . .

"This cultural shift helps explain what otherwise would be inexplicable: the failure to see the rise in family disruption as a severe and troubling national problem."[23]

Nonetheless, in concept it is still true that the state represents the community as a party to each marriage and each divorce, not because the neighbors are trying to pry into private affairs but because of society's enormous stake in the outcome and the offspring of each marriage. To marry is still to make a public commitment that in bringing children into the world, one accepts personal responsibility for those children and for their influence on the kind of community we create over time.

But the adults who have adopted the cultural message of individual autonomy as today's primary value find that their own need for space, flexibility, and personal fulfillment simply trumps the needs of the children in their lives. Ironically, many of these adults justify their attitude by urging that children should also have more autonomy—more freedom to do as they please, without so many adults telling them what to do.

I have seen this adult conflict of interest at work in discussions about legal rights for children. Childrearing makes heavy demands on the time, energy, and financial resources of parents and communities. To escape those demands by giving more "rights" to children is a beguiling invitation, because it provides an easy rationalization for adults whose personal convenience is also best served by the idea that they should leave their children alone.

For example, schoolteachers and administrators may find it not worth the patience required and the frustration involved to provide students with meaningful discipline. Marriage partners may think it unimportant to cooperate with each other for the sake of their children. Divorced and unmarried fathers may feel less obliged to make payments of financial support. Parents may be unconcerned about employment or leisure time interests that conflict with their children's needs.

The growing preference of many adults for a more casual sexual environment also encourages destructive sexual permissiveness among adolescents. For example, a team of distinguished researchers in the field of adolescent pregnancy concluded a large study about rising rates of teen pregnancy with the chilling observation that "for ourselves, we prefer to cope with the consequences of early sex as an aspect of an emancipated society, rather than pay the social costs its elimination would exact."[24]

In other words, the researchers could clearly see ways to reduce teenage pregnancies, but they were not willing to pursue those policies because they don't want to curb the morally permissive atmosphere that American adults have now come to enjoy in the media and elsewhere "as an aspect of an emancipated society."

I once saw a small boy standing alone on a street looking helpless and afraid. He was wearing a big T-shirt bearing the slogan, "Leave me alone." I thought he would make a good poster child to illustrate the irony in the attitude of adults who willingly abandon children to their "right" to be "autonomous."

America's founding fathers had a longer-term view about how to maintain a free and stable society. They spoke in the preamble to the Constitution about "secur[ing] the blessings of Liberty" not only "to ourselves" but also to "our Posterity." To make our own days and those of our posterity "long upon the land" God has given us, it is essential not only for children to honor their parents but for parents to honor their children.

CHAPTER TWENTY-TWO

NO-FAULT DIVORCE
AND THE LOST PLOT

We have seen how no-fault divorce was first introduced in California in 1968 in an attempt at relatively modest reform. The original legislation tried to eliminate the emotionally divisive need to prove that one partner was "at fault" in breaching the marriage covenants. It also added a new justification for granting a divorce: "irretrievable breakdown." But in order to preserve society's interest in—and its ultimate control over—marriage termination, the new law left family court judges with the responsibility to decide whether the marriage was in fact beyond repair. Thus no-fault divorce did not originally give marriage partners the right to simply announce that their marriage was over. Yet the no-fault concept ultimately led to that conclusion.

The 1960s were a time of huge social change, with challenges to state authority that frightened all public leaders from representatives in Congress to school principals and judges. Judges charged with the duty to determine "irretrievable breakdown" found themselves simply unable or unwilling to challenge the claims of people who wanted to get out of their marriages. So within a short time, marriage became essentially terminable at will—first at the will of both parties together and then at the will of only one party.

The state's willingness to take this approach papered over an ironic misunderstanding about what marriage breakdown really meant—and means. It soon became easy for couples to assume the marriage must be over if the state didn't resist ending it and for judges to assume the marriage must be over if the couple didn't resist ending it. In fact, however:

"There is something deceptive about [the phrase 'irretrievable breakdown']. The passive, impersonal structure, the dry legalities of the language, conceal a lie. It suggests that a marriage has an independent organic existence. It exonerates us by portraying us as merely the clinicians pronouncing the body dead. But at what precise point does the breakdown of a marriage become irretrievable? The moment we declare it so, and no sooner. And the marriage doesn't just break down. We disconnect the life support. While it requires will to make a marriage work, it also requires a quite horrifying act of will to bring one to an end."[1]

This development was influenced by many factors. For one thing, the emphasis on individual rights during the 1960s especially prized "the right to be let alone." That idea originally focused on being "let alone" from government control of one's life. But to state-appointed judges, it soon meant deferring to the partner who wanted a divorce rather than to a partner who wanted to help make the marriage succeed. Togetherness is always harder for courts to enforce than separateness because law, like the proverbial bull in the china closet, is inherently better at pulling (or blowing) things apart than it is at keeping them together.

Another purely coincidental factor was that no-fault auto insurance came on the national scene at about this same time. This concept introduced the idea that accidents simply happen, and courts shouldn't waste time trying to fix blame for them. Rather, insurance companies should just pay the bills and save the court costs of the blame game. A failed marriage is hardly like a fender bender, but before long, it was easy to assume, wrongly, that therapy sessions could do for refugees from a divorced family what an auto body shop could do for a wrecked car—repair the damage.

Economic changes also played a role. Over the last several decades, corporations and governments have generally replaced the family as the primary source of economic power and property rights. As part of some evolving patterns about the best way to protect the individual against unfairly losing one's source of economic sustenance, it is now easier for a married person to divorce a spouse than it is for an employer to fire somebody he hired last month. Not that many years ago, by contrast, divorce was very difficult to justify in court and an employer could terminate an employee at will.

Other general forces of cultural change have also had a heavy impact on the way people came to interpret no-fault divorce. Our society has recently experienced a gradual shift from positive to negative attitudes about the very idea of one person's "belonging" to another in a marriage or family. An anonymous letter to the *New Yorker* magazine eloquently captured this development. The writer had just attended the funeral of a woman she called Mary Jones. She was a couple of generations younger than Mary and hadn't known her well, but the nature of Mary's relationship with her husband had left an indelible impression on the young writer, enough to draw her to the funeral.

Every summer since her childhood she had "watched Robert and Mary Jones walking down the beach to the water for a swim: she a tall, big-boned woman, clearly beautiful when young, a person" of both "character and humor." Robert was "a small man, distinguished, . . . upright (in spirit and body), cheerfully earnest, energetic."

The couple were "slightly comical" because of "their difference in size." "They would walk at a leisurely pace, several feet apart, conversing." Their "conversation ranged from serious discussion to banter," often "punctuated with laughter; I remember the laughter most vividly. When they reached the water, they would wade in, still talking, losing their balance somewhat on the rocks underfoot, talk some more, and, finally, sink in and swim around a little—in a semi-upright position that allowed them to continue talking. Their enjoyment of each other was arresting—sharp as pepper, golden. I have seen other happy older couples, but" something about Robert and Mary "came to represent to me an essence of human exchange—something indescribably moving and precious, which comes to fruition only toward the end of a lifelong marriage. Whatever that essence is, I find it dazzling. It has always struck me as one of the great possibilities life has to offer."

Then the writer reflected on the contrast between her image of the Joneses' marriage and our new age of liberation, which is now "forming the values and governing the lives" of our generation. Not that liberation is all bad: "The spirit of emancipation has also touched deep nerves of truth, has also opened windows on life's great possibilities." Still, she's troubled not by the principle of liberation but by its "limitations"—"the blind side of our age" and "the cost of the blindness; of a perhaps fatal stupidity intertwined with our [modern] enlightenment." The "idea of emancipation, after all, has to do with an escape from bonds, not a strengthening of bonds." Our age of liberation somehow makes relationships into political issues. It focuses on "the individual, not the connection between individuals," stressing "terms like 'self-awareness,' 'self-fulfillment,' 'self-discovery,' 'self-determination,' and 'self-sufficiency'—terms that crowd anybody other than the 'self' right out of one's imagination."

Our generation thinks these attitudes are supposed to help relationships. But "when the relationship—no matter how good—gets in the way of self-fulfillment, it is clear which one has to go." That's why it's not just a coincidence that "more and more people are living alone these days, that more are getting divorced, that fewer are getting married, " and that, therefore, "there are going to be fewer and fewer Robert and Mary Joneses."

The writer wanted to hang onto the warmth of Mary's marriage against the "chill of an unknown future." What chilled her was a "sense of the transformation of our society from one that strengthens the bonds between people to one that is, at best, indifferent to them; a sense of an inevitable fraying of the net of connections between people at many critical intersections, of which the marital knot is only one. Each fraying accelerates others," affecting feelings about community, citizenship, and family.

"If one examines these points of disintegration separately," she continued, "they have a common cause—the overriding value placed on the idea of individual emancipation and fulfillment, in the light of which . . . the old bonds are seen not as enriching but as confining. We are coming to look upon life as a lone adventure." And while there is value in this view, we are "carrying it to such an extreme that," if we have no Robert or Mary of our own to return to, our life journey may be "rendered pointless by becoming limitless." And that's why she "hoarded a small, indirect warmth" at Mary Jones's funeral—because Mary reminded her that "we give form and meaning" to our "solitary destinies" through "our associations with others." But as our commitment to these human ties "has been allowed to fade away," we are left "exposed to a new kind of cold."[2]

Part of this cold new world is that people are no longer sure what the word *family* even means. Is *family* a legal term, a social or political one, or just a matter of personal preference? As the government has generally "deregulated" marriage, it increasingly leaves the process of family creation and definition to individual preferences. For example, a growing number of state and private agencies now treat unmarried "domestic partnerships" the same as they treat formal marriages for purposes of health insurance and other benefits.

I remember when the idea of extending spousal benefits beyond traditional definitions of the family was first introduced in San Francisco in the late 1970s as a proposal for city employees. An editorial in that open-minded city's open-minded newspaper thought the idea was preposterous.

But within a short time, delegates to the 1980 White House Conference on the Family came very close to adopting a proposal that would have defined the family as any "two or more persons who share resources, responsibility for decisions, values and goals, and have commitment to one another over time."

These countercultural ideas really were unthinkable as serious public policies when they were first proposed. I recall the day when Sister Barbara B. Smith, then the general Relief Society president for the Church, called me. She knew that I taught family law, and she wanted to know how the law defined the term *family.* She explained that this question had become the most divisive issue in a committee meeting for the 1980 White House Conference on the Family, on whose planning board Sister Smith served. That same divisiveness has only spread its influence in the intervening years.

For some liberated people, even a common family name began to create a kind of psychological claustrophobia. One cartoon a few years back showed a man and woman with their two children standing outside a neighbor's apartment. The apartment owner had just opened the door. The father said with a smile, "Hi! We're the new family from next door. I'm Bill Jones, this is Sally Smith, and these are our kids, Beth Townsend and Jason Connally."

In taking this brief glance back through history, I am struck by the persistent evidence that in many ways, most people in "Mainstreet USA" really didn't want to lose the marriage plot. To some significant degree, public opinion has simply been carried along by noisy, revolutionary forces and turbulent movements that have swept many individuals and families into their path like so much debris in a flood plain. Despite a fundamental increase in the public's tolerance for permissive lifestyle choices, and despite the fact that our runaway interpretation of no-fault divorce has made America the world's most divorce-prone society, most people aren't convinced that a "culture of divorce" is really desirable.

It is quite possible—though very ironic—that the current interpretation of no-fault divorce law, the general movement toward emancipation and self-interest, and even today's confusion about the meaning of *family* have not resulted from society's fully conscious choice. As one study found, the no-fault divorce movement "was the product of a limited elite, including academics and lawyers, and of the therapeutic culture. . . . There is reason to speculate that a majority of the public may remain traditional in its concepts of marriage and the family."[3]

CHAPTER TWENTY-THREE

THE MOST BASIC UNIT:
FOUR REASONS WHY

The Church's Proclamation on the Family urges its readers "to promote those measures designed to maintain and strengthen the family as the fundamental unit of society."[1] The First Presidency has often stated that the family is the basic unit of the Church as well as society: "The home is the basis of a righteous life, and no other instrumentality can take its place nor fulfill its essential functions."[2] Not even the Church can take the place of the family.

Until recently, Western society generally agreed with this concept, offering little additional explanation because the idea was so widely shared. As a result, we felt little need to express the reasons behind these general conclusions. Family patterns universally accepted before the dawn of law and government hardly required full-dress justification.

Now that individualism has severely challenged these traditional assumptions, however, we need to articulate more fully the reasoning behind our beliefs about family life. The need for such articulation was perhaps one reason why the Church issued the

Proclamation on the Family. Let us note at least four root ideas that underlie our convictions about the family's basic role.

The first root is the needs of children. As the Proclamation states, "Children are entitled to birth within the bonds of matrimony, and to be reared by a father and a mother who honor marital vows with complete fidelity."[3]

Research studies have now verified beyond question every child's need for stability and continuity in his or her home environment in order to enjoy optimal, normal development.[4] This research has proved wrong many ideas from the Great Society days of the 1960s, when some government planners believed that many family functions could be better performed by outside agencies. The research also shows that even in a relatively weak family, state intervention may disrupt a child's world so much that it does more harm than good. Unfortunately, those who have encouraged easy divorce or have permitted children to be reared in the homes of unmarried couples have not taken these findings seriously.

Not all formal families are stable and caring, as today's high levels of divorce and abuse amply demonstrate. But the commitments built into long-term marriage do increase a child's chance for stability and continuity. Those factors are so essential to child development that they alone may justify the priority we have traditionally given to permanent kinship units based on marriage.

The second root is that family commitments teach people—both parents and children—how to overcome self-interest and live the civic virtues that make a free society possible. Much of what family members "owe" each other cannot be enforced in a court of law; yet the very idea of family ties has an uncanny power to help people learn to obey such unenforceable duties as responsibility, cooperation, and self-restraint.

A sense of voluntary duty is the lifeblood of a free society. But civic virtue will not exist socially until it has been *learned* individually and voluntarily assumed. The government cannot force people to live a moral life. But living in a real family can instill the moral "habits of the heart" that make secure homes our civic foundation.[5] That is why Elder Neal A. Maxwell often said it is more important to keep pure the headwaters of humanity—the home—than simply to worry about downstream pollution.[6]

That pattern holds true not only for learning to live in society but for learning how to live in heaven. The family home is the Lord's most basic classroom for teaching us, as we apply gospel principles to family interaction, how to become real Christians.

So when family disintegration does foul the headwaters, downstream pollution inevitably follows. As President Gordon B. Hinckley told a 2003 audience in Denver, where the Columbine High School shootings had occurred a few years before:

"There are . . . millions of [young people] whose lives are like smoking candles from which the flame has been blown. . . . They are the bitter fruit of broken families and fractured homes. Most of them have no fathers of whom they know.

"In my judgment the greatest challenge facing this nation is the problem of the family, brought on by misguided parents and resulting in misguided children. . . . The family is the primary unit of society. I believe it was designed by the Almighty. A nation will rise no higher than the strength of its families.

"The children of broken homes look for identity. They want to be a part of something. In their quest so many of them turn to gangs. Here they swagger and fight. . . . The spectacle of children killing children is an abhorrent and terrible thing.

"America now has two million [prison inmates. They] are the products of homes, the place where behavior is learned, where standards are taught, where values are established."[7]

Third, the family helps maintain a free, democratic society, which the Lord Himself "suffered to be established . . . for the rights and protection of all flesh" (D&C 101:77).

Today's mass society seems very personal, even chummy, if national TV is our symbol: all two hundred-plus million of us in one big living room, chatting with our talk show hosts. But where in that vast and, ironically, often lonely crowd do we learn what to do with our hard-won freedoms—what our lives mean and what direction we should take?

Families create a crucial organizational level between the individual and the massive structures of government and business conglomerates. The family is the "little platoon" that gives each individual a sense of personal meaning for his or her life.[8] Other than teaching us our basic citizenship duties, it is not the place of government or the marketplace to tell us what our most personal life purposes should be. Rather, government and business are supposed to maintain the political and economic stability that will allow each of us to pursue the life purpose we draw from such meaning-generating sources as religion and family life.

So we have historically given the family the immensely important power of deciding which personal values children should learn. We would never allow state control over childrearing, as was characteristic of Soviet communism, because that control destroys the diversity and range of free choice that democracy is designed to protect.

Without the decentralized authority that lets families and churches play this mediating role between individuals and society's megastructures, we are vulnerable to totalitarianism, which imposes on society one comprehensive order of meaning. Even if our government remains democratic, however, the nation's family and religious structures can grow weak, as they are now becoming. When that happens, people wander in search of personal purpose, often falling prey to the meaningless addictions of materialism and pleasure-seeking.

Amos foresaw such a famine of meaning, "not a famine of bread, nor a thirst for water, but of hearing the words of the Lord: and they shall wander from sea to sea, and . . . they shall run to and fro to seek the word of the Lord, and shall not find it" (Amos 8:11–12).

Still, in democratic societies, the family is "the major institution within the private sphere, and thus for many people the most valuable thing in their lives. Here they make their moral commitments, invest their emotions, [and] plan for the future."⁹ Here they can also find emotional and spiritual purpose, as well as the most personal forms of fulfillment, often expressed through having and rearing children.

Even apart from childrearing, marriage alone plays a critical role in the democratic structure, creating a legal entity between the individual and the State. As the English writer David H. Lawrence put it:

"The marriage bond . . . is the fundamental connecting link in Christian society. Break it, and you will have to go back to the overwhelming dominance of the State, which existed before the Christian era. . . .

" . . . Perhaps the greatest contribution to the social life of man made by Christianity is—marriage. . . . Christianity established the little autonomy of the family within the greater rule of the State. Christianity made marriage . . . not to be violated by the State. It is marriage, perhaps, which has given man the best of his freedom, given him his little kingdom of his own within the big kingdom of the State, given him his foothold of independence on which to stand and resist an unjust State. Man and wife, a king and queen with one or two subjects, and a few square yards of territory of their own: this, really, is marriage. It is a true freedom."[10]

Fourth, the long-term commitment of marriage is the basis of the most stable expectations in personal relationships. My willingness to marry (like my willingness to have a child) should permit both my family and society to assume that I am invested in this relationship for the long haul, even permanently. Then my wife and children may also invest themselves in the relationship without wondering if that investment is worth their effort, their risk, and their sacrifice.

In unmarried relationships, by contrast, or even in a half-hearted commitment to marriage, each individual may have a different view of the relationship, whether it is a trial marriage, a substitute marriage, or a temporary but convenient place to park. In this noncommittal context, individual partners will inevitably hold back, not giving their all to make the marriage work; and as a result, it often does not work.

The partners to a serious covenant marriage, however, are entitled to count on each other to allow their family to be a place where people can honestly "practice" their Christianity amid commitments so secure that they can learn and grow from their errors without being cast out on grounds of imperfection. The Proclamation on the Family must have contemplated such a family: "Happiness in family life is most likely to be achieved when founded upon the teachings of the Lord Jesus Christ."[11]

CHAPTER TWENTY-FOUR

HOW SAME-SEX MARRIAGE WEAKENS WHAT MARRIAGE MEANS

Because the First Presidency has taken a public position against same-gender marriage, President Gordon B. Hinckley has often been asked about the Church's attitude toward people who feel same-sex attraction. His response is personally compassionate and doctrinally clear:

"We love them as sons and daughters of God. They may have certain inclinations which are powerful and which may be difficult to control. . . . If they do not act upon these inclinations, then they can go forward as do all other members of the Church. . . .

"We want to help these people, to strengthen them, to assist them with their problems and to help them with their difficulties. But we cannot stand idle if they indulge in immoral activity, if they try to uphold and defend and live in a so-called same-sex marriage situation. To permit such would be to make light of the very serious and sacred foundation of God-sanctioned marriage and its very purpose, the rearing of families."[1]

"God-sanctioned marriage between a man and a woman has been the basis of civilization for thousands of years. . . .

"Some portray legalization of so-called same-sex marriage as a civil right. This is not a matter of civil rights; it is a matter of morality . . . that is of critical importance to the future of the family. . . . We are compelled by our doctrine to speak out."[2]

Because gay marriage is fundamentally a moral issue, laws on this subject can alter both personal and public moral attitudes about sex, marriage, and the family. For instance, the "individual autonomy" theory (the idea that people should be free to live as they please) behind the Massachusetts gay marriage case has developed in a way that erodes the place of marriage as a socially guarded institution. By extension, this reduces children and their best interests to incidental, unprotected tangents of adult autonomy. To explain how this happens requires a brief look at how the law classifies various kinds of human behavior.

Same-sex marriage blurs the distinction between what society *tolerates* and what it *endorses*. Opinion polls show that a majority of the American people have grown more tolerant of gay lifestyles, just as they have grown more tolerant of personal choices on many lifestyle issues. Most people today would not consider adult homosexual behavior a crime. But the polls typically show that roughly one-third favor same-sex marriage. The public draws a clear distinction between *tolerating* gay lifestyles and *promoting* them by the legal endorsement inherent in marriage.[3] Said another way, Americans draw a clear line between "passive toleration" and "active support" of homosexual conduct.[4]

Our laws distinguish between toleration and endorsement by maintaining three broad categories of conduct: (1) conduct that is "prohibited," such as robbery; (2) conduct that is "permitted," such as making a contract; and (3) conduct that is especially "protected" (as by special constitutional rights), such as worshipping God or giving a political speech. The Constitution's Bill of Rights gives such high preference to protected conduct that the state may regulate it only if the state can show a truly compelling need for regulation.

Civil rights advocates worked successfully and admirably during the past generation to move the choices of racial minorities and women from being merely "permitted" to being legally "protected" by potent antidiscrimination laws. During the early part of this same era, gays and lesbians were working to convince state legislatures to change the classification of their behavior from being "prohibited" to being "permitted" by repealing laws that had made homosexual acts a crime.

There is a natural line of "tolerance" between prohibited and permitted, and another natural line of "endorsement" between permitted and protected:

PROHIBITED tolerance PERMITTED endorsement PROTECTED

For example, the United States Supreme Court has held that family and kinship-based interests, such as the right to direct the upbringing of one's own children, are constitutionally protected rights. The Constitution therefore not only "tolerates" these choices but affirmatively endorses and protects them—because, the Court has said, the obligations of parenthood, marriage, and biological kinship are fundamental to preserving a civilized order. Such weighty societal obligations are worthy of being highly protected, not merely being tolerated or permitted.

One consequence of the law's protecting marriage is that the state is a party to the marriage; and the state must legally approve both starting and ending it. That's why a state license and ceremony are required to create a legal marriage, and a state court judgment is required to end a marriage. These formalities are not required to create or dissolve other legal contracts. Society actually has a greater stake in the creation and survival of each marriage than it does in the survival of each business agreement, even though a healthy economy obviously needs stable businesses.

Society is now more willing than in the past to tolerate homosexual behavior between adults. Does that mean that same-gender marriage should now move to the "permitted" range, or even the "protected" range? The question is not whether the legal system should no longer consider homosexual acts a crime. That has already happened. The United States Supreme Court now "permits" homosexual relations, but it has stopped short of endorsing them with a protected constitutional right. What makes gay marriage such a big next step is that its official formality not only permits gay conduct but the nature and protocol of state sponsorship also have the effect of endorsing and even promoting that conduct. The credibility of this endorsement arises from the place of marriage in both our law and culture as an important—actually our most important—social institution. From the perspective of prophetic teachings, state endorsement means the government would be promoting serious immorality.

Perhaps because they realize that the public is not really ready to give them that much state support, many gay rights advocates insist that marriage is not really a social institution but a strictly individual choice. That is one reason why the 2003 Massachusetts case that protected gay marriage grounded its reasoning on "principles of respect for individual autonomy."[5] "Autonomy" does not claim to have high social value. Indeed, autonomy arguments often thrive on challenging society's established order. So these advocates urge that the state should disengage from the role of promoting society's interest in marriage and family life.

In the most forceful statement yet by a Supreme Court justice in support of gay rights, Justice Harry Blackmun wrote in 1986 that he would protect homosexual behavior not because it promotes any social value but precisely because it dissents from the established social order: "We protect these rights not because they contribute . . . to the general public welfare, but because they form so central a part of an individual's life," including one's "right to differ as to things that touch the heart of the existing order."[6]

Ironically, however, the Massachusetts judges in the 2003 gay marriage case cited several instances in which homosexual couples who wanted the right to marry already had children in their homes. This little-noticed element in those cases was going a very different direction from Justice Blackmun's assumption that homosexual relationships may not benefit society but should be protected anyway. Once adopted or surrogate children are in the home of gay parents, the parent-child relationship means the marriage is no longer a simple matter of adult personal autonomy.

Though they didn't say so, I believe the lawyers for the Massachusetts gay couples, and the judges who agreed with them, thought that by showing that these couples were raising children (with no comment on how that experience affects children), they hoped to establish same-gender marriage as an acceptable enough childrearing environment to serve society's interest in how children are raised. However, the empirical research makes clear that a child's being with both father and mother is clearly the optimal environment for childrearing, which is why our social policies have always given that environment such high priority.

In 2001, for example, the *New York Times* reported a "powerful consensus" in the social science research that "from a child's point of view . . . the most supportive household is one with two biological parents in a low-conflict marriage."[7] Further, one of the principal goals of the diverse groups who support the current national "marriage movement" is to "make the case that each child has a right to grow up with his or her own mother and father who love the child and love each other, and that supporting [hetereosexual] marriage is society's main way of giving children this right."[8]

Even though this ideal is not always possible because of deaths and unavoidable divorces, children need the stability and role-modeling of being raised by their two biological parents. The further society chooses to depart from the ideal, the greater will be the risk to children and their future. The Proclamation on the Family states that "children are entitled . . . to be reared by a father and a mother." When a mother and father work at it, this pattern warmly invites both boys and girls to grow up understanding the equal but distinct gifts and roles of men and women who "honor marital vows with complete fidelity."[9]

The power of the law to communicate society's endorsement tells us that our system does not and should not protect everything it tolerates. If we merge tolerance with protection, our system will end up removing marriage and childrearing from the most protected legal sphere, because the lowest common denominator effect of "individual autonomy" denies the possibility that some relationships are more significant to society than others. That's what happens when we confuse the distinction between what the law merely "permits" and what it "protects."

So, the closer our society comes to approving gay marriage, the more we will actually reduce our expectation that married people owe anything at all to society, including their utmost effort to succeed in their marriages. That is how gay marriage undermines the sense of personal and social obligation that is fundamental to our thinking about what marriage is and what it means.

Therefore, Robert Bork believes, acceptance of the

Massachusetts court's same-gender marriage theory "would ratify, in the most profound way, the anarchical spirit of extreme personal . . . autonomy that is the driving force behind much of our [current] cultural degradation." If that happens, marriage will be "just one more sexual arrangement among others. The symbolic link between marriage, procreation, and family is broken, and there is a rapid and persistent decline in heterosexual marriages." [10]

Marriage was historically understood in American law, even from a secular viewpoint, as a three-party arrangement, with the state as a conscious party. This understanding has reflected society's high stake in each marriage. Indeed, it is precisely the *public* part of marriage—the high degree of social interest involved in its very concept and function—that distinguishes it from all other relationships and contracts. To marry is to accept a *public* responsibility to the community and its basic social values, especially its values about what is best for children. For this reason, the society itself, through its legislatures, has retained the primary role in determining which relationships, which privileges, and which duties reflect the kind of marriage that satisfies society's long-term interest in creating the culture of the future.

Our present legal definition of marriage has not yet really altered this time-honored understanding, but our recent public conversations have obscured it, and the outcome of the same-sex marriage debate could obliterate it.

PART IV

CONCLUSION

CHAPTER TWENTY-FIVE

HE SATISFIETH THE LONGING SOUL

Society may be losing the plot of the great Love Story. But the plot has always been there, like a great, towering mountain that beckons us to climb its heights. The mountain may often seem hidden today, behind storms and swirling clouds. But it isn't lost. The plot is in the story of Adam and Eve and the great love stories both prophets and poets have known and told since ancient times. This plot gives us the clear prototype for covenant marriage, teaching us how God's plan will lead us through the dense mist to the summit of clear peace.

The chapters of Part III tried to penetrate today's social fog, in the hope of clarifying the historical and cultural background for our more personal discussion of covenant marriage. This chapter takes a concluding upward glance, to the place where the mountain spikes beyond the clouds to the clear view that will let us see forever.

Sometimes I have been assigned to interview people who earlier made mistakes that led to the loss of their priesthood and temple blessings and who now want to come back into full

Church fellowship and reclaim their blessings. In these intimate conversations, I sometimes ask, "What motivated your desire to come back?" Most of the answers are variations on a central theme. That theme was illustrated by one man who had been working all alone as a sheepherder after being separated by his wrong choices from his family. He said he'd sit alone and look into his campfire each night, thinking about his wife and his children. He would say to himself, over and over, "I want to be with my family, eternally, more than I want anything else." That powerful vision gave him the courage and strength to repent and return.

Harry Triffitt was fighting in a torrent of rain and blood one night on New Guinea during World War II. Shrapnel from enemy shells ripped into his stomach, and he lay dying in a muddy foxhole. As he pleaded with God to send a rescue crew, he closed his eyes and a dreamlike picture of his sweetheart flooded his mind's eye. The image of returning to her and raising a family together gave him the will to live until a British officer named Abel scooped him onto a stretcher. Harry returned home to marry the girl of his dream, and soon they joined the Church. More than fifty years later, he is a stake patriarch, and their posterity is among the strength of the Devonport Australia Stake. Harry was kept alive—physically and spiritually—by his dream of family love. That dream saved him as a young man, and then it focused his sense of direction and nourished his lifelong growth.

The mental image of his wife gave Viktor Frankl the strength to survive the agony of a Nazi concentration camp: "As we stumbled on for miles, . . . dragging one another up and onward, . . . my mind clung to my wife's image. . . . Her look was more luminous than the sun. . . .

" . . . For the first time in my life . . . I grasped the meaning of the greatest secret that human poetry and human thought and belief have to impart: *The salvation of man is through love and in love.*" Therefore, "he who has a *why* to live for can bear with almost any *how.*"[1]

His "why" was the vision of being together with his companion. Full of such hope, he could live with the awful "how" of imprisonment.

President Gordon B. Hinckley spoke eloquently about the "girl of his dreams," both in his youth and in his later years, in his first general conference address after his wife, Marjorie, passed away: "My children and I were at her bedside as she slipped peacefully into eternity. As I held her hand and saw mortal life drain from her fingers, I confess I was overcome. Before I married her, she had been the girl of my dreams, to use the words of a song then popular. She was my dear companion for more than two-thirds of a century, my equal before the Lord, really my superior. And now in my old age, she has again become the girl of my dreams."[2]

A Young Women leader taught the Laurels in a very remote area with few Church members. The slim prospects for eternal companions discouraged her girls terribly. She taught them to cultivate a vision of their future home and marriage, urging them to pray actively for their future companions, who were surely alive somewhere. She taught them to live worthy to fulfill such a dream, every day, every night. All six of her Laurels ultimately found and married faithful young men in the temple.

We must nourish a vision that draws on our doctrinal understanding of the past and the future to give us patience and purpose in the present. Even then, of course, that dream is only part of what we must do. A "vision without effort is daydreaming, effort without vision is drudgery; but vision, coupled with effort, will obtain the prize."[3] Some people believe in the vision of an eternal family, but they aren't willing to pay the price to fulfill the dream. Without doing that work, that sometimes very heavy lifting, the vision is just dreaming. Part II considered some of the work—the tasks—that bring reality to the vision. For now, just picture the vision—the extension of the wedding pictures we saw earlier.

Mount Cook is New Zealand's highest peak, the tallest mountain in the huge South Pacific region. I once saw this mountain, its rugged granite edges softened by layers of fresh snow, rising in strength against a clear blue sky. For the next few days, the mountain was enshrouded by dense clouds. I soon learned that Mount Cook is usually hidden by fog and mist. We were fortunate to have seen it on our first day there. Like the view on a wedding day, our view of the sky and the mountain that day stretched endlessly, stunningly clear.

Yet the very next day, we saw many people arrive, stay a day or two and then depart, not really sure whether there was a famous mountain behind those clouds. Some had traveled many miles to see the mountain, but they never did. I sensed that some of them wanted their money back! I understood their disappointment, but I knew the mountain was there. I had "seen the vision."

Sometimes our dream of joyful marriage and family life is obscured by fog and dense clouds. The mists in Lehi's dream tell us that this obscurity is natural in this telestial world—there are even good reasons for the mixture of misery and joy these mists symbolize.

I testify that we can experience the fulfilment of our desire for eternal love, if we really want it, so long as we don't want anything else more. The longing of the heart for this fulness is a central vision of the gospel. It is also the source of great spiritual power, especially on those cloudy days or years when our dreams seem impossible.

Even when love wounds us, that is because love matters so much. The deep hurt is the mirror image of the deep joy that still awaits us. The ache we feel wouldn't be so bad if it didn't come from something so good.

Our longing to belong forever to a loving family comes from God, and He has promised its fulfillment, if we are faithful: "For he satisfieth the longing soul, and filleth the hungry soul with goodness" (Psalm 107:9). His promise is sure.

I conclude where we started—with wedding pictures. The first is a verbal picture from the story of an Austrian couple, Immo and Helmi Luschin, former president and matron of the Bern Switzerland Temple. In the early years of their marriage, their relationship intuitively carried the early hallmarks of the great and ancient Love Story, even though they had not yet heard of the restored gospel.

One night Immo and Helmi were immersed in one of their stimulating, long—really never-ending—conversations. Speaking with a conviction that left no room for doubt, Immo told Helmi he just didn't believe the Catholic priest who had told them their marriage would end at death. "We shall be together forever," said Immo.

Helmi was amazed. "How could this be possible?" she asked.

"I do not know," said Immo. "But one thing I know for sure. If they don't have this kind of provision yet, they must invent it for our sake."[4]

Some years later, Immo and Helmi met the missionaries. In his first conversation with them, Immo asked, "During our marriage, my wife and I have both felt that we should also be together in heaven, even though we fail to see at the moment how this is possible. What stand do you, or rather, does your church take?"

As the elders answered this and other questions, their gospel teachings rang so true that Immo began to feel "as if I was approaching my old home town after many years of absence."⁵ His love for Helmi was leading him home. That has remained true ever since, even as he now waits for her, beyond time, in their permanent home.

The final picture is from the end of another long and fruitful marriage. It captures covenant hearts in the full flower of their maturity, still laced with a natural mixture of opposition and joy.

John Haslem Clark lived in Manti, Utah. The following is the closing entry from his journal, with a short addition by his wife, Therissa Cox Clark. Written between 1922 and 1925, their language captures the intimate spiritual companionship of a modern

Adam and Eve. John begins writing about Therissa and then falls naturally into writing directly to her. Her reply fully blends their voices, their pens, and their hearts.

"The folks have been here today, but have gone to their homes. The clatter of racing feet, the laughter and babble of tongues have ceased. We are alone, *We two*. We two whom destiny has made one. Long ago, it has been sixty years since we met under the June trees. I kissed you first. How shy and afraid was your girlhood. Not any woman on earth or in heaven could be to me what you are. I would rather you were here, woman, with your gray hair than any fresh blossom of youth. Where you are is home. Where you are not is homesickness. As I look at you I realize that there is something greater than love, although love is the greatest thing in earth. It is loyalty. For were I driven away in shame you would follow. If I were burning in fever your cool hand would soothe me. With your hand in mine may I pass and take my place among the saved of Heaven. Being eight years the eldest—and as the years went by and I felt that the time of parting might be near—it was often the drift of our thought and speech: how could either of us be left alone. Alone, after living together for 56 years. I scarcely dared think of it and though a bit selfish comforted myself thinking [that] according to our age I would not be the one left alone."[6]

Therissa's reply appears about two years later on the same page, as if she were writing in her own journal:

"Almost two years and a half since the last writing, and its following events are so sad, so heartbreaking for this, his life's companion that this pen has been laid down many times ere this record is made. Loss and loneliness is ever present and will be with me to the end. It matters not where I may be or who is with me, the same sad loneliness envelops me and [I] can scarcely live without making others sad. Will time soften this sadness, will I be able to leave the Old Home and not feel that he is waiting for me, calling me? I am only content at home where I feel that he is watching over me, his presence always with me.

"On March 11, 1923, John Haslem Clark passed away after an illness of only one week. He seemed so like himself, talking and active. We had no thought that the end was near until he passed into unconsciousness a few hours before his death. Oh, may we all be as clean and pure, ready to go before our Maker."[7]

Because John and Therissa's headwaters ran pure, their posterity can sing a hymn of grateful praise. I sing that hymn, because I am John and Therissa's great-grandson. Their daughter Claire was my grandmother, a gracious woman with a covenant-keeping heart. From my earliest days, I remember her voice, her face, her hands, and the hope I felt from her.

Eight years after this journal entry, Therissa was able to join John. Sometimes I try to imagine their reunion, sensing from their writing how their fifty-six years together made them feel about each other. Perhaps they just walked together, through the familiar palaces, walks, and gardens until one of them whispered, "I am here again." I wonder what dances they joined, what songs they sang, as the community of family and friends there welcomed them into "that same sociality which exists among us here . . . , only . . . coupled with eternal glory" (D&C 130:2).

When I compare Wal Richards's wedding pictures with a picture of John and Therissa, I think of them as bookends—the early days and the later days of being together, with volumes from the book of life in between. Placed next to each other, the bookend pictures have a kind of "before" and "after" relationship: "*After* much tribulation come the blessings" (D&C 58:4).

Newlyweds cannot really grasp, as beautiful as their own

wedding day might be, what it takes a lifetime of sacrifice to understand. Knowing this helps me see better what it means, and what it is worth, to keep striving in our own marriage until we, like John and Therissa, also know the eternal contentment of "where you are is home."

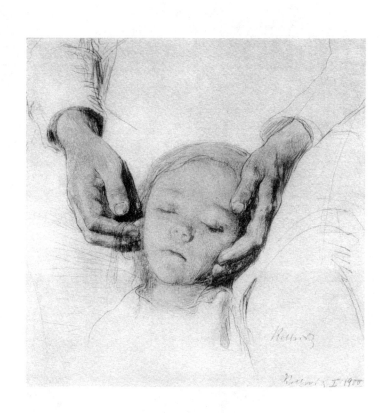

FROM A GRANDMA'S HEART

MARIE K. HAFEN

Daily, hourly, even minute by minute, I feel after you. And with my spiritual senses, I see you in your kitchens, I see you in your classrooms and with your friends. I see you with your parents and with each other. I see you there wherever you are, and I see the light in your faces. Though most days I am away from you, my heart turns to you always. And I want so much for that light to stay in your faces. I want so much for you to turn those faces to your parents and to your grandparents. And I want for your grandparents' and great-grandparents' faces to be turned to you. I want the light to burn brighter. The world would douse that light if it could.

From where I stand in the accumulation of seasons, I can look backward to your ancestors and forward to your children. From here, for now, in the face of the world's pressure but in the light of the Lord's promise, this is what I want you to know.

I want you to know that you have an ancestor named Lydia Knight, who kept her face turned to our Father and to her husband and children. The light in her own face never dimmed, even when her husband died and Brigham Young said it would be better for her family if they gave up their oxen and wagons so another family could make the trek west. Saying yes meant that she and her children would have to wait three years for their turn. "Brother Brigham," she said, "I will do whatever you ask."

I want you to know, my grandchildren, that it would have been much easier for her to return with her seven children to her good yet unbelieving parents. But she did not turn back. She kept facing west toward Zion.

Lydia Knight lived what Vilate Raile wrote in her poem "Pioneers":

> They cut desire into short lengths
> And fed it to the hungry fires of courage.
> Long after, when the flames died,
> Molten gold gleamed in the ashes;
> They gathered it into bruised palms
> And handed it to their children
> And their children's children.[1]

As your senses deepen, I trust that this poem will move you as it moves your grandpa and me. My desire for you is that you'll feel such courage in the heat of these Noah-like latter days, and that no matter how sore the buffetings of the world make you, I pray that your hands will stay clasped with those you love.

Your grandpa has explained in this book why what the world is telling you about husbands and wives, and mothers and fathers, and families is wrong. The world would want you to believe that it doesn't matter so much if mothers and fathers raise their children together, it doesn't matter so much if a man and a woman are married to each other, it doesn't matter so much if parents teach their children what is right and wrong, and it doesn't matter so much what people choose to do in their own private lives. This is what the world believes, but the world is wrong.

If the world has its way, there will be more children with no sense of right and wrong than there will be children who are followers of righteousness. Much of the world around you will tell you that sacrificing for the Lord and for your family is not as important as your parents tell you it is. The world is wrong. It matters terribly. And if parents don't look to their children and kindle within them the fire of sacrifice, the earth's purpose is "utterly wasted" (D&C 138:48).

I want you to know that your great-grandparents gained the courage to say no to themselves when their desires were selfish. By making good choices, they fed their righteous desires, which became the courage to say yes to whatever would lead them physically and spiritually to Zion. If the demands of their particular trails were knee buckling and breath taking, they would bend their knees to pray; and then, even though their feet were blistered, they would take the next steps forward until the breath came. They did not flinch nor shrink because they had faith in the joy and peace of Zion.

Though you are young, I see growing in you—in your faces— the same light I sense from Lydia. With her will and the Lord's grace she dredged gold from the ashes of her campfires: the gold is the love and strength born of sacrifice, which gives birth to joy and peace. With sore, roughened hands she passed this gathered gold to her children. Then she watched them turn and, often with gut-wrenching sacrifices, pass it to their children. Always, the sacrifices turned hearts to the Lord.

I too feel what Malachi must have felt in his last recorded prophecy (Malachi 4:5–6). I want for you what he wanted— hearts turned, softened—hearts that care enough about babies and children to take on the soul-stretching work of raising them up to put on the "beautiful garments" of Zion (2 Nephi 8:24).

I have such hope for you when I see on a couch in a family room a young father, his arm around his resting wife. He is holding on one shoulder his sleeping fuzzy-headed baby son, their long-haired three-year-old daughter asleep on her mother's lap. The mother strokes the child's face and hair. It is a circle of love and commitment, a picture of joy that cannot be matched.

I will cut my desires into short day-by-day lengths, and I will feed those lengths to the hungry fires of courage because I want nothing more than for my sacrifices to be accepted, my gold to be purified, even if my hands are bruised. I want you, my children's children, and your children, to know that no matter how hard it gets, it is worth it. It is worth everything—holding nothing back from each other nor from the Lord. Without each other, there is no real reason to build the fire. And without the fire, life falls cold and dark, without purpose, and without meaning.

I want to give you all the gold I have. I yearn to reach out to each of you and place the gold from my bruising but sanctifying experiences into your hands. If I choose well, if I always say yes to what He asks—by covenant—if I sacrifice with my whole heart, I will have purified gold to give to you.

What is the sacrifice? It is all of my heart, might, mind, and strength placed on the altar and burnished by the fire of the covenant that refines the gold, the gold that is passed from generation to generation. Being true to the refined love you are handed and then answering back with your own love keeps the fire burning that makes your faces even lighter.

What is the joy? The joy is in that love. Because I have felt and do feel that love for you, I have felt that joy. And I want you to feel that joy for yourselves.

More than anything, I want you to know and feel for yourselves that this love is made pure because of Jesus. It is possible to know this kind of love only when we are willing to give everything we have for Him, no matter what. That is our covenant with Him, and His with us.

Without His sacrifice, there would be no resurrection. Without Him, there would be no priesthood to act for Him. Without the priesthood, there would be no authority. Without His authority, there would be no temples. Without temples, there would be no sealing of hearts together in a love that will last forever. With Him, we have the promise of eternity. Because of Him, my heart is fully turned to you.

NOTES

PREFACE

1. "For the Beauty of the Earth," *Hymns,* no. 92.

2. Ibid.

3. "No Nation Can Rise Higher Than the Strength of Its Families," 6.

4. "President Hinckley Notes His 85th Birthday," 6; italics added.

5. "Follow the Prophet," *Children's Songbook,* 110.

6. Maxwell, *Moving in His Majesty and Power,* 53.

7. President Gordon B. Hinckley taught: "There are some who, for reasons unexplainable, do not have the opportunity of marriage. To you I should like to say, don't spend your time and wear out your lives wandering about in the wasteland of self-pity. . . .

   " . . . There are tremendous opportunities for you if you are prepared to take advantage of them. Nearly all of the honorable vocations of life are now open to women. Do not feel that because you are single God has forsaken you. The world needs you. The Church needs you. . . .

   "Be prayerful, and do not lose hope. . . . Live the very best life of which you are capable, and the Lord . . . in his eternal season will give you answer to your prayers." "Live Up to Your Inheritance," 82–83.

   President Ezra Taft Benson said: "I also recognize that not all women in the Church will have an opportunity for marriage and motherhood in mortality. But if those of you in this situation are worthy and endure faithfully, you can be assured of all blessings. . . .

"I assure you that if you have to wait even until the next life to be blessed with a choice companion, God will surely compensate you. Time is numbered only to man. God has your eternal perspective in mind.

"I also recognize that some of our sisters are widowed or divorced. My heart is drawn to you. . . . The Brethren pray for you, and we feel a great obligation to see that your needs are met. Trust in the Lord. Be assured He loves you and we love you." "To the Single Adult Sisters of the Church," 97.

Chapter One
Wedding Pictures

1. See *Time* (Pacific edition), 27 Apr. 1998, 30.
2. "I Dreamed a Dream," from the musical *Les Misérables,* by Alain Boublil and Claude Michel Schönberg. Lyrics by Alain Boublil, Herbert Kretzmer, Jean-Marc Natel. © Alain Boublil Music Ltd. Reprinted by permission.
3. Mother Teresa of Avila, quoted in "The Great Liberal Death Wish," *Imprimis,* May 1979, Hillsdale College, Michigan; cited in Maxwell, *But for a Small Moment,* 34.
4. Taylor, *Deseret News Weekly,* 28 Dec. 1859, 337; or *Journal of Discourses,* 7:318.
5. Young, Journal, 17 Feb. 1847.
6. Young, *Journal of Discourses,* 4:268.

Chapter Two
Adam, Eve, and the Great Love Story

1. Quoted in Hafen, *Disciple's Life,* 531.
2. See Pastan, "Meditation by the Stove," line 16.
3. Review of Booker, *Seven Basic Plots,* in *New York Times,* by Michiko Kakutani; cited in *International Herald Tribune,* 19 Apr. 2005, 12.
4. Benz, quoted in Keele, "Mozart's *Magic Flute,*" 43.
5. Benz, quoted in ibid., 44.
6. Ibid., 58.
7. Ibid., 58, 62.
8. Ibid., 65.
9. Ibid., 52, 70.
10. Keele, *In Search of the Supernal,* 278–79. The libretto—the script and words to the opera's songs—was written by Hugo von Hofmannsthal, "one of the finest lyric poets and dramatists in the German language." Keele, *In Search of the Supernal,* 259.
11. Ibid., 298.

12. Ibid., 315.

13. Ibid., 321, 324.

14. Ibid., 326–27.

15. Keele, "Mozart's *Magic Flute*," 71.

16. Quaker proverb.

CHAPTER THREE
NOW PEOPLE ARE CONFUSED

1. "Follow the Prophet," *Children's Songbook,* 110.

2. Wilkins, "Marriage on the Brink," 15 Feb. 2004.

3. Ibid.

4. Lyall, "In Europe, Lovers Now Say: Marry Me, a Little," 1.

5. Knox, "Nordic Family Ties Don't Mean Tying the Knot," 15.

6. Rich, "Viagra and the Sanctity of Marriage," 8.

7. Rich, "What's Love Got to Do with It?" section 2, page 1, column 4.

8. See *State of Our Unions,* 18, at marriage.rutgers.edu.

9. *Marriage in America,* 7. "Illegitimacy rates, after doubling every decade from 1960 to 1990, appear to have leveled off [at] 33 percent." Gallagher, "What Marriage Is For." The thirteenfold increase in nonmarital births is documented in Wardle, "Is Marriage Obsolete?" 189, 196.

10. Faust, "Challenges Facing the Family," 1.

11. Glendon, *Abortion and Divorce in Western Law,* 63.

12. Fukuyama, "Great Disruption," 55.

13. *Encyclopedia of Mormonism,* 1:392.

CHAPTER FOUR
HOW WE LOST THE PLOT

1. Gallagher, *Abolition of Marriage,* 4. See generally Waite and Gallagher, *Case for Marriage.*

2. Tribe, *American Constitutional Law,* sections 988–89.

3. *Roe v. Wade,* United States, 1973.

4. Schlesinger, "How Gay Marriage Thrust Two Outsiders onto Center Stage."

5. Quoted in Hafen and Hafen, "Abandoning Children to Their Autonomy," 450.

6. Dolgin, "Family in Transition," 1519, 1520.

7. Ibid., 1570.

8. Ibid., 1571.

9. "The trend towards getting married later has helped reduce the nationwide

[United States] divorce rate from 4.7 per 1,000 people in 1990 to 4 in 2001. However, the figure still dwarfs the European Union's rate of 1.9." Ward, "South Finds Families That Pray Together May Not Stay Together," 3.

10. Moir, "New Class of Disadvantaged Children," 63.

11. *Lawrence v. Texas,* United States, 2003.

12. *Goodridge et al. v. Department of Public Health et al.,* Massachusetts, 2003.

13. "Court Upholds Ban on Same-Sex Adoptions," 23 July 2004, citing world-netdaily.com/news/article.asp. The United States Supreme Court refused to hear an appeal from this decision. Biskupic, "Ban on Adoption by Gays Left Intact."

14. Berry, *Sex, Economy, Freedom and Community,* 125, 137–39; italics added.

15. Chesterton, "Superstition of Divorce," *Collected Works,* 4:239.

16. Moir, "New Class of Disadvantaged Children," 63 n. 2, 65; italics omitted.

17. For a brief historical summary of the movement and for a statement of its goals as of 2004, see *What Next for the Marriage Movement?* www.americanvalues.org.

18. Heaton, "Factors Contributing to Increasing Marital Stability in the United States," 392–409.

19. Gallagher, "What Marriage Is For," 22.

20. Stuart, "Three Weddings and a Contract," 22.

21. Saulny, "Here Comes the Bride, Again."

22. McDannel and Lang, *Heaven,* 308.

23. Bellah et al., *Habits of the Heart,* 86.

24. See Hafen and Hafen, *Belonging Heart,* 3–20.

25. See Hafen, *Disciple's Life,* 528.

26. Thornton, "Changing Attitudes," 873, 891.

27. Wilson, *Marriage Problem,* 4–5.

28. Schneider, "Moral Discourse and the Transformation of Family Law," 1803, 1860; italics added.

29. James, *Essays on Faith and Morals,* 23–28.

30. Kimball, *Marriage and Divorce,* 12–16; italics added; or "Marriage and Divorce" (address); see also *Teachings of Spencer W. Kimball,* 305. President Gordon B. Hinckley has similarly said, "There is no greater happiness than is found in the most meaningful of all human relationships—the companionships of husband and wife and parents and children." "Marriage That Endures," 4.

Chapter Five
Marriage in Eternal Perspective

1. Shakespeare, *Macbeth,* act 5, scene 5, lines 22–31.
2. "I Am a Child of God," *Children's Songbook,* 2–3; or *Hymns,* no. 301.
3. Oaks, "Parental Leadership in the Family," 7.
4. See McDannell and Lang, *Heaven,* 309.
5. Ibid., 308.
6. Ibid., 313, 320.
7. "Families Can Be Together Forever," *Children's Songbook,* 188; or *Hymns,* no. 300.

Chapter Six
The Doctrinal Pattern of Adam and Eve

1. Ballif, *Lamentation and Other Poems,* 3–6.
2. Eliot, "Little Gidding," part 5, lines 26–29.
3. McConkie, *Doctrinal New Testament Commentary,* 1:548; see also 546–49, 604–8.

Chapter Seven
A Hireling's Contract or a Shepherd's Covenant?

1. Hales, "Eternal Family," 65.
2. Faust, "Gift of the Holy Ghost," 33.
3. Benson, "Marriage of Adam and Eve."
4. Young, *Discourses of Brigham Young,* 410.
5. "The Lord Is My Shepherd," *Hymns,* no. 108.
6. Sorokin, *Society, Culture, and Personality,* 99–108.
7. Ibid.
8. Packer, "Marriage," 15.
9. Peck, *Road Less Traveled,* 81, 159.

Chapter Eight
Good Shepherds

1. McKay, *Man May Know for Himself,* 72.
2. Peck, *Road Less Traveled,* 15, 16.
3. Ibid., 18.

Chapter Nine
The Wolf of Adversity

1. Hinckley, "What God Hath Joined Together," 72.
2. Christensen, "Marriage and the Great Plan of Happiness," 65.
3. Roethke, "The Waking," in *Collected Poems,* 108.
4. Hafen, "Joy Cometh in the Morning," 30, 35.
5. Whitney and Kramer, "No Man Is an Island"; see also John Donne, *Meditation 17.*

Chapter Ten
Shared Afflictions

1. Tolstoy, *War and Peace,* 616–17.
2. "I Need Thee Every Hour," *Hymns,* no. 98.

Chapter Eleven
The Wolf of Personal Imperfection

1. Hinckley, "Our Solemn Responsibilities," 50–51.
2. Ibid., 50.
3. Ellsworth, *Latter-day Plague,* 19–20.
4. Kimball, "Jesus: The Perfect Leader," 5.
5. Lasater, "Shepherds of Israel," 74.

Chapter Twelve
Charity

1. Hafen, "From Criticism to Cooperation to Charity," 42–43.
2. Quoted in Warner, "Honest, Simple, Solid, True," 36–37.
3. Erickson and Erickson, *When Life Doesn't Seem Fair,* 214–18.
4. "Mending Our Marriage," 49.

Chapter Thirteen
The Wolf of Excessive Individualism

1. Morson, "Prosaics," 515, 523.
2. Packer, "Our Moral Environment," 66.
3. Brinley, "What Our Temple Marriage Means to Us," 98–99.

Chapter Fourteen
Abiding Alone, Abiding Together, and Bringing Forth Fruit

1. Gibran, *Prophet,* 19–20.
2. Albom, *Tuesdays with Morrie,* 65.

3. Kilpatrick, "Faith and Therapy," 25–26.

4. Ellis, "Psychotherapy and Atheistic Values," 635, 638 (table 2).

5. Hunter, "Opening and Closing of Doors," 59.

6. Kimball, "Lord's Plan for Men and Women," 4.

CHAPTER FIFTEEN
THE BONDS THAT LIBERATE

1. Gibran, *Prophet,* 35.

2. Novak, "Family Out of Favor," 37; italics added.

3. Lincoln, First Inaugural Address.

4. Faust, "Refiner's Fire," 53.

CHAPTER SIXTEEN
GLIMPSES OF COVENANT MARRIAGE

1. Mukherjee, "Mother Teresa," 88, 90.

2. Norris, "Hudson's Geese," in *Collected Poems,* 174.

3. Kimball, Conference Report, Oct. 1962, 58.

4. Anderson, *Joan of Lorraine,* act 2.

5. Poelman, "God's Love for Us Transcends Our Transgressions," 27–28.

6. Kimball, *Miracle of Forgiveness,* 250.

7. Kimball, *Marriage and Divorce,* 24–25; or "Marriage and Divorce" (address); see also *Teachings of Spencer W. Kimball,* 304–11.

8. Hinckley, "What God Hath Joined Together," 73–74.

9. Haight, "Marriage and Divorce," 12.

10. Packer, "Marriage," 15.

11. Faust, "Father, Come Home," 35.

CHAPTER SEVENTEEN
EQUAL PARTNERS

1. First Presidency and Council of the Twelve Apostles, "The Family: A Proclamation to the World," 102.

2. Dooley, "Baptist Seminary Says Faculty Must Sign Statement."

3. Tertullian, *De Cultu Feminarum* I.12, as quoted in Pagels, *Adam, Eve, and the Serpent,* 63; italics omitted.

4. Widtsoe, *Evidences and Reconciliations,* 194.

5. Ibid., 193.

6. Smith, Conference Report, Oct. 1967, 121–22.

7. I thank Donald W. Parry for help with the Hebrew translation. See also Campbell, "Mother Eve," 39.

8. Packer, "For Time and All Eternity," 22.

9. *Apocryphon of John* 31, 1–6, in *The Nag Hammadi Library,* 98–116, quoted in Pagels, *Adam, Eve, and the Serpent,* 67–68.

10. Pagels, *Adam, Eve, and the Serpent,* 67.

11. Campbell, *Power of Myth,* 37–39.

12. Kimball, "Blessings and Responsibilities of Womanhood," 301, 302.

13. Kimball, in "A Treasury of Quotations for Women," 432.

14. Bushman, "Joseph Smith's Visions," 14.

15. Oaks, "Men, Women and Priesthood in the Family and in the Church."

16. Hafen, *Disciple's Life,* 14–15.

17. L'Engle, *Irrational Season,* 98.

CHAPTER EIGHTEEN
THE MORAL INFLUENCE OF WOMEN

1. First Presidency and Council of the Twelve Apostles, "The Family: A Proclamation to the World," 102.

2. Holland and Holland, *On Earth As It Is in Heaven,* 85.

3. World Bank, *World Development Report 1991,* 49–58. See also Bellah et al., *Habits of the Heart,* 37–39.

4. See de Tocqueville, *Democracy in America,* 1:298–342.

5. Shakespeare, *Macbeth,* act 1, scene 5, lines 16–17, 48–57.

6. Quoted in Holland, "'Because She Is a Mother,'" 35.

7. Quoted in Bahr and Bahr, *Another Voice, Another Lens.*

8. Summers, *God's Police,* 70.

9. "Feminism's Identity Crisis," 58.

10. First Presidency and Council of the Twelve Apostles, "The Family: A Proclamation to the World," 102.

11. Papazoglou, "Despising Our Mothers, Despising Ourselves," 11.

12. Whitfield, "Sensitive Directions for Children's Moral Development." "A huge volume of recent evidence from psychology and neuroscience [shows] that strong, overt parental love is essential for the brain to develop normally during infancy. . . .

   "Research . . . shows that babies who live with stressed or depressed mothers were more likely to respond to difficulties in later life by releasing unhealthy levels of stress hormones, such as cortisol." Review of Gerhardt, *Why Love Matters,* in *Financial Times,* 7–8 Aug. 2004, W4.

13. "Large-Scale Study Shows Reality for Mothers," Motherhood Study, summarized at www.motherhoodproject.org.

14. Kass, "End of Courtship," 45, 63.

15. Popenoe, *Life without Father,* 173–74.
16. Popenoe, "Case for Marriage and the Nuclear Family," 6.
17. Quoted in Fukuyama, "Great Disruption," 72.
18. Margaret Mead, cited in Popenoe, *Life without Father,* 185.
19. Popenoe, "Case for Marriage and the Nuclear Family," 6.
20. See Popenoe, *Life without Father,* 164–88.
21. Yeats, "The Second Coming," lines 1–4.
22. Gollan, "How Feminine Intuition Can Help the Profit Margin," 13.
23. Quoted in Summers, *God's Police,* 337.
24. See ibid., 354–55.
25. Ibid., 352, 51.
26. Ibid., 354.
27. Ibid., 50.

CHAPTER NINETEEN
THE MORAL INFLUENCE OF MEN

1. Packer, "Relief Society," 73–74.
2. Gutmann, "Paternal Imperative," 118, 119.
3. Petersen, *Hugh Nibley,* 353, 358.
4. First Presidency and Council of the Twelve Apostles, "The Family: A Proclamation to the World," 102.
5. Gutmann, "Paternal Imperative," 119–20.
6. Ibid., 120.
7. "I Am a Child of God," *Children's Songbook,* 2–3; or *Hymns,* no. 301.
8. Faust, "Fathers, Mothers, Marriage," 4.
9. Gutmann, "Paternal Imperative," 120.
10. Ibid., 122.
11. Ibid.
12. Lasch, *Haven in a Heartless World,* 123.
13. Ibid., 186, 125.
14. See Hafen, *Broken Heart,* 155–73.
15. Gutmann, "Paternal Imperative," 123.
16. Song performed some years ago by the Lamanite Generation, Brigham Young University, Provo, Utah.
17. Gutmann, "Paternal Imperative," 124.
18. Ibid.
19. Ibid., 121.

CHAPTER TWENTY
THE CLADDAUGH RING

1. Berry, *Sex, Economy, Freedom and Community,* 125.
2. Ibid., 138.
3. Hinckley, quoted in "'Continue Bright, Strong the Links of Your Generations,'" 13.
4. Myer, "Birth Dearth," 54, 56.
5. Fornos, "Population Crisis Still Looms," 6.
6. Dyer, "Global Phenomenon Is Being Born with Disappearing Babies," A13.
7. Myer, "Birth Dearth," 56–57.
8. Landler, "Western Europe Fears What It Needs," 3.
9. Doi, "From Boom to Bust," W1.
10. Ben Wattenberg, quoted in Neuhaus, "Where Have All the Children Gone?" 59.
11. See sources cited in Myer, "Birth Dearth," 59–63.
12. State interior minister Otto Schily, quoted in Berth and Schneider, "Germans No Longer Want Children," 1; translation by the author.
13. Biedenkopf, "Panic Rules," 24 Apr. 2004.
14. Bowring, "West Ignores Low Birthrates at Its Peril," 6.
15. Conversation with Lindsay Dil of Auckland, New Zealand, about 30 Mar. 2004.
16. About 12 percent of the Australian population was over age sixty-five in 1999. That figure will rise to 25 percent in fifty years. Of present caregivers for the elderly, more than 70 percent are married; 2 percent are living in unmarried relationships. Gobbo, address to Australian Regional Conference of World Congress of Families II.
17. Unpublished data compiled by Europe Central Area Translation Office shows a decline in active LDS children in Denmark, Finland, Norway, Sweden, Germany, Austria, and Switzerland (German-speaking stakes) from 5,581 to 4,113 between 1996 and 2003.
18. Carlson, "Depopulation," 6.
19. Ibid., 8; italics omitted.
20. Conversation with Allan Carlson in Melbourne, Australia, 6 Aug. 1999.
21. De Tocqueville, *Democracy in America,* 2:105–6; see also Bellah et al., *Habits of the Heart,* 37–39.
22. First Presidency and Council of the Twelve Apostles, "The Family: A Proclamation to the World," 102.

23. Packer, "Do Not Fear," 79.

24. Clark, "To Them of the Last Wagon," 10.

CHAPTER TWENTY-ONE
CHILDREN AND THE SOCIAL INTEREST IN MARRIAGE

1. Whitehead, "Dan Quayle Was Right," 55.

2. Ibid., 47.

3. *Marriage in America,* 1, 4, 6, 8.

4. Ibid., 6.

5. Ibid.

6. Ibid.

7. Cloud, "What Can the Schools Do?" 39.

8. Ibid.

9. Ibid., 38.

10. *Marriage in America,* 6.

11. *USA Today,* 12 Apr. 1999, www.usatoday.com.

12. *Marriage in America,* 8.

13. "Fatherless Boys Grow Up into Dangerous Men," A22; quoted in Hinckley, "Bridges to the Future," 22 Apr. 2003.

14. *Propositions,* 8.

15. *Why Marriage Matters,* 8, 9, 10, 14, 15, 17.

16. Conversation with Dr. W. Dean Belnap, Frankfurt, Germany, 17 Aug. 2003.

17. *Hardwired to Connect,* 5.

18. Ibid., 40.

19. Devlin, *Enforcement of Morals,* 61.

20. First Presidency and Council of the Twelve Apostles, "The Family: A Proclamation to the World," 102.

21. Whitehead, "Dan Quayle Was Right," 82.

22. Ibid., 58; italics added.

23. Ibid., 52.

24. M. Zelnik, J. Kantner, and K. Ford, *Sex and Pregnancy in Adolescence* (1979), 182, quoted in Hafen, Book Review, 435.

CHAPTER TWENTY-TWO
NO-FAULT DIVORCE AND THE LOST PLOT

1. Taylor, "Death of a Marriage," 13.

2. "Talk of the Town," 21–22.

3. Moir, "New Class of Disadvantaged Children," 66.

CHAPTER TWENTY-THREE
THE MOST BASIC UNIT

1. First Presidency and Council of the Twelve Apostles, "The Family: A Proclamation to the World," 102.
2. David O. McKay, as quoted in *Encyclopedia of Mormonism,* 2:486.
3. First Presidency and Council of the Twelve Apostles, "The Family: A Proclamation to the World," 102.
4. See sources cited in Hafen, "Constitutional Status of Marriage," 474.
5. See de Tocqueville, *Democracy in America,* 1:298–342.
6. See Maxwell, Conference Report, Oct. 1970, 97.
7. Hinckley, "Bridges to the Future," 22 Apr. 2003.
8. Edmund Burke, quoted in Hafen, "Constitutional Status of Marriage," 479.
9. Quoted in ibid., 480.
10. David H. Lawrence, quoted in ibid., 483.
11. First Presidency and Council of the Twelve Apostles, "The Family: A Proclamation to the World," 102.

CHAPTER TWENTY-FOUR
HOW SAME-SEX MARRIAGE WEAKENS WHAT MARRIAGE MEANS

1. Hinckley, "What Are People Asking about Us?" 70.
2. Hinckley, "Why We Do Some of the Things We Do," 54.
3. Since the Massachusetts case in late 2003, opinion polls have shown that most Americans oppose same-gender marriage, though the level of opposition has varied over time. A March 2005 *USA Today*/CNN/Gallup Poll reported 68 percent were opposed. A more recent poll released in May 2005 reported 56 percent opposed, 39 percent in favor, and 5 percent undecided. Another 2005 poll found that 90 percent said gays and lesbians should have equal employment rights. Jones, "Gay Marriage Debate Still Fierce One Year Later." An Associated Press report on this same poll indicated 37 percent in favor with 50 percent opposed and 11 percent neutral, with a sampling error of plus or minus 3.6 percent. "Poll: Half of Americans Disapprove of Same-Sex Marriages," *USA Today,* 15 May 2005; also reported briefly in *International Herald Tribune,* 16 May 2005, 5. A 1996 national poll earlier found that 33 percent of those sampled believed that same-sex marriages should be legalized. *Newsweek,* 3 June 1996, 27. The same poll found that 84 percent believe gays should have equal access to job opportunities.
4. Bernstein, "When One Person's Civil Rights Are Another's Moral Outrage," section 4, page 6; Barney, "Shaky Ground," A1.

5. Paragraph 4 of majority opinion, *Goodridge et al. v. Department of Public Health et al.,* Massachusetts, 2003.

6. *Bowers v. Hardwick,* United States, 1986, 199, 204, 211 (Justice Blackmun dissenting).

7. Hardin, "2-Parent Families Rise After Change in Welfare Laws," quoted in *What Next for the Marriage Movement?* 4.

8. Culture Changers, goal 6 through 2006, *What Next for the Marriage Movement?* 20 Dec. 2004, MarriageMovement.org.

9. First Presidency and Council of the Twelve Apostles, "The Family: A Proclamation to the World," 102.

10. Bork, "Necessary Amendment," 17, 19.

CHAPTER TWENTY-FIVE
HE SATISFIETH THE LONGING SOUL

1. Frankl, *Man's Search for Meaning,* 48–49, 9.

2. Hinckley, "Women in Our Lives," 82.

3. Monson, Conference Report, Apr. 1972, 72.

4. Rector and Rector, *No More Strangers,* 49.

5. Ibid., 52, 53.

6. Clark, Journal, 22–23, entry dated 13 Nov. 1922; edited slightly for readability.

7. Ibid., 23, entry dated Aug. 1925.

EPILOGUE
FROM A GRANDMA'S HEART

1. Vilate Raile, "Pioneers," in *Legacy Remembered,* 19.

SOURCES

BOOKS

Albom, Mitch. *Tuesdays with Morrie: An Old Man, a Young Man, and Life's Greatest Lesson.* New York: Doubleday, 1997.

Anderson, Maxwell. *Joan of Lorraine: A Play in Two Acts.* Washington, D.C.: Anderson House, 1947.

Bahr, Kathleen S., and Howard M. Bahr. *Another Voice, Another Lens: Making a Place for Sacrifice in Family Theory and Family Process.* Virginia F. Cutler Lecture, Brigham Young University, 13 Nov. 1997. Monograph.

Ballard, M. Russell. *Counseling with Our Councils: Learning to Minister Together in the Church and in the Family.* Salt Lake City: Deseret Book, 1997.

Ballif, Arta Romney. *Lamentation and Other Poems.* Privately printed, 1989.

Bellah, Robert N., et al. *Habits of the Heart: Individualism and Commitment in American Life.* Berkeley: University of California Press, 1985.

Berry, Wendell. *Sex, Economy, Freedom and Community.* New York: Pantheon Books, 1993.

Brinley, Douglas E. "What Our Temple Marriage Means to Us." In *LDS Marriage and Family Relations: Student Manual.* Department of Church History and Doctrine, Brigham Young University. Dubuque, Iowa: Kendall Hunt, 1998.

Campbell, Joseph. *The Power of Myth, with Bill Moyers.* Ed. Betty Sue Flowers. New York: Doubleday, 1988.

Chesterton, G. K. "The Superstition of Divorce." In vol. 4 of *The Collected*

Works of G. K. Chesterton. 35 vols. San Francisco: Ignatius Press, 1986–2005.

Children's Songbook of The Church of Jesus Christ of Latter-day Saints. Salt Lake City: The Church of Jesus Christ of Latter-day Saints, 1989.

De Tocqueville, Alexis. *Democracy in America.* Trans. Henry Reeve. Ed. Francis Bowen and Phillips Bradley. 2 vols. New York: Vintage Books, 1945.

Devlin, Patrick. *The Enforcement of Morals.* New York: Oxford University Press, 1972.

Eliot, T. S. *Four Quartets.* London: Folio Society, 1968.

Ellsworth, Sterling G. *Latter-day Plague: Breaking the Chains of Pornography—Causes, Cures, Preventions.* Provo, Utah: Maasai Publishing, 2002.

Encyclopedia of Mormonism. Ed. Daniel H. Ludlow et al. 4 vols. New York: Macmillan, 1992.

Erickson, Bruce, and Joyce Erickson. *When Life Doesn't Seem Fair.* Salt Lake City: Bookcraft, 1995.

Faust, James E. "Challenges Facing the Family." In *Worldwide Leadership Training Meeting: The Priesthood and the Auxiliaries of the Relief Society, Young Women, and Primary.* Salt Lake City: The Church of Jesus Christ of Latter-day Saints, 2004.

Frankl, Viktor E. *Man's Search for Meaning: An Introduction to Logotherapy.* 4th ed. Boston: Beacon Press, 1992.

Gallagher, Maggie. *The Abolition of Marriage.* Washington, D.C.: Regnery, 1996.

Gibran, Kahlil. *The Prophet.* New York: Alfred K. Knopf, 1936.

Gilligan, Carol. *In a Different Voice: Psychological Theory and Women's Development.* Cambridge, Mass.: Harvard University Press, 1982.

Glendon, Mary Ann. *Abortion and Divorce in Western Law.* Cambridge, Mass.: Harvard University Press, 1987.

Hafen, Bruce C. *A Disciple's Life: The Biography of Neal A. Maxwell.* Salt Lake City: Deseret Book, 2002.

———. *The Broken Heart: Applying the Atonement to Life's Experiences.* Salt Lake City: Deseret Book, 1989.

Hafen, Bruce C., and Marie K. Hafen. *The Belonging Heart: The Atonement and Relationships with God and Family.* Salt Lake City: Deseret Book, 1994.

Hafen, Marie K. "From Criticism to Cooperation to Charity." In *Clothed in Charity: Talks from the 1996 BYU Women's Conference.* Salt Lake City: Deseret Book, 1997.

Hardwired to Connect: The New Scientific Case for Authoritative Communities. New York: Institute for American Values, 2003.

Holland, Jeffrey R., and Patricia T. Holland. *On Earth as it Is in Heaven.* Salt Lake City: Deseret Book, 1989.

Hymns of The Church of Jesus Christ of Latter-day Saints. Salt Lake City: The Church of Jesus Christ of Latter-day Saints, 1985.

James, William. *Essays on Faith and Morals.* Ed. Ralph Barton Peery. Cleveland: World Publishing, 1962.

Journal of Discourses. 26 vols. London: Latter-day Saints' Book Depot, 1854–86.

Keele, Alan. *In Search of the Supernal: Preexistence, Eternal Marriage, and Apotheosis in German Literary, Operatic, and Cinematic Texts.* Muenster, Germany: Agenda Verlag, 2003.

Kimball, Spencer W. "Blessings and Responsibilities of Womanhood." In *LDS Women's Treasury: Insights and Inspiration for Today's Woman.* Salt Lake City: Deseret Book, 1997.

———. In "A Treasury of Quotations for Women." *LDS Women's Treasury: Insights and Inspiration for Today's Woman.* Salt Lake City: Deseret Book, 1997.

———. *Marriage and Divorce.* Salt Lake City: Deseret Book, 1976.

———. *The Miracle of Forgiveness.* Salt Lake City: Bookcraft, 1969.

———. *The Teachings of Spencer W. Kimball: Twelfth President of The Church of Jesus Christ of Latter-day Saints.* Ed. Edward L. Kimball. Salt Lake City: Bookcraft, 1982.

Lasch, Christopher. *Haven in a Heartless World: The Family Besieged.* New York: Basic Books, 1977.

L'Engle, Madeleine. *The Irrational Season.* Large print ed. New York: Walker and Company, 1984.

Marriage in America: A Report to the Nation. New York: Institute for American Values, 1995. Monograph.

Maxwell, Neal A. *But for a Small Moment.* Salt Lake City: Bookcraft, 1986.

———. *Moving in His Majesty and Power.* Salt Lake City: Deseret Book, 2004.

McConkie, Bruce R. *Doctrinal New Testament Commentary.* 3 vols. Salt Lake City: Deseret Book, 1965–73.

McDannell, Colleen, and Bernhard Lang. *Heaven: A History.* New Haven, Conn.: Yale University Press, 1988.

McKay, David O. *Man May Know for Himself: Teachings of David O. McKay.* Comp. Clare Middlemiss. Salt Lake City: Deseret Book, 1967.

Moir, Donald S. "A New Class of Disadvantaged Children." In D. Allen and

J. Richards, *It Takes Two: The Family in Law and Finance.* Toronto, Ontario, Canada: C. D. Howe Institute, 1999.

Norris, Leslie. *Collected Poems.* Bridgend, Wales: Seren Books, 1999.

Pagels, Elaine. *Adam, Eve, and the Serpent.* New York: Random House, 1988.

Pastan, Linda. "Meditation by the Stove." In *Carnival Evening: New and Selected Poems, 1968–1998.* New York: W. W. Norton, 1998.

Peck, M. Scott. *The Road Less Traveled: A New Psychology of Love, Traditional Values, and Spiritual Growth.* New York: Touchstone, 1998.

Petersen, Boyd Jay. *Hugh Nibley: A Consecrated Life.* Salt Lake City: Greg Kofford Books, 2002.

Popenoe, David. *Life without Father.* New York: Free Press, 1996.

Raile, Vilate. "Pioneers." In *A Legacy Remembered: The Relief Society Magazine 1914–1970.* Salt Lake City: Deseret Book, 1982.

Rector, Hartman, and Connie Rector. *No More Strangers.* Salt Lake City: Bookcraft, 1971.

Roethke, Theodore. *The Collected Poems of Theodore Roethke.* Garden City, New York: Doubleday, 1966.

Shakespeare, William. *Macbeth.* Ed. Barbara A. Mowat and Paul Werstine. New Folger Library edition. New York: Washington Square Press, 1992.

Sorokin, Pitirim. *Society, Culture, and Personality.* 2d ed. New York: Cooper Square Publishers, 1962.

Summers, Anne. *God's Police.* Australia: Penguin Books, 1994.

Tolstoy, Leo. *War and Peace.* Trans. Louise and Aylmer Maude. Vol. 51 of *Great Books of the Western World.* Ed. Mortimer J. Adler. 2d ed. Chicago: Encyclopedia Brittanica, 1990.

Tribe, Laurence. *American Constitutional Law.* Mineola, N.Y.: Foundation Press, 1978.

Waite, Linda J., and Maggie Gallagher. *The Case for Marriage.* New York: Doubleday, 2000.

Why Marriage Matters: Twenty-One Conclusions from the Social Sciences. New York: Institute for American Values, 2002. Monograph.

Widtsoe, John A. *Evidences and Reconciliations.* Salt Lake City: Bookcraft, 1987.

Wilson, James Q. *The Marriage Problem: How Our Culture Has Weakened Families.* New York: HarperCollins, 2002.

World Bank. *The Challenge of Development: World Development Report 1991.* Oxford: Oxford University Press, 1991.

Yeats, W. B. *The Poems.* Ed. Richard J. Finneran. Vol. 1 of *The Collected Works of W. B. Yeats.* Ed. Richard J. Finneran and George Mills Harper. New York: Macmillan, 1989.

Young, Brigham. *Discourses of Brigham Young.* Sel. John A. Widtsoe. Salt Lake City: Deseret Book, 1976.

PERIODICALS

Benson, Ezra Taft. "To the Single Adult Sisters of the Church." *Ensign,* Nov. 1988, 96–97.

Bernstein, Richard. "When One Person's Civil Rights Are Another's Moral Outrage." *New York Times,* 16 Oct. 1994, section 4, page 6.

Berth, Felix, and Jens Schneider. "Germans No Longer Want Children." *Suddeutsche Zeitung,* 3 May 2005, 1.

Biedenkopf, Kurt. "Panic Rules." *Die Welt,* 24 Apr. 2004.

Biskupic, Joan. "Ban on Adoption by Gays Left Intact." *USA Today,* usatoday.com, 11 Jan. 2005.

Blankenhorn, David. "Fatherless Society." *Quadrant,* December 1997, 9.

Bork, Robert H. "The Necessary Amendment." *First Things,* Aug./Sept. 2004, 17.

Bowring, Philip. "Pensions in Danger: The West Ignores Low Birthrates at Its Peril." *International Herald Tribune,* 23–24 Oct. 2004, I-6.

Christensen, Joe J. "Marriage and the Great Plan of Happiness." *Ensign,* May 1995, 64.

Clark, J. Reuben, Jr. "To Them of the Last Wagon." *New Era,* July 1975, 8. Reprint. Address originally delivered at general conference, 5 Oct. 1947.

Cloud, John. "What Can the Schools Do?" *Time,* 3 May 1999, 38.

"'Continue Bright, Strong the Links of Your Generations.'" *Church News,* 11 Sept. 1999, 13.

"Court Upholds Ban on Same-Sex Adoptions." Meridianmagazine.com, 23 July 2004, citing worldnetdaily.com/news/article.asp.

Barney, Dennis. "Shaky Ground: Gay Rights Confront Determined Resistance from Some Moderates." *Wall Street Journal,* 7 Oct. 1994, A1.

Doi, Ayako. "From Boom to Bust." *Financial Times Weekend,* 20–21 Mar. 2004, W1.

Dolgin, Janet. "The Family in Transition: From Griswold to Eisenstadt and Beyond." *Georgetown Law Journal* 82, no. 4 (1994): 1519.

Dooley, Tara. "Baptist Seminary Says Faculty Must Sign Statement Saying Wives Must 'Submit Graciously' to Husbands." *Salt Lake Tribune,* 24 Oct. 1998.

Dyer, Gwynne. "Global Phenomenon Is Being Born with Disappearing Babies." *Salt Lake Tribune,* 3 May 2004, A13.

Ellis, Albert. "Psychotherapy and Atheistic Values: A Response to A. E. Bergin's Psychotherapy and Religious Values." *Journal of Consulting and Clinical Psychology* 48 (1980): 635.

Faust, James E. "Father, Come Home." *Ensign,* May 1993, 35.

———. "Fathers, Mothers, Marriage." *Ensign,* Aug. 2004, 3.

———. "The Gift of the Holy Ghost—A Sure Compass." *Ensign,* May 1989, 31.

———. "The Refiner's Fire." *Ensign,* May 1979, 53.

"Feminism's Identity Crisis." *Newsweek,* 31 Mar. 1986, 58.

First Presidency and Quorum of the Twelve Apostles. "The Family: A Proclamation to the World." *Ensign,* Nov. 1995, 102.

Fornos, Werner. "Population Crisis Still Looms." *International Herald Tribune,* 14 Jan. 2004, 6.

Fukuyama, Francis. "The Great Disruption." *Atlantic Monthly,* May 1999, 72.

Gallagher, Maggie. "What Marriage Is For." *Weekly Standard,* 4–11 Aug. 2003, 22.

Gollan, Paul. "How Feminine Intuition Can Help the Profit Margin." *Sydney Morning Herald,* 28 Jul. 1998, 13.

Gutmann, David. "The Paternal Imperative." *American Scholar* 67, no. 1 (Winter 1998): 118.

Hafen, Bruce C. Book Review. *Harvard Law Review* 100, no. 2 (Dec. 1986): 435.

———. "The Constitutional Status of Marriage, Kinship, and Sexual Privacy—Balancing the Individual and Social Interests." *Michigan Law Review* 81, no. 3 (Jan. 1983): 463.

Hafen, Bruce C., and Jonathan O. Hafen. "Abandoning Children to Their Autonomy: The United Nations Convention on the Rights of the Child." *Harvard International Law Journal* 37 (Spring 1996): 449.

Haight, David B. "Marriage and Divorce." *Ensign,* May 1984, 12.

Hales, Robert D. "The Eternal Family." *Ensign,* Nov. 1996, 64.

Heaton, Tim B. "Factors Contributing to Increasing Marital Stability in the United States." *Journal of Family Issues* 23, no. 3 (2002): 392.

Hinckley, Gordon B. "Live Up to Your Inheritance." *Ensign,* Nov. 1983, 81.

———. "Marriage That Endures." *Ensign,* July 2003, 3.

———. "Our Solemn Responsibilities." *Ensign,* Nov. 1991, 49.

———. "What Are People Asking about Us?" *Ensign,* Nov. 1998, 70.

———. "What God Hath Joined Together." *Ensign,* May 1991, 71.

————. "Why We Do Some of the Things We Do." *Ensign,* Nov. 1999, 52.

————. "The Women in Our Lives." *Ensign,* Nov. 2004, 82.

Holland, Jeffrey R. "'Because She Is a Mother.'" *Ensign,* May 1997, 35.

Hunter, Howard W. "The Opening and Closing of Doors." *Ensign,* Nov. 1987, 58.

Jones, Charisse. "Gay Marriage Debate Still Fierce One Year Later." *USA Today,* Internet edition, 17 May 2005.

Kass, Leon R. "The End of Courtship." *Public Interest* 126 (Winter 1997): 39.

Keele, Alan F. "Toward an Anthropology of Apotheosis in Mozart's *Magic Flute.*" *BYU Studies* 43, no. 3 (2004): 43.

Kilpatrick, William. "Faith and Therapy." *First Things,* Feb. 1999, 25–26.

Kimball, Spencer W. Conference Report, Oct. 1962, 58

————. "Jesus: The Perfect Leader." *Ensign,* Aug. 1979, 5.

————. "The Lord's Plan for Men and Women." *Ensign,* Oct. 1975, 2.

————. "Marriage and Divorce." Brigham Young University Speeches of the Year, Provo, Utah, 7 Sep. 1976.

Knox, Noelle. "Nordic Family Ties Don't Mean Tying the Knot." *USA Today,* 16 Dec. 2004, 15, www.usatoday.com/news/world.

Landler, Mark. "Western Europe Fears What It Needs: People from the East." *International Herald Tribune,* 5 May 2004, 3.

Lasater, John R. "Shepherds of Israel." *Ensign,* May 1988, 74.

Lyall, Sarah. "In Europe, Lovers Now Say: Marry Me, a Little." *Sydney International Herald Tribune,* 16 Feb. 2004, 1.

Maxwell, Neal A. Conference Report, Oct. 1970, 97.

"Mending Our Marriage." *Ensign,* Oct. 1996, 44.

Monson, Thomas S. Conference Report, Apr. 1972, 69.

Morson, Gary Saul. "Prosaics: An Approach to the Humanities." *American Scholar,* Autumn 1988, 515.

Mukherjee, Bharati. "Mother Teresa: The Saint." *Time,* 14 June 1999, 88.

Myer, Michael. "Birth Dearth." *Newsweek,* 27 Sep. 2004 (international edition), 54.

Neuhaus, Richard John. "The Public Square: Where Have All the Children Gone?" *First Things,* May 2005, 59.

"No Nation Can Rise Higher Than the Strength of Its Families." *Church News,* 3 Oct. 1998, 6.

Novak, Michael. "The Family Out of Favor." *Harper's Magazine,* April 1976, 37.

Oaks, Dallin H. "Parental Leadership in the Family." *Ensign,* June 1985, 7.

Packer, Boyd K. "Do Not Fear." *Ensign,* May 2004, 77.

———. "For Time and All Eternity." *Ensign,* Nov. 1993, 21.

———. "Marriage." *Ensign,* May 1981, 13.

———. "Our Moral Environment." *Ensign,* May 1992, 66.

———. "The Relief Society." *Ensign,* May 1998, 72.

Papazoglou, Orania. "Despising Our Mothers, Despising Ourselves." *First Things,* Jan. 1992, 11.

Poelman, Ronald E. "God's Love for Us Transcends Our Transgressions." *Ensign,* May 1982, 27.

"Poll: Half of Americans Disapprove of Same-Sex Marriages." *USA Today,* 15 May 2005, Internet edition.

"President Hinckley Notes His 85th Birthday." *Church News,* 24 June 1995, 6.

Propositions 12, Fall 2001.

Review of Christopher Booker, *The Seven Basic Plots: Why We Tell Stories* (Continuum, 2005), in *New York Times,* by Michiko Kakutani. Cited in *International Herald Tribune,* 19 Apr. 2005, 12.

Review of Sue Gerhardt, *Why Love Matters: How Affection Shapes a Baby's Brain* (London: Brunner-Routledge, 2004), in *Financial Times,* 7–8 Aug. 2004, W4.

Rich, Frank. "Viagra and the Sanctity of Marriage." *International Herald Tribune,* 31 Jan.–1 Feb. 2004, 8.

———. "What's Love Got to Do with It?" *New York Times,* 1 Feb. 2004, section 2, page 1, column 4.

Saulny, Susan. "Here Comes the Bride, Again, and Again . . ." *New York Times,* 10 July 2003, section A, page 1, column 3.

Schlesinger, Jacob M. "How Gay Marriage Thrust Two Outsiders onto Center Stage." *Wall Street Journal,* 23 Feb. 2004.

Schneider, Carl. "Moral Discourse and the Transformation of Family Law." *Michigan Law Review* 83 (1985): 1803, 1860.

Smith, Joseph Fielding. Conference Report, Oct. 1967, 121.

Stuart, Sarah. "Three Weddings and a Contract." *Sunday Telegraph* (Australia), 18 Oct. 1998, 22.

"The Talk of the Town." *New Yorker,* 30 Aug. 1976, 21.

Taylor, John. "The Death of a Marriage." *Sunday Telegraph* (Australia), 30 May 1999, 13.

Taylor, John. *Deseret News Weekly* 43, no. 9 (28 Dec. 1859): 337.

Thornton, Arland. "Changing Attitudes toward Family Issues in the United States." *Journal of Marriage and the Family* 51 (1989): 873.

Time (Pacific edition), 27 Apr. 1998, 30.

USA Today, 12 Apr. 1999, www.usatoday.com

Ward, Andrew. "South Finds Families That Pray Together May Not Stay Together." *Financial Times,* 24 Jan. 2005, 3.

Wardle, Lynn. "Is Marriage Obsolete?" *Michigan Journal of Gender Law* 10 (2003): 189.

Warner, C. Terry. "Honest, Simple, Solid, True." *Brigham Young Magazine,* June 1996, 36.

Whitehead, Barbara Dafoe. "Dan Quayle Was Right." *Atlantic Monthly* 271, no. 4 (April 1993): 47.

Wilkins, Richard G. "Marriage on the Brink." www.meridianmagazine.com, 15 Feb. 2004.

OTHER

Benson, RoseAnn. "The Marriage of Adam and Eve: Covenant Ritual, Literary, and Legal Patterns." Unpublished manuscript.

Bushman, Richard. "Joseph Smith's Visions." God, Humanity, and Revelation Conference. Yale University, 27 Mar. 2003. Unpublished manuscript.

Campbell, Beverly. "Mother Eve: Mentor for Today's Woman: A Heritage of Honor." Address to Collegium Aesculapium, Salt Lake City, 2 Apr. 1993.

Carlson, Allan. "Depopulation and the New World Social Order." Address to Australian Regional Conference, World Congress of Families II. Melbourne, Australia, 7 Aug. 1999.

Clark, John Haslem. Journal. Typescript in possession of author.

Gobbo, Sir James. Australian Regional Conference of World Congress of Families II, Melbourne, Australia, 6 Aug. 1999.

Hafen, Fran Clark. "Joy Cometh in the Morning." Unpublished manuscript.

Hinckley, Gordon B. "Bridges to the Future." Remarks at University of Denver, 22 Apr. 2003.

"I Dreamed a Dream." From the musical *Les Misérables,* by Alain Boublil and Claude Michel Schönberg. Lyrics by Alain Boublil, Herbert Kretzmer, Jean-Marc Natel. © Alain Boublil Music Ltd.

"Large-Scale Study Shows Reality for Mothers." *The Motherhood Study,* summarized at www.motherhoodproject.org.

Lincoln, Abraham. First Inaugural Address, 1861.

Oaks, Dallin H. "Men, Women, and Priesthood in the Family and in the Church." General Authority Training, Salt Lake City, 29 Mar. 2001. Unpublished manuscript.

Popenoe, David. "The Case for Marriage and the Nuclear Family: A Biosocial Perspective." Unpublished manuscript.

State of Our Unions, at marriage.rutgers.edu.

What Next for the Marriage Movement? New York: Institute for American
    Values, posted to MarriageMovement.org, 12 Dec. 2004.
Whitfield, Richard. "Sensitive Directions for Children's Moral Development."
    Presentation to World Congress of Families, Prague, Czech Republic, 20
    Mar. 1997.
Whitney, Joan, and Alex Kramer. "No Man Is an Island," 1950. Retrieved Aug.
    2005 from website: members.tripod.com/jrmeads_515/tipssep.htm
Young, Brigham. Journal. Archives of The Church of Jesus Christ of Latter-day
    Saints, Salt Lake City. (Ms/1234/Bx75/Fd.34)

INDEX